# 中小学生认知发展与学习心理学
# Psychology of School Children's Cognition and Learning

何心勇 著

·郑州·

图书在版编目(CIP)数据

中小学生认知发展与学习心理学 / 何心勇著
郑州：河南大学出版社,2025.5. --ISBN 978-7-5649-6261-6

Ⅰ.G442
中国国家版本馆 CIP 数据核字第 20258V2L49 号

责任编辑　屈琳玉
责任校对　陈晓林
封面设计　翟淼淼

| | |
|---|---|
| 出版发行 | 河南大学出版社 |
| | 地址：郑州市郑东新区商务外环中华大厦2401号　邮编：450046 |
| | 电话：0371-86059750(高等教育与职业教育出版分社) |
| | 　　　0371-86059701(营销部)　网址：hupress.henu.edu.cn |
| 排　版 | 郑州市今日文教印制有限公司 |
| 印　刷 | 郑州市今日文教印制有限公司 |
| 版　次 | 2025年5月第1版　　　　　　　　　印　次　2025年5月第1次印刷 |
| 开　本 | 787 mm×1092 mm　1/16　　　　　　印　张　19.5 |
| 字　数 | 645千字　　　　　　　　　　　　　定　价　63.00元 |

本书为

河南省高教学会 2021 年河南省高等教育研究项目

"新文科视阈下地方高校外语教师教育类通识课程教材改革

与实践（2021SXHLX088）"

阶段性研究成果

2023 年许昌学院应用型教材建设项目

"Psychology of School Children's

Cognitive Development and Learning（PX-49232901）"

2024 年许昌学院教学改革项目

"新文科背景下高校英语师范专业心理学教材建设与实践（PX-60243345）"

2024 年许昌学院第四批应用型课程建设项目

"中学班级管理（PX-62243480）"

阶段性研究成果

# 序　言

《教师教育课程标准(试行)》的颁布实施,从国家层面对教师教育机构设置和教师教育课程体系提出明确要求。在此背景下,教育学、心理学等教师教育类课程与教材受到前所未有的重视。教育教学改革与实践往往需要依托教材建设来具体落实与体现。因此,在新文科建设、新人才培养及教育教学改革的大背景下,应用型教材的建设与实践显得尤为迫切。

本书针对高校英语教育专业教师教育课程长期存在采用汉语教材、由非英语专业教师教授、师生重视程度不足的问题,创新性地提出了"五个融合,十个促进"的编写模式。这一模式从教材编写、教学过程到课程评价形成了完整的闭环,打通了产、学、研、用的通道。通过采用英文教材、双语授课及引入真实案例,有效提升了学生的学习兴趣、专业能力、应用能力及就业能力,为课程改革提供了新思路。以下从五个维度具体阐释"五个融合,十个促进"的编写模式。

第一,本书引用了大量中国灿烂的历史文化案例,并结合心理学原理进行深刻分析,既激发了英语师范生的爱国热情,又丰富了他们的心理学专业知识。通过"思政促进专业的方向性,专业促进思政的生长性",确保教材的方向性,彰显党和国家的意志,实现了"思政与专业融合",进而引领学生树立正确的价值观。

第二,本书针对目前国内英语师范生缺乏教师教育类课程英文版教材的问题,顺应新文科倡导的学科交叉融合理念,打破专业壁垒,编写了英文版心理学教材。"专业学习促进教师教育课程的完善,教师教育课程优化促进专业能力的提高",两者相互促进、相得益彰,充分彰显了专业特色,实现了"专业与教师教育课程的融合"。

第三,根据教学实践,本书注重引导打通产、学、研、用的通道,通过"理论促进生活实践,实践促进理论学习",实现"理论与实践融合"。具体表现为创新教学场景和创新实践成果,如下图所示。

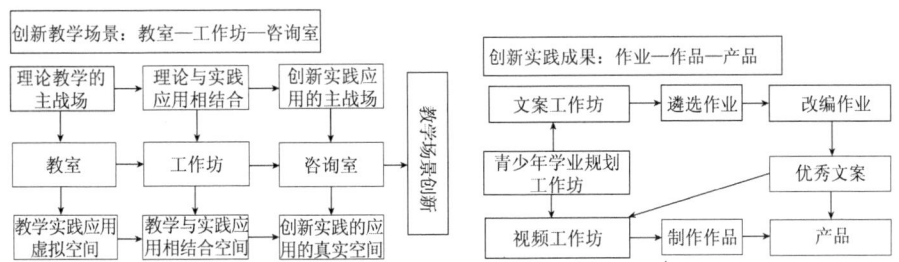

第四,基于教学实践,本书注重引导实现"课上与课下融合",更多体现为"虚拟空间"与"现实空间"的融合,"学习、研究"与"实践、应用"的融合,以及"课堂、工作坊"与"生活、咨询室"的融合。通过创新实践环节,实现"课上学习促进课下应用,课下应用

深化课上学习"。课堂既是理论学习的主阵地，也是模拟演练的空间，学生把课堂所学理论知识与生活、学习中的案例相结合进行课堂现场模拟，使课堂成为知识学术氛围与生活工作气息交织的殿堂，为课下创作优质作品提供理论和实践基础。课下才是学生学习实践应用的重要环节。每个学习共同体围绕"作业→作品→产品"的目标努力，一起头脑风暴，寻找解决问题的方案，撰写文案，最终完成作业，如下图所示。

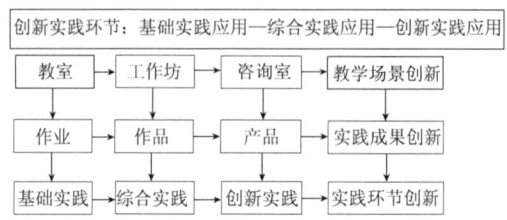

第五，本书每一章节内容都紧密围绕教师招聘考试和教师资格证考试所涉及的相关心理学概念、规律、原理展开，并辅以丰富案例，有效激发学生的学习兴趣与积极性，提高教师资格证等考试的通过率，进而提高毕业生的就业率，真正做到"课堂促进考试通过率，考试助推课堂学习效率"，实现"课程与考证融合"，为高校新文科下"新人才"的培养提供参考。

本书内容涵盖以下章节：第一章介绍认知过程。鉴于英语师范生缺乏普通心理学知识，而国内同类汉语教材往往忽视这一点，本书第一章着重介绍认知过程，包括感觉、知觉、记忆、思维、想象等，以弥补知识缺口，为后续学习夯实基础。第二、三章探讨中小学生认知发展状况。第四章系统阐述不同流派的学习理论及其教学启示。第五章详细分析学习动机及其在教学中的应用。第六章介绍学习迁移及其在促进学习中的作用。第七章探讨学习策略的有效运用。第八章介绍不同的学习风格。

编者衷心希望这本英文版教材能够满足英语教师教育课程改革的迫切需求。同时，编者也深知编写教材是一项艰苦而长期的工作，由于水平与能力有限，书中难免存在疏漏与偏差，恳请各位专家、学者及广大读者不吝赐教，提出宝贵意见与建议。

何心勇
2024 年 10 月 19 日

# Catalogue

Chapter 1　Process of Cognition ………………………………………………… ( 1 )
　1.1　Sensation ……………………………………………………………… ( 1 )
　1.2　Perception …………………………………………………………… ( 5 )
　1.3　Memory ……………………………………………………………… ( 14 )
　1.4　Image ………………………………………………………………… ( 25 )
　1.5　Imagination …………………………………………………………… ( 28 )
　1.6　Speech ………………………………………………………………… ( 30 )
　1.7　Thinking ……………………………………………………………… ( 31 )
Chapter 2　Cognitive Development of Primary School Children …………… ( 45 )
　2.1　Jean Piaget's Cognitive-Stage Theory ……………………………… ( 45 )
　2.2　Lev Vygotsky's Sociocultural Theory ……………………………… ( 47 )
　2.3　Sensory development of primary school children ………………… ( 48 )
　2.4　Perceptual development of primary school children ……………… ( 50 )
　2.5　Memory development of primary school children ………………… ( 52 )
　2.6　Thinking development of primary school children ……………… ( 55 )
　2.7　Imagination development of primary school children …………… ( 60 )
　2.8　Attention development of primary school children ……………… ( 60 )
　2.9　Language development of primary school children ……………… ( 63 )
Chapter 3　Cognitive Development of Middle School Children ……………… ( 69 )
　3.1　Development of middle school children's sensation, perception and
　　　　observation …………………………………………………………… ( 70 )
　3.2　Development of middle school children's memory ……………… ( 72 )
　3.3　Development of middle school children's thinking ……………… ( 76 )
　3.4　Development of middle school children's imagination …………… ( 85 )
　3.5　Development of middle school children's attention ……………… ( 86 )
　3.6　Development of middle school children's speech ………………… ( 87 )
Chapter 4　Theories of Learning ………………………………………………… ( 90 )
　4.1　Learning ……………………………………………………………… ( 90 )
　4.2　Learning classification ……………………………………………… ( 92 )
　4.3　Behaviorism learning theory ………………………………………… ( 97 )
　4.4　Cognitive learning theory …………………………………………… (117)

|   |   |   |
|---|---|---|
| 4.5 | Constructivist learning theory | (132) |
| 4.6 | Humanistic learning theory | (142) |

## Chapter 5  Learning Motivation and Cultivation ········ (150)

|   |   |   |
|---|---|---|
| 5.1 | Overview of learning motivation | (150) |
| 5.2 | Classification of learning motivation | (152) |
| 5.3 | Functions of learning motivation | (156) |
| 5.4 | Relationship between learning motivation and learning effect | (158) |
| 5.5 | Theories of learning motivation | (160) |
| 5.6 | Stimulation and cultivation of learning motivation | (181) |

## Chapter 6  Learning Transfer and Cultivation ········ (193)

|   |   |   |
|---|---|---|
| 6.1 | Concept of learning transfer | (193) |
| 6.2 | Classification of learning transfer | (193) |
| 6.3 | Theory of learning transfer | (197) |
| 6.4 | Factors (Conditions) affecting learning transfer | (204) |
| 6.5 | Strategies of promoting school children's effective transfer | (207) |

## Chapter 7  Learning Strategies and Cultivation ········ (211)

|   |   |   |
|---|---|---|
| 7.1 | Concept of learning strategies | (211) |
| 7.2 | Characteristics of learning strategies | (212) |
| 7.3 | Classification of learning strategies | (213) |
| 7.4 | Cognitive strategies | (216) |
| 7.5 | Meta-cognitive strategies | (228) |
| 7.6 | Resource management strategies | (232) |
| 7.7 | Training and teaching of learning strategies | (235) |

## Chapter 8  Learning Styles and Cultivation ········ (242)

|   |   |   |
|---|---|---|
| 8.1 | Concept and characteristics of learning styles | (242) |
| 8.2 | Theories of learning styles | (243) |
| 8.3 | Factors of learning styles | (250) |
| 8.4 | Learning styles and their learning characteristics | (252) |
| 8.5 | Identification on cognitive styles | (264) |
| 8.6 | Individualized instruction according to learning styles | (271) |

|   |   |
|---|---|
| Appendix I | (276) |
| Appendix II | (280) |
| Appendix III | (282) |
| Appendix IV | (284) |
| Appendix V | (290) |
| References | (296) |

# Chapter 1　Process of Cognition

*In ancient China, during the Warring States period, a philosopher named Zhuangzi encountered a butterfly fluttering around him. As he watched it dance gracefully, he felt a profound sense of peace. Suddenly, he questioned whether he was Zhuangzi dreaming of being a butterfly or a butterfly dreaming of being Zhuangzi. This moment sparked a deep reflection on identity, reality, and perception.*

Zhuangzi's story encapsulates the intricate process of cognition. It highlights how our thoughts and perceptions shape our understanding of reality. Just as Zhuangzi grappled with the nature of his existence, we constantly engage in a cognitive process. In this chapter, we will delve into the process of cognition, exploring how we acquire, process and utilize information. By understanding the cognitive mechanisms at play, we can enhance our ability to learn, think critically, and navigate the complexities of our world, much like Zhuangzi navigating the realms of dreams and reality.

As the saying goes, you can never earn money beyond the realm of your cognition. What's cognition? In psychological research, individual psychological activities are generally divided into three categories: psychological processes, individual psychology, and psychological states, among which the psychological process is the dynamic process of a person's psychological phenomena, including the cognitive process, the emotional process, and the volitional process. The human brain accepts input information from the outside world, processes it, transforms it into internal mental activities, and then dominates human behavior. The process is one of information processing, that is, the cognitive process. Cognition refers to the process that people acquire knowledge or apply knowledge or the process of information processing, which is the most basic psychological process of people, including sensation, perception, memory, thinking, imagination, and language.

## 1.1　Sensation

*Once upon a time, four blind men met an elephant. They wanted to know what the elephant looked like, so they began to feel it. The first blind man felt the elephant's tusk and said, "The elephant is like a spear." The second blind man touched the elephant's ear and shouted, "The elephant is like a big fan." The third felt the elephant's leg and exclaimed, "The elephant is a big pillar." The fourth touched the elephant's tail and shouted, "The elephant is a rope." So the four blind men quarreled.*

The story reflects the relationship between sensation and perception. From a sensory perspective, every blind man is right, and they are all wrong from a perceptual perspective. What is sensation? What is perception? What are the specific contents of sensation and perception? First, this section mainly talks about sensation.

### 1.1.1 Definition of sensation

Sensation is the reflection of the human brain on the special properties of objective things that directly affect the sense organs. Sensation is the simplest psychological phenomenon and the starting point of knowledge. Sensation is also the basis of all knowledge and experience and is a necessary condition for human normal psychological activities. Human knowledge of the world begins with sensory perception. Our five sense organs constitute the main sensory systems through which an individual relates to the outside world and maintains contact with it. We can get information about the individual properties of things by sensation, such as color, lightness and darkness, softness and hardness, taste, tone of things, etc.

### 1.1.2 Types of sensation

Sensation is divided into external sensation and internal sensation. External sensation refers to the sensation of receiving external stimuli and reflecting the individual attributes of external things, such as vision, hearing, smell, taste, and tactile sense, among which vision plays a leading role in human sensations. Internal sensation refers to the sensation of receiving internal stimuli and reflecting internal changes of the body, which is also called organic sensation, including equilibrium sensation, kinesthesis, visceral sensation, and so on.

### 1.1.3 General laws of sensation

The sensation caused by a stimulus acts directly on a certain sense, but the human senses only respond to a certain range of stimuli. The range and the corresponding sensory capacity are called sensory thresholds and sensitivity, respectively.

1. Relationship between sensitivity and sensory threshold

1) Sensitivity and sensory threshold

**Sensitivity** refers to the ability of the sensory organs to sense suitable stimuli. Human sensitivity is not fixed, and the development of sensitivity depends on a person's living conditions and practical activities, such as a tea doctor's tea tasting skills or a skilled steelmaker's sharp eyes. **Sensory threshold** is the amount of stimuli just enough to induce sensation or differential sensation. Sensitivity is measured by the size of the sensory threshold. The relationship between sensitivity and sensory threshold is numerically inversely proportional. The higher the sensitivity, the lower the sensory threshold; the lower the sensitivity, the higher the sensory threshold. According to the definitions of sensitivity and sensory threshold, sensitivity belongs to a kind of ability, and sensory threshold belongs to a kind of value or range.

2) Absolute sensitivity and absolute sensory threshold

The minimum stimulus intensity that can just cause sensation is called the absolute threshold. *For example, the grandpa's absolute threshold is 8 in Figure 1-1*. The ability of human senses to perceive the minimum stimulus intensity is called absolute sensitivity. *For example, the grandson's absolute sensitivity is higher than grandpa's in Figure 1-1*.

Figure 1-1 Sensitivity and sensory threshold

3) Differential sensitivity and differential sensory threshold

The minimum difference between stimuli that can just cause differential sensation is called the **differential sensory threshold**, also known as the just noticeable difference (JND). The ability to sense the minimum difference between stimuli is called **differential sensitivity**.

2. Law of sensations

Due to the interaction of the same or different sensations, sensation has different characteristics, including adaptability, contrast, continuity, compensativeness, and relevance.

1) Adaptability

Adaptability is mainly manifested in sensory adaptation. Sensory adaptation refers to the phenomenon in which sensitivity changes due to the continuous action of a stimulus on the receptor. Adaptation is manifested in all senses, but it differs across various types of senses.

**Visual adaptation** mainly includes bright adaptation and dark adaptation. Dark adaptation refers to the process of improving visual sensitivity when lighting stops or when an individual turns from a bright place to a dark place. **Bright adaptation** refers to the process of decreasing visual sensitivity when lighting starts or when an individual turns from a dark place to a bright place.

When you go to a dance party, you may initially feel that the music is too loud. After a while, you will feel that the music is not as loud as it seemed at first. This phenomenon belongs to **auditory adaptation.**

If you enter an orchid room for a long time, you will no longer smell its fragrance, and if you enter an abalone shop for a long time, you will not notice its stench. This phenomenon belongs to **olfactory adaptation.**

*"Too many lice to itch"* belongs to **pain adaptation**. Pain adaptation is difficult to occur, so pain sensation becomes a signal of noxious stimuli and has biological significance.

2) Contrast

Contrast refers to **sensory contrast**, which is the phenomenon in which the same receptor receives different stimuli and changes its sensitivity. Sensory contrast can be divided into simultaneous contrast and successive contrast. **Simultaneous contrast** occurs when several stimuli act on the same receptor at the same time. *For example, if you place a small gray square on a white background, it looks darker; if you place the same gray square on a black background, it appears brighter.* **Successive contrast** occurs when several stimuli successively act on the same receptor. *If you eat oranges after eating sugar, you will find them very sour. If you put your hand in hot water and then in warm water, you will feel that the warm water is very cold. Eating a piece of candy after taking medicine, you won't feel the bitterness.*

3) Continuity

Continuity is mainly manifested in **sensory afterimages**, also known as sensory aftereffects, which refer to the sensory phenomenon that remains temporarily after the stimulation stops. The **visual aftereffect**, also known as the visual afterimage, is very significant. Visual afterimages can be divided into *positive and negative* *afterimages*. If you look at a glowing light bulb for a few seconds and then close your eyes, you will see a light source similar to the light bulb appearing against a dark background in front of you. This is the positive afterimage. After the positive afterimage, if you turn your eyes to a white background, you will find black spots on the bright background, which is the negative afterimage. Color vision afterimages are generally negative afterimages. If you stare at a green flower for about a minute and then look at a white wall, you will see a red flower on the white wall; if you look at a yellow flower first, the afterimage will be blue.

4) Compensativeness

Compensativeness is mainly shown in the mutual compensation of different sensations. The sensitivity of any kind of receptor will change due to the influence of other receptors acting simultaneously or successively. The weak stimulation of one receptor increases the sensitivity of other receptors, while strong stimulation reduces the sensitivity of other receptors. Sensory compensation means that the function of other sensory systems compensates after the function of one sensory system is lost. A person who is blind may have more acute hearing through practical activities. A deaf person can "use their eyes instead of their ears".

5) Relevance

Relevance mainly refers to synesthesia. **Synesthesia** is a phenomenon in which one type of sensory stimulation evokes a simultaneous experience in another sense. *Red gives a warm feeling. Purple gives a noble feeling. Blue gives a sense of tranquility. Black gives a heavy feeling. The weather feels a bit cold.* Different sounds also create different synesthesia, such as cheerful songs and heavy songs. "*The moonlight in the lotus pond is not uniform; but light and shadow create a harmonious melody, like a famous tune played on a violin*" (*Moonlight in the Lotus Pond* by Zhu Ziqing).

## 1.2 Perception

Sensation is a person's understanding of individual attributes of things. However, we not only need to know the color and taste of an apple, but also need to distinguish it from other things as a whole and understand that it is a fruit beneficial to human health. Our recognition of the totality of things is perception.

### 1.2.1 Definition of perception

**Perception**, produced on the basis of sensation, is the reflection of the human brain on the overall attributes of objective things that directly act on the sense organs, such as a coat, a flag, a house, an apple, a song, a piece of music, and so on. Perception comes from sensation and is higher than sensation.

## 1.2.2 Types of perception

According to the different analyzers that play a leading role in the process of perception, perception can be divided into visual perception, auditory perception, olfactory perception, tactual perception, and so on. According to the different objects reflected by the human brain, perception can be divided into object perception and social perception. According to whether the perceptual object conforms to objective reality and the accuracy of reflecting that reality, perception can be divided into fine perception, fuzzy perception, illusion, and hallucination. Next, we mainly introduce object perception, social perception, and illusion.

1. Object perception

Object perception can be divided into space perception, time perception, and motion perception.

**Space perception** refers to the reflection of the spatial characteristics of objects in the human brain, including shape perception, size perception, depth perception, and orientation perception.

**Time perception** is a reflection of the time relationship of objective things (the speed, continuity, and sequence of the movement of things). In time perception, hearing, vision, touch, and other senses all participate and play different roles. The factors that affect a person's time perception are:

1) The nature of sensory channels. In terms of accuracy in judging time, hearing is the best, followed by touch, and vision is the least accurate.

2) The number and nature of the occurrence of events within a period of time. In a given period, the more frequently events happen, and the more complex the nature of the events is, the shorter people tend to estimate the time is; while if the number of events is small and their nature is simple, people tend to estimate that the time is longer. If the content of a lecture is rich and fascinating, the audience will feel that time passes quickly; on the contrary, if the content of the report is poor and boring, the audience will estimate that the time is longer. In contrast, when a person recalls the same period, the richer their experience is, the longer they think the time is; the simpler their experience is, the shorter they feel the time is.

3) People's interests and emotions. When you are interested in something, you will feel that time passes quickly and underestimate the time. Conversely, if something is

disgusting or indifferent, you will feel that time passes slowly and overestimate it. When you look forward to something, you will feel that time passes slowly. On the contrary, if you don't want something to happen, you will feel how time flies. For example, time goes slowly when you have to wait for your girlfriend; time flies too fast when you are dating your girlfriend and don't want it to end too early.

**Motion perception** is the perception of the movement of an object's spatial position, which directly depends on the speed of the object's movement. If the speed of an object's movement is too slow, or the distance it moves per unit time is too small, people cannot produce motion perception. Motion perception is divided into real motion perception and apparent motion perception. **Real motion perception** refers to the perception caused by the continuous displacement of an object from one place to another at a specific speed or acceleration. **Apparent motion perception** refers to the phenomenon where, under certain conditions, people perceive objectively stationary objects as moving or perceive discontinuous displacements as continuous motion. Apparent motion perception mainly includes forms such as stroboscopic movement, induced movement, autokinetic movement, and aftereffects of movement (Table 1-1).

Table 1-1 The main forms of apparent motion perception

| Forms | Definitions | Classic cases |
| --- | --- | --- |
| Stroboscopic movement | Stroboscopic movement refers to the continuous movement from one stimulus to another when two stimuli are presented one after the other at a certain spatial interval and time interval. | *The principle of the production of films, cartoons, etc. Turning a picture storybook quickly.* |
| Induced movement | Induced movement refers to the phenomenon in which the movement of one object causes the movement of adjacent stationary objects. | *The relatively stationary moon appears to be moving due to the motion of the floating clouds.* |
| Autokinetic movement (Autokinetic effect) | Autokinetic movement refers to the phenomenon in which a person feels that a light spot is moving after staring at a faint and stationary light spot for a moment against a dark background. | *Looking at the stars in the night sky on a moonless night, you will feel that the stars are flashing.* |
| Movement aftereffect | After staring at an object moving in one direction, if you turn your gaze to a stationary object, you will see that the stationary object seems to move in the opposite direction. This phenomenon is called the movement aftereffect. | *After we gaze at the waterfall for a while, we look at the cliff next to it, and the cliff seems to move upward.* |

2. Social perception

Social perception, also known as social cognition, is a person's perception of others, groups, and themselves in life practice. Common social perception biases include the social stereotype effect, halo effect, primacy effect, recency effect, and projection effect (Table 1-2).

Table 1-2 Common social perception biases

| Classifications | Definitions | Examples |
| --- | --- | --- |
| Social stereotype effect | An individual generalizes the characteristics or motivations of a group of people, attributes the generalized characteristics of the group to everyone in the group, and believes that each of them has those characteristics, while ignoring the individual differences among group members. This phenomenon is called the social stereotype effect. | *The French are romantic. The English are gentlemen. Northerners are bold. Boys are responsible for earning money; girls are responsible for beauty. Young people are enthusiastic, lively, and more open; older people are more conventional and conservative. Birds of a feather flock together.* |
| Halo effect | When we think someone has a certain characteristic, we make similar judgments about their other characteristics. | *Students think that a teacher who is attractive in appearance has strong teaching abilities. A fair face covers a hundred wrongs.* |
| Primacy effect | The primacy effect refers to the phenomenon in which the information acquired initially has a greater impact on the formation of an overall impression than the information acquired later. | *People pay attention to first impressions when interacting, such as in interviews and blind dates.* |
| Recency effect | The recency effect refers to the phenomenon in which the information acquired recently has a greater impact on the formation of an overall impression than the information acquired previously. | *The deepest impression of my friends, whom I haven't seen for many years, in my mind is what he looked like when I said goodbye to him for the last time.* |
| Projection effect | Projection effect refers to the psychological phenomenon in which an individual infers that others have the same characteristics as himself due to his own certain characteristics. | *A pot calls the kettle black. Measure the heart of a gentleman with the mind of a petty person.* |

### 3. Illusion

Illusion is a distorted and incorrect perception of objective things, a special case of perception. Illusions include size illusion(Figure 1-2), shape illusion, orientation illusion(Figure 1-3), time illusion, spiral illusion, twisted cord illusion, movement illusion(Figure 1-4), tilt illusion, and so on. The reasons for illusions include not only objective and subjective factors but also physiological and psychological factors.

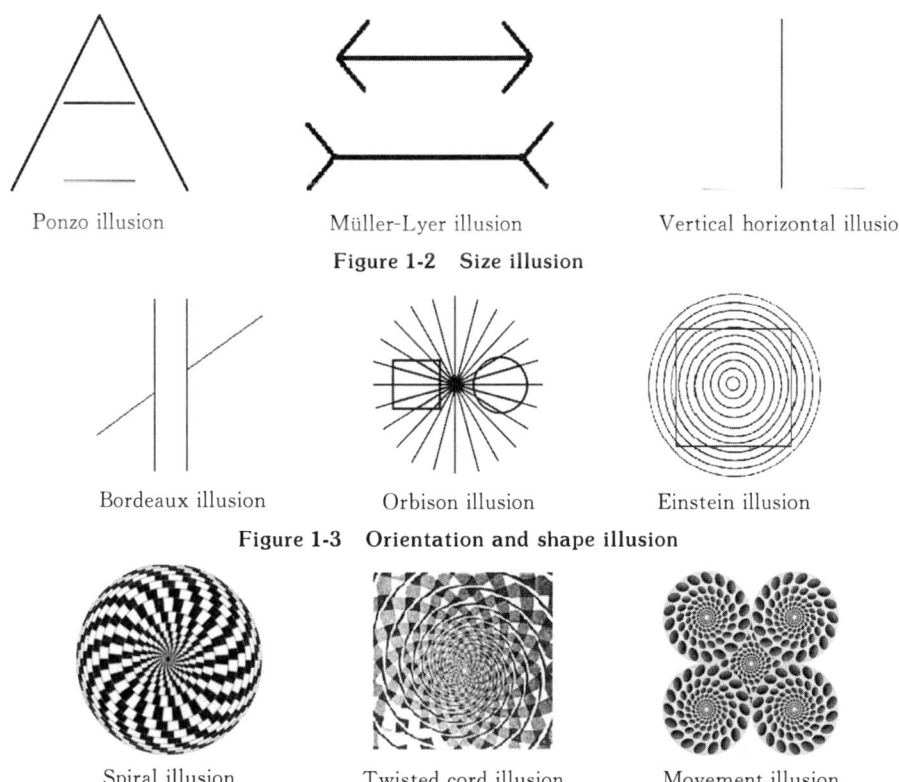

Figure 1-2  Size illusion

Figure 1-3  Orientation and shape illusion

Figure 1-4  Spiral, twisted cord and movement illusion

## 1.2.3  Laws of perception

### 1. Perceptual selectivity

**Perceptual selectivity** means that the perceptual system will automatically divide stimuli into objects and backgrounds, distinguishing perceptual objects from the background preferentially when faced with many objects. The stimulus that is clearly reflected is called the object of perception, while the stimulus that is vaguely reflected is called the background of perception. The object of perception is relative to the background and can be converted to each other (Figure 1-5).

Figure 1-5  Ambiguous figures

Perceptual selectivity is affected by both subjective and objective factors. Objective factors that affect perceptual selectivity include intensity law, difference law, activity law, contrast law, and combination law. **Intensity law** means the size, color, and sound of stimuli should reach the sensory threshold. The stronger the stimulus within the threshold range, the easier it is to be selected for perception. *It is easy for people to perceive thunder and lightning because of their high perception intensity, but it is difficult to detect the activities of insects, such as the walking sound of ants.* **Difference law** refers to the difference between the object and the background. The difference law states that the greater the contrast between the object and the background in color, shape, sound, and so on, the easier the object is to highlight from the background and be perceived first. On the contrary, the smaller the contrast between the object and the background, the easier the object is to disappear in the background and be difficult to perceive. *The teacher corrects the homework with a red pen. The key part of the blackboard newspaper written with colored chalk is the easiest to be picked up. Military camouflage and the protective color of insects make the difference between the object and the background smaller, so the military and insects are not easy to find. A spot of red in the green sea is easy to perceive.* "儿童急走追黄蝶,飞入菜花无处寻" *indicates that it is difficult for the children to find yellow butterflies in the yellow flowers.* **Activity law** means that moving objects are easier to perceive than stationary ones. *Meteors in the night sky and neon advertisements are easy to perceive. The magician uses one hand to make obvious movements to attract the attention of the audience, while the other hand is playing tricks to achieve his purpose.* **Contrast law** emphasizes the difference between two or more objects. Two things that are significantly different or even opposite to each other are easily perceived. **Combination law** means that things that are close in space, continuous in time, the same in shape, and consistent in color are easy to form a whole and be clearly perceived.

Subjective factors that affect perceptual selectivity include purpose law, existing knowledge and experience, needs, motivations, interests, and so on. Purpose law emphasizes people's subjective purpose. Purpose law states that the clearer the purpose, the clearer the perception. *Children have been to the zoo many times with their parents since childhood, but they have no deep and clear impression of many animals in the zoo because they have no specific purpose each time. If the biology teacher leads the students to visit the zoo, the purpose of observation will be more prominent, and the students will have a clearer and deeper impression of the animals in the zoo.* The richness of an individual's existing knowledge and experience affects perceptual selectivity. An individual's needs, motivations, interests, hobbies, stereotypes, emotional states, etc., affect perceptual selectivity.

## 2. Perceptual wholeness

**Perceptual wholeness** refers to the process in which people integrate various attributes of objective things that directly act on the sensory organs into a unified whole according to their own knowledge and experience. *For example, a small sign can indicate a great trend; the falling of one leaf heralds autumn; a glimpse reveals the whole leopard.* Perception is the integrated process of sensory information based on knowledge and experience. Perceptual wholeness is when people integrate the attributes of all parts of a thing to grasp the thing as a whole. Perceptual wholeness not only helps to improve a person's intuitive ability and speed but may also hinder and interfere with the reflection of partial and detailed features.

Perceptual wholeness often depends on the following four factors: 1) characteristics of perceptual objects, such as proximity, similarity, closure, continuity, and other factors (Figure 1-6). 2) the intensity relationship between the components of the perceptual object. 3) the structural relationship between the parts of the perceptual object. The same parts in different structural relationships will become different perceptual wholes. If the same notes are composed in different sequences and in different beats and melodies, different tunes are formed. If the relationship between the components of the tune remains unchanged, and the tune is just played with different instruments or sung by different people, our perception of the wholeness of the tune will not change. 4) perceptual wholeness mainly depends on the subjective state of the perceiver, the most important of which is knowledge and experience.

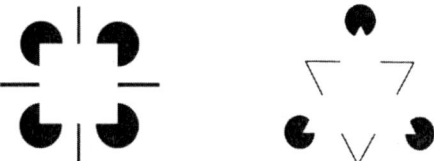

Figure 1-6  Subjective contours

What components are easy to combine into a shape? Psychologists have proposed the following principles for graphic organization: proximity, similarity, symmetry, good continuation, common fate, closure, orientation, line orientation, and simplicity(Figure 1-7).

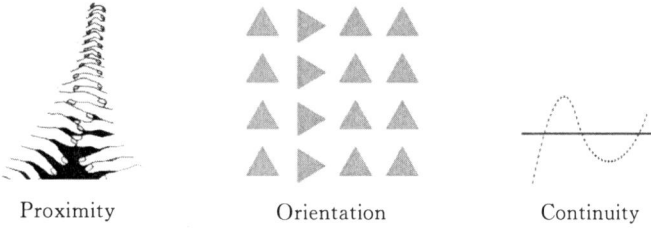

Proximity　　　　　　Orientation　　　　　　Continuity

Line orientation    Simplicity    Closure

Figure 1-7  Principles of graphic organization

3. Perceptual understandability

**Perceptual understandability**, also known as perceptual organization, refers to the processing procedure in which a person processes and deals with the perceived things based on knowledge and experience, and makes generalizations and explanations with words. Perception is deeply related to memory and experience. The understanding of things is achieved through the thinking activities in the process of perception, and thinking is closely related to language. The guidance of language can help a person understand the object of perception more quickly and completely. For example, in Figure 1-8, we can see some black spots, but we can't tell what they are at once. When someone says it's a dog, these spots will immediately appear as the outline of a dog. Furthermore, there are a thousand Hamlets in a thousand readers' eyes.

In the process of perception, people strive to make some explanation of the perceptual object based on their existing knowledge and experience, giving it certain meaning. Therefore, perceptual understandability is closely related to people's existing knowledge and experience. The richer the knowledge and experience, the more profound the understanding and the more complete and precise the perception.

Figure 1-8  Hidden graphics

Knowledge and experience play a role in the understandability and wholeness of perception. In perceptual wholeness, experience helps us to put incomplete things into a whole; in perceptual understandability, different people have different understandings of the same thing due to their varied experiences.

4. Perceptual constancy

The **perceptual constancy** means that a person's perceptual image remains relatively unchanged when the objective things themselves stay the same, even as the perceptual conditions change within a certain range. There are mainly four types of perceptual constancy (Table 1-3). For example, whether in the morning, noon, or evening, our national flag is always regarded as Chinese red. Perceptual constancy includes the following forms.

Table 1-3  Types of perceptual constancy

| Types | Concepts | Examples |
| --- | --- | --- |
| Shape constancy | When the same object is observed from different angles, although the projection of the object on the retina may change greatly, people can still perceive it as the same shape. | *No matter whether a door is open or closed, although its projection on the retina may change greatly, people always perceive the door as a rectangle (Figure 1-9).* |
| Size constancy | A person's perception of the size of an object does not change with distance. | *When the distance varies, the size of a person's height projected on the retina changes greatly, but people can still perceive it according to the actual size (Figure 1-10; Figure 1-11).* |
| Brightness constancy | When lighting conditions change, the perception of relative brightness or visual lightness of objects remains unchanged. | *The lightness reflected by white paper in sunlight and moonlight differs by 800,000 times, but people always perceive the paper as white with the same brightness.* |
| Color constancy | When an object is illuminated by colored light, its surface color remains relatively unchanged. | *When you illuminate the surface of a white object with red light, you see not red but white under that light.* |

**Figure 1-9  Shape constancy**

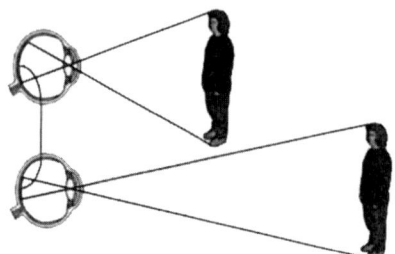

Figure 1-10  Size of retina image                Figure 1-11  Size constancy

## 1.3 Memory

Memory, the interesting psychological phenomenon, will be introduced in this section. Firstly, what memory is will be discussed. Then we will discuss the quality and classification of memory; at last, we will talk about the processes and laws of memory.

### 1.3.1 Definition of memory

**Memory** is the process in which we encode, store, and retrieve information. The human brain perceives past events, thinks about past problems and theories, experiences past feelings and emotions, practices past actions, etc., all of which can become the content of memory. Because of the existence of memory, the past and present of our psychological activities can be connected, and thus our psychological activities can become a continuous, developing, and unified whole.

### 1.3.2 Quality of memory

A person's memory should be evaluated based on their memory qualities — agility, persistence, accuracy, and readiness.

**1. The agility of memory**

The agility of memory is the characteristic of speed and efficiency of memory. *At the end of the Eastern Han Dynasty, Yang Xiu invited Zhang Song to read the "New Book of Mengde" by Cao Cao. Zhang Song only read it once and said, "The 7-year-old children in Xichuan can recite it; how can it be called a new book?" So, Zhang Song recited all the content of the "New Book of Mengde" word by word. After hearing about it, Cao Cao burned the "New Book of Mengde".* Zhang Song's memory possesses four kinds of qualities: agility, persistence, accuracy, and readiness.

## 2. The persistence of memory

The persistence of memory is the retention feature of memory. *At the end of the Eastern Han Dynasty, Cao Cao asked Cai Wenji, "I heard that there used to be many ancient books in your house. Can you still remember them now?" Cai Wenji said, "My father left me more than 4,000 volumes of books, but because of the war and displacement, very few have been preserved. Now I can write down only about 400." So, Cai Wenji wrote down the contents of the ancient books and sent them to Cao Cao without any mistakes.*

## 3. The accuracy of memory

The accuracy of memory is the correct and precise characteristic of memory. The accuracy characteristic of memory is extremely important, and the other qualities of memory are of no value without accuracy. *For example, Cai Wenji could write down the books without any mistakes, and Zhang Song could recite all the content of the "New Book of Mengde" word by word, which indicates they had an excellent characteristic of accuracy in memory.*

## 4. The readiness of memory

The readiness of memory is the characteristic of the retrieval and application of memory. The readiness of memory is embodied in phrases like *"words flowing from the mouth as from the pen of a master"*, *"replying in a stream of eloquence"*, *"finishing a piece of writing in one go"*, and so on.

### 1.3.3 Classification of Memory

1) Memory can be divided into immediate memory, short-term memory, and long-term memory according to the length of time the memory material remains in the mind.

**Immediate memory** (sensory memory) refers to the memory that sensory information will be preserved for a very short time after the objective stimulus stops working. It is the beginning stage of the memory system. Although this type of memory holds a large amount of information, it lasts for a short period, approximately 0.25-2 seconds. When an individual is slightly distracted, immediate memory disappears immediately; if noticed, it can transition to short-term memory.

**Short-term memory** (working memory) refers to the memory in which the information in the human brain is processed and encoded within one minute. *For example, if you try to remember a phone number, you can repeat it a few times and then dial immediately. However, once you dial the phone, you may forget that number immediately because it is only stored in short-term memory and not* *converted into long-term memory.* In fact, the specific amount of information (the capacity of short-term memory) that can be held in short-term memory has been identified as $7\pm2$ "chunks" of information. A chunk is a grouping of information that can be stored in short-term memory. *For example, a chunk can be a group of seven individual letters and numbers, permitting us to hold the seven-digit phone number (296-8966) in short-term memory.*

A chunk may also consist of larger categories, such as words or other meaningful units. For example, consider the following list of 22 letters: G A Y B U Z L K W E P O G U O A H H M X O P. Because the list of individual letters exceeds seven items, it is difficult to recall the letters after one exposure. But suppose they were presented as follows: GAY BUZL KWE POG UOA HHM XOP. In this case, even though they are still 22 letters, you'd be able to store them in short-term memory since they represent only 7 chunks. Information in short-term memory, if experiencing rehearsal or application, can develop into long-term memory (Robert S. Feldman, 2015).

Working memory expands the concept of short-term memory (Baddeley & Hitch, 1974). Working memory refers to a memory system with limited capacity that temporarily stores and processes information during information processing. *For example, when completing the calculation task $22+40+18+12$, you must first remember the results of $22+40=68$ and $18+12=30$ to proceed smoothly to the next calculation; 68 and 30 are stored in working memory.*

**Long-term memory** refers to the memory in which information is fully processed and maintained in the mind for more than a minute or even a lifetime. Long-term memory has such a large capacity that it is almost impossible to fill it with what we learn in a lifetime. *For example, the Tang poems you learned in kindergarten, such as "Ode to the Goose" and "Compassion for the Farmers", are still remembered to this day.*

2) Memory can be divided into imaginal memory, episodic memory, semantic memory, emotional memory, and movement memory according to the content of memory.

**Imaginal memory** is a memory in which a person takes the image of things he has perceived as the content. Imaginal memory stores past experiences in the mind in the form of images. Visual memory and auditory memory are important in imaginal memory. The persons and objects we have seen, the scenes we have experienced, the music we have heard, the tastes we have tasted, and the objects we have touched all belong to imaginal memory. *For example, after visiting the Great Wall, a vivid* *image is left in the mind.*

**Episodic memory** is a kind of memory based on personally experienced events (situations) that happened at a certain time and place. The information received and stored in episodic memory is related to specific times and places, and episodic memory uses personal experience as a reference. *For example, you remember a conference you attended or a place you visited.*

**Semantic memory**, also known as word-logic memory, is an individual's memory based on various organized knowledge. The contents of semantic memory include definitions, theorems, formulas, and rules that reflect the nature and laws of objective things. *For example, the Pythagorean theorem and Newton's Three Laws.* Semantic memory is unique to human beings. Semantic memory is relatively stable because it is restricted by general rules, knowledge, concepts, and words, and is seldom disturbed by external factors.

**Emotional memory** is the memory based on emotions or feelings that an individual has experienced. Emotional memory is the process in which individuals retain past emotional experiences in their memory and re-experience these emotions and feelings under certain conditions. *For example, Peter still remembers the joy of being the English subject representative in Grade 4 in primary school.*

**Movement memory** is the memory based on the movement state or action image of the body. It is a form of imaginal memory, but the object of memory is not the intuitive image of static characters, objects, or natural scenery, but the movement image of various actions. The movement image formed by past movements or operational actions is a prerequisite for movement memory. If there is no movement image, there is no movement memory. The information stored in movement memory is easy to retrieve and not easy to forget. *For example, gymnastic movements and dance movements retained in the mind belong to movement memory.*

3) Memory can be divided into declarative memory and procedural memory according to the different content of information processing and storage or the different nature of memory content.

**Declarative memory** refers to the memory of facts and events. It can be acquired at one time through language teaching, and its retrieval often requires the participation of consciousness. *For example, all kinds of textbook knowledge and common sense of daily life we learn in class belong to this kind of memory.*

**Procedural memory** refers to the memory of how to do things, including the memory of perceptual skills, cognitive skills, and movement skills. Procedural memory often takes many attempts to acquire gradually. Procedural memory often does not require the participation of consciousness. It pertains to habits and skills, such as knowing how to throw a ball or an infant's kicking upon seeing a familiar mobile. *We may have read some books about swimming and remembered some essentials of swimming movements, which belong to declarative memory. Later, we will turn swimming knowledge into swimming skills and truly learn to swim after continuous practice. This memory is procedural memory.*

4) According to the degree of conscious participation, memory can be divided into explicit memory and implicit memory, both of which belong to long-term memory.

**Explicit memory** refers to the memory that is displayed when an individual needs to consciously and actively collect certain experiences to complete the current task. *For example, free recall, clue recall, and recognition.*

**Implicit memory** refers to the memory that our experience automatically affects the current task without the need for conscious participation or intentional recall. In implicit memory, a person is not aware of the information extraction, nor is he aware of the content of the extraction. Implicit memory mainly refers to procedural memory, such as learning continuous movements like cycling, skiing, and dancing. Once implicit memory is formed, it can remain stable for a lifetime; so when you learn to ride a bicycle as a child, even if you don't ride it for many years in the future, you can still ride it immediately many years later.

### 1.3.4 Process of memory

The memory process includes three links: memorization, retention, and reproduction (recognition and recall). From the perspective of information processing, memory is the process of encoding, storing, and retrieving information. The input and encoding of information is the process of memorization, the storage of information is the process of retention, and the extraction of information is the process of recognition or recall.

The three basic links of the memory process are interdependent and closely related. Without memorization, it is impossible to retain knowledge and experience; without memorization and retention, it is impossible to recall or recognize what has been experienced. Memorization and retention are the premise of recognition and recall, and recognition and recall are the results of memorization and retention that can further consolidate and strengthen the content of memorization and retention.

1. Memorization

Memorization is the process in which individuals acquire knowledge and experience, which is the first link in the memory process.

1) Memorization can be divided into voluntary memorization and involuntary memorization according to the purpose of memorization.

**Involuntary memorization** means that we memorize something naturally without a predetermined purpose in advance and do not need to use any method or will to help us memorize things. A person can get a lot of information through involuntary memorization, but the content is often accidental, fragmented, and lacks systematicness due to the lack of purpose. The content of involuntary memorization generally has two characteristics: the stimulation that acts on a person's sensory organs is of great significance or attracts attention; involuntary memorization aligns with his needs and interests and can produce a more profound emotional experience.

**Voluntary memorization** is memorization with a clear purpose and the use of certain methods. In the process of memorization, a certain amount of willpower is required. The attitude of voluntary memorization is proactive, the object of memorization is clear, the content is systematic, and the effect is firm and lasting. Voluntary memorization requires the cooperation of high attention, strong willpower, and positive thinking activities. Therefore, under the same conditions, the effect of voluntary memorization is better than that of involuntary memorization. Voluntary memorization is the main way for people to acquire and accumulate systematic knowledge and master science and technology. Students' learning activities mainly rely on voluntary memorization.

2) According to the nature of the memorizing materials and the difference in memorizing methods, memorization can be divided into rote memorization and meaningful memorization.

**Rote memorization** refers to memorization carried out by means of repetition according to the external relationship of materials. However, it is necessary for rote memorization in the following situations: materials that the learner needs to memorize are meaningless or have no internal relationship, such as memorizing meaningless syllables, names of places or persons, historical dates, etc.; although the materials may be meaningful, the learner lacks the necessary understanding of the materials, so he can memorize them first only by rote and gradually understand them with the accumulation of knowledge and experience. *For example, children learn Tang poetry, and students in Grade One recite multiplication tables.*

**Meaningful memorization** refers to memorization based on understanding and using existing knowledge and experience according to the internal relationship of materials. The effect of meaningful memorization is better than that of rote memorization in terms of comprehensiveness, accuracy, consolidation, and speed.

The main factors that affect the effect of memorization are the purpose and task of memorization; the attitude and emotional state during memorization; the nature of activities and tasks; the quantity and nature of materials; and the methods of memorization.

2. Retention

**Retention** refers to the process of consolidating the acquired knowledge and experience in the human brain, which is the second link of memory. Retention is not a static process of intactly retaining the materials in mind but a dynamic process full of changes. This change is manifested in two aspects: quantitative changes in retention and qualitative changes in retention and memory recovery.

Quantitative changes in retention generally show that the content of memory decreases over time, and even has been forgotten. It can also be manifested as memory recovery. **Memory recovery** means that the retention amount of the material measured after a period is greater than that measured immediately after memorization. Memory recovery usually occurs in the following situations: memory recovery happens more commonly to children than to adults; the memory recovery of materials that are difficult to learn is more likely to occur than that of materials that are easy to learn; and the memory recovery of materials that you are not proficient in is more likely to occur than materials that you are very proficient in.

Qualitative changes in retention are manifested in two aspects. On the one hand, the unimportant details of the memory content tend to disappear, while the main content and prominent features can be better retained so that the memory content is concise, generalized, and reasonable. On the other hand, some features and clues of the memory content are selectively preserved, while some features are added to make the memory content easier to understand.

3. Forgetting

1) Definition of forgetting

**Forgetting**, a psychological process opposite to retention, refers to the phenomenon of inability to recall or recognize the memorized materials, or incorrect recall or recognition. Forgetting is a natural, normal, and reasonable psychological phenomenon. Forgetting does not mean that the memorized information is completely lost, but that the retained information cannot be successfully retrieved when needed. According to the viewpoint of information processing, forgetting is the failure or error of information retrieval.

2) Types of forgetting

Forgetting can be divided into temporary forgetting (false forgetting) and permanent forgetting (true forgetting) according to the time of forgetting. **Temporary forgetting** means that the content that has been transferred into long-term memory cannot be retrieved temporarily but may be recovered under appropriate conditions. *For example, when someone asks you whether you know Peter, and you do know Peter, but you can't remember him for a moment, you may be able to recall him afterwards.* **Permanent forgetting** refers to the forgetting caused by the disappearance of memory materials without revision in the stages of immediate memory and short-term memory.

Forgetting can be divided into active forgetting and passive forgetting according to the initiative and willingness to forget. Active forgetting means that people consciously force themselves not to recall events that cause particularly painful experiences and feelings, or consciously distort them in some way to make them no longer appear, which is also called intentional forgetting. *For example, Zhou Botong, the old urchin in "Legend of the Condor Heroes", forced himself to forget the "Nine Yin Sutra".* Passive forgetting refers to the forgetting caused by fading, interference, decay, attenuation, and so on.

According to the content of forgetting, it can be divided into partial forgetting and overall forgetting.

3) Laws of forgetting

From 1844 to 1879, German psychologist Ebbinghaus conducted experimental studies of forgetting and proposed the famous forgetting curve (Figure 1-12). This curve shows that forgetting starts immediately after learning, and the speed of forgetting is very fast in the initial period. With the passage of time, the speed of forgetting gradually slows down, and forgetting almost ceases after a long time. It can be seen that the process of forgetting is uneven, showing a trend of fast first and slow later, more first and less later, and exhibiting negative acceleration. The rate of

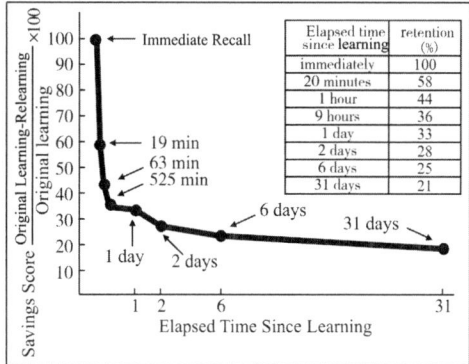

Figure 1-12 Ebbinghaus forgetting curve

forgetting slows down nine hours later and continues to decline even after many days.

4) Factors affecting forgetting process

First, the nature and amount of learning materials affect the forgetting process. Generally speaking, both too much and too little material are not conducive to the memory of knowledge. The nature of learning materials refers to the type, length, difficulty, and significance of the materials. Meaningful materials are forgotten more slowly than meaningless materials; figurative and intuitive materials are forgotten more slowly than abstract materials; the forgetting process of longer and more difficult materials aligns more closely with Ebbinghaus's forgetting curve, and materials with moderate length and difficulty have the best retention effect. Materials that can arouse the learner's interest, meet their needs and motivation, elicit strong emotional experiences, and are of great significance in their work, study, and life are generally not easy to forget(Figure 1-13).

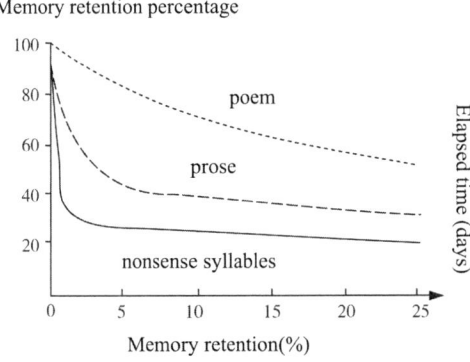

Figure 1-13　Memory retention percentage

Second, the serial position effect affects the forgetting process. **Serial position** refers to the different positions of learning materials in serial memory during serial learning. **The serial position effect** refers to the trend that the memory effect of materials close to the beginning and end is better than that of the middle part. The beginning and end of the list have better memory effects, known as the primacy effect and the recency effect respectively (refer to Table 1-2). It is generally easier to remember the beginning and end of a text, while the middle part is easy to forget because the beginning is only interfered with by retroactive inhibition, not by proactive inhibition, and the end is only interfered with by proactive inhibition, not by retroactive inhibition. In contrast, the middle part is affected by both retroactive and proactive inhibition, making it the easiest to forget.

Third, the degree of learning affects the forgetting process. Too much and too little learning are called over-learning and under-learning respectively. The memorization of materials that has not reached the standard of error-free recitation is referred to as under-learning. Under-learned materials are easy to forget. **Over-learning** refers to continuing to learn after reaching the point of being able to recite. The effect of learning is best when over-learning reaches 50%, meaning the proficiency of learning reaches 150%. When it exceeds 150%, the effect does not increase and may lead to boredom, fatigue, and ineffective labor. *For example, if it takes you 30 minutes to learn an English text just enough to recite and recall correctly, and you continue to learn for another 15 minutes, this is over-learning, and your over-learning is 50%.*

Fourth, the persistence and importance of memory tasks affect the forgetting process. Generally speaking, tasks requiring long-term memorization are conducive to prolonging the retention time of materials in the mind. Unimportant and unreviewed content is easy to forget.

Fifth, the methods of memorization affect the forgetting process. The effect of comprehension-based meaningful memorization is much better than that of rote memorization.

Sixth, time affects the forgetting process. According to the forgetting law, the speed of forgetting is fast in the initial stage of memory and then gradually slows down. The amount of retained learning content decreases over time.

Seventh, emotion, motivation, and attitude affect the forgetting process.

5) Causes of forgetting

First, **decay theory**. Decay theory, also known as trace decay theory, is the oldest explanation for the cause of forgetting. It originated with Aristotle and was further developed by Thorndike and the Pavlov school. According to this theory, forgetting is caused by the decay of memory traces, which occurs automatically over time. It is suitable for explaining sensory memory and short-term memory but is difficult to prove through experiments, because the decay of retention over time after memorization may result from the decay of memory traces or from the interference of other materials.

Second, **interference theory**. Interference theory holds that forgetting is caused by the interference of other stimuli between learning and memory. Once the interference is eliminated, the memory can be restored, and the memory trace does not fade. Interference theory can be illustrated by proactive inhibition and retroactive inhibition. Proactive inhibition is the interference effect of pre-learned material on the memorization and recall of post-learned material; retroactive inhibition is the interference effect of post-learned material on the retention and recall of pre-learned materials.

Third, **repression theory**. According to repression theory, forgetting is caused by the repression of emotion or motivation. If the repression is lifted, the memory can be recovered. This theory was discovered by Freud when he hypnotized patients. He believed that individuals cannot recall certain memories because they are artificially repressed into the subconscious due to the pain they cause. *For example, forgetting caused by exams.*

Fourth, **retrieval failure theory**. We all have this experience: we can't recall something, but we know that we know it. This phenomenon, where you know something but can't recall it, is called **"tip of the tongue" or "TOT"**. From the perspective of information processing, forgetting occurs when it is difficult to extract the required information temporarily. Forgetting may result from inaccurate coding, loss of retrieval cues, or cue errors. Once we have the right cue, the information we need can be extracted after searching. This is the theory of retrieval failure.

Fifth, **assimilation theory (cognitive structure theory)**. Ausubel believed that forgetting is a process of organizing knowledge and simplifying cognitive structure. When people learn higher-level concepts and laws, they can use them to replace lower-level concepts, simplifying their cognitive load, which is a form of positive forgetting. In meaningful learning, if the original knowledge structure is not consolidated, if the discrimination between old and new knowledge is unclear, or if new concepts that appear similar but are different in essence replace original concepts, memory errors occur. This is a form of negative forgetting.

4. Reproduction (recognition and recall)

**Recognition** refers to the psychological process in which people can still recognize something they have perceived, thought about, and experienced when it is presented again. *For example, when good friends meet again, they can recognize each other at a glance. Another example is revisiting an old place, where everything feels familiar.* Recognition is the primary form of memory and is an easier and simpler way of restoring experience than recall.

**Recall** is a process in which people re-present the things they experienced in the past when they are not in front of them. Recall is the highest form of memory and a more complex way of restoring experience than recognition. There is no essential difference between recognition and recall; only the degree of retention differs.

According to whether there is a predetermined purpose, task, and will, as well as the degree of effort, recall can be divided into unintentional recall and intentional recall. **Unintentional recall** refers to recall that has no predetermined purpose and does not require any will or effort. *For example, free association, where you occasionally think of a past experience.* **Intentional recall** refers to the conscious recall of past experiences with the task of recalling and making a certain effort. *For example, a schoolchild recalling information while reviewing for an exam or students answering the teacher's questions in class.*

According to the different conditions and methods of recall, recall can be divided into direct recall and indirect recall. **Direct recall** refers to the reproduction of past experiences directly triggered by the current context. *For example, memories revive at the sight of familiar places.* **Indirect recall** refers to the reproduction of past experiences recollected through a series of intermediate links or associations. *For example, recalling where you left your keys based on hints and inferences.*

When a person has difficulty with intentional recall, especially indirect recall, they must make efforts to overcome certain difficulties before they can retrieve the past experience. This kind of intentional recall that requires effort to overcome difficulties is called remembrance.

True-or-false questions and multiple-choice questions in a test are forms of recognition assessment. Ask-and-answer questions and fill-in-the-blank questions are forms of recall assessment. Due to the different levels of recognition and recall, human recognition memory is generally better than recall memory. Under normal circumstances, if you can recall someone or something, you must be able to recognize them; however, if you can recognize someone or something, you may not be able to recall them. Therefore, recognition cannot be used as a reliable indicator for assessing the firmness of memory.

## 1.4 Image

Image is the figure formed in the mind based on perception (Lin Chongde et al., 2003). In other words, an image refers to the figure of something that appears in the mind or the psychological representation similar to a picture. Images are based on what has been perceived before. Image plays an important role in memory and imagination.

### 1.4.1 Classification of image

1) According to the different degrees of image creation, images can be divided into memory images and imaginative images. **Memory image** refers to the image of things that can still be reproduced in the mind when the things perceived in the past

do not appear in front of us. *For example, if you mention a teacher, his image, voice, and smile will appear in your mind.* **Imaginative image** refers to the new image created by a person in the process of imagination, which is produced based on the analysis, synthesis, association, exaggeration, personification, typification, and other processing and transformation of memory images. *For example, sphinx, mermaid, etc.*

2) According to the main sensory channels through which images are produced, images can be divided into visual images (*for example, remembering a mother's smiling face*), auditory images (*for example, thinking of the sound of a guitar*), motion images (*for example, remembering dance moves*), and so on.

3) According to the perceptual range of images, images can be divided into individual images and general images. **Individual image** refers to the image of a specific object after multiple perceptions, which reflects the characteristics of the individual object. *For example, the image of the desk with the Chinese character "早" used by Lu Xun belongs to the individual image.* **General image** is the image of a certain kind of things kept in memory, which reflects the common characteristics of a certain kind of things. *For example, there must be a desk image in our mind, which is abstracted from the images of many different desks, including the desks we have used in different periods, as well as the desks we have seen and used by others.* Comparatively speaking, the level of generalization of individual images is lower than that of general images.

4) Eidetic image is a special form of memory image. **Eidetic image** refers to the vivid, lifelike, clear, and concrete image of objects that have been seen after they are removed from the visual field. Eidetic image is almost as vivid and lifelike as the direct perception of things, but it is not sensory perception, although eidetic image seems to be the same as perception.

### 1.4.2 Characteristics of image

1) **Intuition**: Image is directly observable, visible, and approximate in our mind. The vivid and concrete image of an object is produced in the human mind, as if some characteristics of the object are directly seen or heard. For example, eidetic image.

2) **Generality**: Image is the result of a person's multiple perceptions. It does not represent the individual characteristics of objects but the general outline and main characteristics of objects.

3) **Operability**: A person can zoom in, zoom out, scan, and decompose the formed image in his mind. He is able to manipulate and rotate images of objects in

the mind, just as he is able to manipulate and rotate actual objects in the real world through external actions. Cooper and Shepard (1973) proved the operability of images through the Mental Rotation Experiment (Lin Chongde et al., 2003) (Figure 1-14; Figure 1-15).

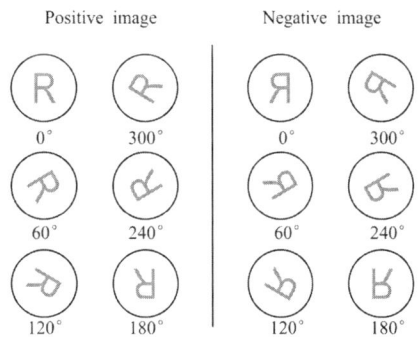

Figure 1-14　Presentation of stimuli in mental rotation experiment

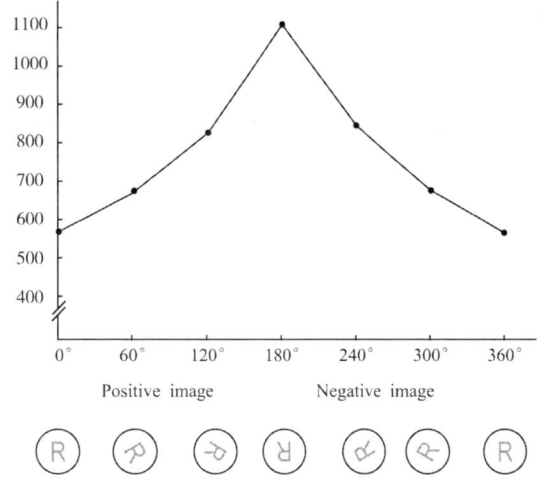

Figure 1-15　Letter stimuli rotated at different angles and the time required to determine whether it is a positive or negative image

Source:彭聃龄,《普通心理学》,北京师范大学出版社,2018,第258—259页.

### 1.4.3　Functions of Image

1) Image is an important form of representation of knowledge. All things in the world have images, which are stored in the human mind in the form of images.

2) Image provides the perceptual basis for the conceptual form. Image is intuitive and similar to perception; it is also general and similar to thinking. Therefore, image is the intermediate link between perception and thinking, and it is the transitional stage from perceptual knowledge to rational knowledge. For example, children often use specific images such as cats, dogs, chickens, and ducks

to illustrate the concept of animals.

3) Image promotes problem-solving. In teaching, imaginal training can improve teaching quality and develop students' thinking abilities. Primary school children in the lower grades need the help of images when performing addition and subtraction operations, so they often use the form of "What is one apple plus two apples?" in learning. When middle school students solve geometry problems, they need support from images.

4) Image promotes language understanding. Research proves that images can promote and facilitate the understanding of sentences and idioms.

## 1.5  Imagination

**Imagination** is a psychological process in which the human brain processes and transforms the stored images to form new images.

### 1.5.1  Classification of imagination

1) According to the purpose and planning of imagination, imagination can be divided into unintentional imagination and intentional imagination. Unintentional imagination, also known as involuntary imagination, is the imagination that is produced involuntarily without a predetermined purpose. *For example, when you look up at the unpredictable clouds in the sky, you will have images of cotton, an elephant, and other things in your mind; when you see the ice flowers on the windows in winter, you will feel that they are like footprints or leaves, which are concrete manifestations of unintentional imagination.* Dreams are an extreme manifestation of unintentional imagination, such as daydreaming. **Intentional imagination**, also known as voluntary imagination, is the imagination that is consciously carried out with a predetermined purpose. It is a form of conscious activity. This kind of imagination possesses certain predictability and directionality. People have always controlled the direction and content of imagination in the process of imagination. *For example, the characters that are conceived by writers and various assumptions put forward by scientists belong to intentional imagination.*

2) According to the different degrees of creation, intentional imagination can also be divided into reproductive imagination and creative imagination. Fantasy is a special form of creative imagination. **Reproductive imagination** is a process of forming corresponding new images in the mind according to the description and indication of words or symbols. *For example, when we read the descriptions of Ah Q in "The*

*True Story of Ah Q"*, *the specific character — Ah Q — will appear in our minds; mechanical manufacturing workers imagine the main structure of the machine according to the drawings they see; construction workers can imagine the future high-rise buildings according to the design drawings.* **Creative imagination** is a process of independently creating new images in the mind by using the images accumulated in the past according to certain purposes and tasks. *For example, Lu Ban, inspired by thatch that cut his hand, invented the saw. Newton studied physics and found three laws. Darwin studied biology and wrote "The Origin of Species".*

3) **Fantasy** is a kind of imagination that is combined with life desire and points to the future. Compared with general creative imagination, fantasy has the following two characteristics: Fantasy reflects a person's desire and is the image that he yearns for; fantasy is often the preparatory stage for creative activities. Fantasy can be divided into the following three forms: **Scientific fantasy** is a form of scientific foresight, a preparatory stage and driving force for the development of creative imagination, and a positive fantasy with progressive significance and realistic possibility. *For example, the scientific fantasy that people made more than a century ago to travel in the sky and in the sea has become a reality today.* **An ideal** is a positive fantasy that conforms to the law of development of things and has realistic possibilities. *If you want to become a scientist or an artist and contribute to the prosperity of your country, it is the ideal of many contemporary young people.* **An idle dream** is a negative fantasy that goes against objective reality and cannot be realized at all. Idle dreams often make people divorced from reality. People who fall into idle dreams for a long time often do nothing and accomplish nothing.

## 1.5.2 Processing methods of imagination

There are various ways for people to process and reorganize images in their minds. In scientific invention and artistic creation, the processing strategies of imagination are usually shown as bonding, exaggeration, personification, typification, and so on (Table 1-5).

Table 1-5 Processing methods of imagination

| Types | Definitions | Examples |
| --- | --- | --- |
| Bonding | Bonding refers to the process of combining the attributes, elements, characteristics, and parts of two or more objective things together to form a new image. | *The image of Monkey King, Zhu Bajie, Ox-Head and Horse-Face, mermaids, and the Dragon King.* |

**Continued table**

| Types | Definitions | Examples |
|---|---|---|
| Exaggeration | Exaggeration refers to changing the normal characteristics of objective things, exaggerating and emphasizing certain traits, making them larger, smaller, more numerous, and more colorful. | The image of the thousand-handed Avalokitesvara. |
| Personification | Personification refers to the process of adding human characteristics to external things to personalize them. | The image of the thunder god and the lightning goddess. |
| Typification | Typification refers to the process of creating new images based on the common and typical characteristics of a class of things. | The image of Ah Q in Lu Xun's novel. |

### 1.5.3 Functions of imagination

The functions of imagination is shown in the table below (Table 1-6).

Table 1-6　Functions of imagination

| Functions | Explanation |
|---|---|
| Foresight function | The imagination can predict the results of activities and guide the direction of activities. |
| Supplementary function | People can supplement the time and space limitations of their cognitive activities, go beyond the narrow range of individual experience, and gain more knowledge with the help of imagination. |
| Vicarious function | In real life, when people's certain needs can not be met, they can get some psychological compensation and satisfaction with the help of imagination. |
| Adjustment function | Imagination can regulate the physiological activity process of the body, and it can change the functional activity process of the peripheral part of the individual. |

## 1.6　Speech

Speech refers to the process in which people use language to communicate. Speech is purposeful, open, regular, discrete, social and individual.

### 1. Types of speech

The types of speech is shown in the table below (Table 1-7).

Table 1-7 Types of speech

| Types | | | Concepts | Characteristics | Examples |
|---|---|---|---|---|---|
| External speech | Oral speech | Dialogue speech | Dialogue speech refers to the speech activities of direct communication between two or more people. | Situationality, reactiveness, and conciseness. | Chat; discussion |
| | | Monologue speech | Monologue speech refers to a long and coherent speech that is carried out alone and related to the narration of thoughts and emotions. | Extensibility, preparation and planning. | Report; speech |
| External speech | Written speech | | A person expresses his thought with the help of words, and accepts the influence of others' words with the help of reading. | Randomness, preparation and planning | Writing articles |
| Internal speech | | | Self-questioning and self-answering or silent speech activity. | Concealment and conciseness | Silent reading |

2. Speech perception

**The perception of oral speech** involves the articulation and intelligibility of language. Articulation and intelligibility refer to the percentage of listeners' understanding of the speaker's speech or the percentage of listeners' correct listening.

**The perception of written speech** is when people receive the information provided by written materials through the visual system and make correct judgments and distinctions about words. Perception of written speech also includes word recognition and reading.

3. Speech comprehension

**Speech comprehension** refers to a proactive process in which people construct meaning in the mind with the help of auditory or visual language materials. It can be divided into the following three levels: vocabulary comprehension or vocabulary identification is the first level of speech comprehension; sentence comprehension is the second level of speech comprehension; text or discourse comprehension is the third level of speech comprehension.

## 1.7 Thinking

Thinking is the generalized and indirect reflection of the human brain on the essential attributes and internal relations of objective things.

### 1.7.1 Characteristics of thinking

According to the concept of thinking, thinking has two characteristics: generality and indirectness.

1. Generality

The generality contains two meanings: first, to extract the common features and essential features of the same kind of things and to summarize them. *For example, trees with different shapes and sizes that can bear jujubes are called "jujube trees." Jujube trees, apple trees, and pear trees are called "fruit trees" according to the commonness of root, stem, leaf, and fruit.* Second, to generalize the connections and relationships between the things that are perceived many times, and to draw a conclusion about the internal connections between the things. *For example, every time you see a "moon halo," it will be "windy," and if the foundation stone is "wet," it will "rain," so you can draw the conclusion that "the moon halo means it will be windy, and the moist foundation stone means it will rain."*

2. Indirectness

The indirectness means that thinking can reflect the things that the senses cannot grasp directly or are not in front of the eyes with the help of some media and brain processing. *For example, with the help of Zhang Heng's seismometer, the direction and location of earthquakes can be determined. For another example, physicians cannot directly see the diseases of the patient's internal organs but can indirectly judge the patient's condition through thinking processing by means of auscultation, laboratory tests, pulse detection, temperature testing, blood pressure measurement, B-ultrasound, CT examination, and other means. Seismologists can analyze and predict the earthquake situation according to the abnormal phenomena of animals or the data from other instruments.*

### 1.7.2 Quality of thinking

1. Extensiveness and profundity of thinking

**The extensivenss of thinking** refers to the open-mindedness and the ability to expose the connections of things from various angles and multiple aspects and to think about the problem comprehensively. **The profundity of thinking** refers to the ability to think deeply about problems, to be good at grasping the essence of things through the superficial phenomena of things, and to reveal the inner connections between things. *For example, the ability to see the essence through phenomena.*

## 2. Independence (originality) and criticality of thinking

**The independence (originality) of thinking** refers to the ability not to be influenced by others, not to blindly follow others' opinions, not to rely on existing methods and conclusions, and not to be arbitrary, not to insist on one's own way, not to be stubborn, and to give full play to one's subjective initiative to discover, think, deal with, and solve problems independently. Everyone has originality in thinking, but the degree of performance and the timing of originality differ. Originality of thinking is the advanced manifestation of intelligence. The flexibility of thinking is the condition and foundation of the originality of thinking.

**The criticality of thinking** refers to being good at critically evaluating others' thoughts and achievements, absorbing others' strengths, advantages, and essence of thoughts, discarding others' weaknesses, shortcomings, and dross of thoughts, and excelling at thinking rigorously and meticulously, calmly and objectively evaluating and consciously controlling one's own thinking activities, not easily being affected by their own emotions and preferences.

## 3. Flexibility and agility of thinking

**The flexibility of thinking** refers to thinking about problems flexibly. It is manifested as being able to think about problems from different angles and using different methods. When conditions change, thinking can adapt to the changes, and original plans and schemes can be changed in time to find new solutions to problems.

**The agility of thinking** refers to the rapidness and correctness of thinking activities and the ability to make quick decisions. The agility of thinking, different from rashness, requires not only fast speed of thinking but also high accuracy of thinking.

## 4. Logicality and preciseness of thinking

**The logicality and preciseness of thinking** mean that thinking is clear, the organization is clear, and the logic law is strictly followed when considering and solving problems. That is, the questioning is clear, the reasoning is rigorous, the primary and secondary are clear, the argument is sufficient, the goal is specific and persuasive, and the evidence for the conclusion is overwhelming. The logicality and preciseness of thinking is the central link of thinking qualities and the concentrated embodiment of all thinking qualities.

### 1.7.3 Classifications of thinking

1) Thinking can be divided into intuitive-action thinking, concrete image thinking, and abstract logical thinking according to the content of thinking, the nature of the task, the level of development, and the way of solving problems.

**Intuitive-action thinking** is a thinking process that takes concrete and practical actions as the "pillars". The tasks to be solved by intuitive-action thinking are always intuitive and specific. *For example, students in the lower grades of primary school often help their thinking through actions such as counting their fingers when they solve math problems. For another example, if there is something wrong with your e-bike, you must first check the corresponding parts of the e-bike to determine whether the tire is flat or the bearing is broken, and then repair it.* The thinking activities of solving intuitive and concrete problems through practical operations belong to intuitive-action thinking.

**Concrete-image thinking** is a thinking process that takes intuitive figures and images as the "pillars." Images are the material of thinking, and the thinking process is often manifested in the generalization, processing, and operation of the images. Concrete-image thinking has the characteristics of visualization, integrity, and operability. *For example, when a sculptor creates a sculpture, he always thinks about the image of the work he wants to create first in his mind and then completes the work according to the image in his mind.*

**Abstract-logical thinking** refers to the thinking that reflects the essential attributes and internal laws of things in the form of concepts, judgments, and reasoning in the process of thinking. The concept is the "pillar" of abstract-logical thinking. It is a thinking process that takes words as an intermediary to reflect reality. Abstract-logical thinking is a typical form of human thinking and the most essential feature that distinguishes human thinking from animal thinking. *For example, middle school students often use abstract logical thinking to solve math problems in the form of concepts, judgments, and reasoning.*

2) Thinking can be divided into empirical thinking and theoretical thinking according to whether the thinking process is guided by daily experience or

theory.

**Empirical thinking** is the thinking of judging problems based on daily experience. *For example, according to their own experience, preschool children believe that "birds are flying animals", which belongs to empirical thinking.* Due to the lack of knowledge and experience, empirical thinking can easily produce one-sidedness and even draw misinterpreted or wrong conclusions.

**Theoretical thinking** is the thinking of analyzing and judging problems based on scientific principles, theorems, laws, and other theories. *For example, "Psychology is the subjective reflection of objective reality in the human brain", which is the result of theoretical thinking.* Theoretical thinking can often grasp the essence of things and solve problems correctly. Teachers use theoretical thinking to teach scientific theories, and students use theoretical thinking to learn rational knowledge.

3) Thinking can be divided into analytical thinking and intuitive thinking according to whether the conclusion has clear thinking steps and the clarity and logic of consciousness in the thinking process.

**Analytical thinking** is the thinking that follows strict logical procedures and laws, deduces step by step, and then obtains logical and correct answers or makes reasonable conclusions. Analytical thinking also reflects the objective world in the form of concepts, judgments, and reasoning. *For example, the process of obtaining the answer through multi-step reasoning and demonstration when students solve mathematical problems.* Analytical thinking has procedural characteristics.

**Intuitive thinking** is the thinking that makes reasonable guesses, assumptions, or sudden understandings of the answer to the question without step-by-step analysis. Intuitive thinking is illogical and jumping and has no specific steps. Intuitive thinking has the characteristics of agility, directness, brevity, abruptness, and speculativity. *For example, when a football player grasps the layout loopholes of the opposing players on the field in an instant, he takes no time to kick the ball into the goal, which is the performance of intuitive thinking.* The phenomenon of inspiration is the result of intuitive thinking.

4) Thinking can be divided into convergent thinking and divergent thinking

according to the directionality of thinking.

**Convergent thinking** is a form of thinking that starts from existing information, follows logical rules, and obtains the best answer to a problem based on familiar knowledge and experience. It concentrates thinking in one direction when people solve problems, thereby forming a unique and definite answer. The process of convergent thinking is the process of solving problems by generating logical conclusions based on known information and using familiar rules. It's a way of thinking with direction, organization, and scope. *For example*, $\because A>B, A<C, C>B, C<D, \therefore B<D$.

**Divergent thinking** is a thinking form that starts from existing information, thinks in different directions, reorganizes the knowledge in memory, and produces diverse answers. Their ideas spread in various possible directions to obtain a variety of answers when people solve problems. The process of divergent thinking is the process of generating a variety of information from the existing information.

5) According to the degree of creativity of thinking, it can be divided into re-productive thinking and creative thinking.

**Re-productive thinking**, also known as conventional thinking, refers to the way of thinking in which people use their acquired knowledge and experience to solve problems with customary methods and fixed patterns according to ready-made plans and procedures. *For example, students use learned formulas to solve the same type of problems.* This kind of thinking has a low level of creativity.

**Creative thinking** refers to the thinking activities in which people reorganize existing knowledge and experience, propose new programs or procedures, and create new results. *For example, the development of new large-scale tool software and the proposal of new scientific theories all require creative thinking.* Creative thinking usually possesses the following characteristics:

① **Novelty and uniqueness.** Creative thinking is different from general thinking activities. It requires breaking out of habitual problem-solving methods, reorganizing or reconstructing existing knowledge and experience, and creating thinking achievements that were previously unknown to individuals or unprecedented in society. Therefore, novelty and uniqueness are the most essential characteristics of creative thinking.

② **Crystallization of many kinds of thinking.** Creative thinking is not only the unity of divergent thinking and convergent thinking but also the unity of image thinking and abstract thinking, but it is more manifested in divergent thinking. Creative thinking takes divergent thinking as the core. Divergent thinking has the characteristics of fluency, flexibility, and originality. Therefore, the characteristics of divergent thinking can also represent the characteristics of creative thinking.

③ **Active participation of creative imagination.** The active participation of creative imagination is an important part of creative thinking because creative imagination provides new images of things and makes the achievements of creative thinking concrete. Therefore, the creation of new images in literary works, the proposal of new hypotheses in scientific research, and the invention of new machines are inseparable from creative imagination.

④ **State of inspiration.** The state of inspiration, another typical feature of creative thinking, refers to the mental state in which a new image, a new concept, and a new thought suddenly appear in the process of creative thinking. Inspiration is a sudden insight phenomenon triggered by accidental factors when people focus on solving the problem in their thinking. Any creative thinking is inseparable from inspiration.

### 1.7.4 Forms of thinking

The form of thinking is relative to the content of thinking. All kinds of human thinking contents have certain forms. Because human thinking activities are extremely complex, the same thinking contents can be expressed in different thinking forms, and different thinking contents can also be expressed in the same thinking forms. The forms of thinking include concepts, judgments, and reasoning.

#### 1. Concept

Concept is the thinking form that the human brain reflects the essential attributes of objective things and summarizes and reflects the things with these attributes. Concept is the result of thinking, which is formed on the basis of representation. Concept is the most basic form of thinking and the basic component of human knowledge. ① The connotation and denotation of the concept are different. Connotation represents the essential characteristics of things that the concept can reflect, and denotation represents all the individuals and examples that the concept can include. The richer the connotation of a concept and the greater the amount of information, the less denotation the concept can include. ② Concepts are hierarchical and can be divided into different levels. *For example, "bird" is a concept, "parrot" is a concept, and their levels are different.*

1) Learning process of the concept

All thinking is ultimately expressed in concepts and their related forms, so people can use concepts to deduce the invisible characteristics of things. The concept is not unchanging, and it is constantly formed and developed in the process of human social history. Everyone should master these developmental concepts to gain the knowledge and experience accumulated by predecessors. We can carry out normal psychological activities and participate in social activities on the basis of concepts. The learning process of concept includes two links: concept acquisition and concept application.

① **Concept acquisition. Concept formation** refers to the process in which an individual repeatedly contacts a large number of common characteristics or common attributes of the same kind of things or phenomena and confirms them through positive examples or negative examples. The sign of concept formation is to grasp the essential characteristics of the concept and apply it in practice. Discovery learning is the main way of concept formation, which generally goes through three stages. First, abstraction. The first step to forming a concept is to understand the attributes or characteristics of objective things. Therefore, we must abstract various characteristics and attributes of specific things. Second, classification. In addition to extracting common attributes and features from specific things, the formation of concepts also needs to classify similar attributes and features. In the process of classification, we must induce the similarities or commonalities of some attributes and characteristics of objective things and ignore the differences of non-essential features or attributes between things. Third, discrimination. Discriminating objective things is an important step in the formation of concepts. Discrimination permeates the whole process of concept formation, from discovering the attributes or features of objective things (abstraction) to identifying these attributes and features (classification), and then transitioning to understanding the differences between the attributes or features of objective things (discrimination).

**Concept assimilation** is a way of using the original concepts in learners' cognitive structure to directly prompt them about the key characteristics of concepts in the way of definitions, enabling them to obtain the concepts. The main form of students' concept acquisition is concept assimilation, and reception learning is a typical way of concept assimilation.

② **Concept application.** Once acquired, the concept can play a role in cognitive activities and thus have an impact on cognitive activities. This is the concept application. The concept application is generally reflected in two levels: first, application at the level of perception. It refers to the application of acquired concepts to help identify specific similar things and classify them into this category. Second, application at the level of thinking. It refers to using concepts to judge and reason about things or reorganizing concepts to meet the needs of solving problems.

2) Changes of wrong concepts

**Conceptual change** is the embodiment of the interaction between new and old experience and the transformation of existing experience by new experience. Conceptual change must first trigger learners' cognitive conflict. Cognitive conflict refers to the state that people feel confused, tense, and uncomfortable when a contradiction arises between their original concept and new experience. Cognitive conflict can be divided into three categories: ① cognitive conflict in direct experience and cognitive conflict in indirect experience; ② conflict between realistic concepts and potential concepts; ③ tit-for-tat cognitive conflict and compatible cognitive conflict.

In order to promote the change of wrong concepts, teaching generally includes three links: ① reveal and gain insight into students' original concepts; ② trigger cognitive conflict; ③ encourage students to adjust their original views and form new concepts through analysis and discussion. The specific implementation measures are as follows: ① create an open and mutually acceptable classroom atmosphere; ② listen and gain insight into students' experience world; ③ trigger cognitive conflict; ④ encourage students to communicate and discuss with each other.

3) Mastery of scientific concepts

Concept mastery refers to the process in which learners transform existing concepts in the mind into individual concepts with the help of words. Whether the concept can be correctly applied is the most reliable sign to measure whether the students really master the concept.

Students' mastery of scientific concepts is affected by many factors, including the following aspects: ① past experience, namely the influence of daily concepts and experience; ② provision of variants; ③ the use of words to help students correctly grasp the concept with the help of word description or language description; ④ accuracy of definitions.

Teaching is the main way to guide students to acquire scientific concepts. Teachers should pay attention to the following aspects when helping students master concepts in the teaching process: ① take perceptual materials as the basis for concept mastery; ② make rational use of existing knowledge and experience; ③ provide conceptual examples, cooperate and use positive and negative examples, and make appropriate use of comparison; ④ highlight relevant features, control the quantity and intensity of irrelevant features, and make full use of "variants" correctly; ⑤ correctly use language expression, clearly prompting the essential characteristics of the concept; ⑥ form a correct concept system and apply it to practice.

2. Judgment

Judgment is a form of thinking that uses concepts to affirm or deny that things have certain attributes and is the reflection in the mind of the connections and relationships between things.

Judgments are mostly made in the form of sentences with the help of language and vocabulary. They are usually expressed in sentences composed of two or more words plus "yes", "no", or "maybe". *For example, "He is a steward" is a positive judgment, while "He is not a steward" is a negative judgment.*

Judgment is divided into direct judgment and indirect judgment. Generally, direct judgment is expressed in the way of perception or specific actions and does not need to be accompanied by the judgment of a complex thinking process, such as "A banana is yellow". Indirect judgment reflects certain internal relations of things, which requires complex thinking in terms of time, space, conditions, or cause and effect of things. Flight attendants will judge the needs of passengers through their expressions, behaviors, and languages. *For example, if a passenger bends over to cover his stomach and moans, the steward will judge that the passenger may have an abdominal issue through analysis.*

### 3. Reasoning

Reasoning is a thinking form of deriving new judgments from known judgments. Reasoning is the basic way for people to know objective things indirectly. Reasoning can be divided into inductive reasoning and deductive reasoning. **Inductive reasoning** is a reasoning process from specific things to general laws. *For example, iron can conduct electricity, copper can conduct electricity, and aluminum can conduct electricity. The conclusion that "metal can conduct electricity" is induced.* **Deductive reasoning** is a reasoning process from general laws to special or concrete things. *For example, all mammals are viviparous, and tigers are mammals, so the conclusion that "tigers are also viviparous" is deduced.*

Reasoning consists of two parts: premise and conclusion. Two requirements for obtaining correct reasoning must be met. One is that the reasoning materials should be true and reliable, and the other is that the reasoning process should be logical. If the reasoning materials are untrue and unreliable, or the reasoning process violates logic, "false reasoning" will occur. From the perspective of psychological factors, there are often two reasons for reasoning errors. One is the effect of atmosphere. That is, the atmosphere formed by the premise makes people draw wrong conclusions regardless of logical steps. The other is the influence of emotional bias. That is, although knowing that the conclusion is wrong, people still believe that the conclusion is correct because the conclusion meets their own emotional requirements.

## 1.7.5 Process of thinking

The general process of thinking includes analysis and synthesis, comparison and classification, abstraction and generalization, systematization and concretization. Analysis and synthesis are the basic processes of thinking, and other processes are derived from them.

### 1. Analysis and synthesis

**Analysis** refers to the decomposition of things or objects into parts or attributes in the mind. *For example, a tree is divided into roots, stems,* *leaves, flowers, etc.*

**Synthesis** is the combination of individual parts or attributes of things or objects in the human brain. *For example, making a short play by connecting one's past and present experiences. The children built a small house out of several building blocks.*

2. Comparison and classification

**Comparison** refers to the thinking process of comparing various things and phenomena in the human brain to determine their similarities, differences, and relationships. There is no identification without comparison. Only through comparison can people distinguish the similarities and differences between things, distinguish the advantages and disadvantages of things, identify things, and classify them into certain categories.

**Classification** is a process of thinking that distinguishes things into different kinds according to their similarities and differences. Comparison is the basis of classification. Things can be divided into larger categories according to their commonalities; things can be divided into smaller categories according to their differences.

3. Abstraction and generalization

**Abstraction** is the process of extracting the common and essential features of various things or phenomena in the human brain and discarding the individual and non-essential features. *For example, summarizing the common and essential characteristics of pigeons, eagles, chickens, ducks, etc., that is, "feather" and "animal"; discarding those non-essential characteristics such as "flying", "color", and "size", etc. This is the abstraction process.*

**Generalization** is a thinking process in which the human brain abstracts and synthesizes the common and essential characteristics of things. *For example, people collectively call those "feathered animals" birds, which is the process of generalization.* Generalization has different grades and levels. Experience generalization is the generalization of the primary level, and scientific generalization is the generalization of the advanced level.

4. Systematization and concretization

**Systematization** refers to the thinking process in which the human brain induces things with the same essential characteristics into a certain category system. *For example, students who have mastered the concept of numbers can* *induce them as rational numbers after they have mastered the knowledge of integers, fractions, and decimals.*

**Concretization** refers to the process in which the human brain popularizes the general characteristics and laws after abstract generalization to the specific affairs of the same kind. *For example, the process of using a mathematical formula to solve a specific application problem.*

The process of cognition is a journey of exploration and discovery. Through this intricate journey, we gather information, form beliefs, and make decisions that guide our interactions and behaviors. As we progress in this journey, let us remain open-minded and eager to learn, for cognition is an endless pursuit that enriches our lives and helps us grow as individuals. Ultimately, the process of cognition is not just about acquiring knowledge but about growing as individuals and contributing meaningfully to society.

## Ⅰ. Review and reflection

- real motion perception
- apparent motion perception
- social stereotypes
- halo effect
- primacy effect
- recency effect
- projection effect
- intensity law
- difference law
- activity law
- combinatorial law
- objective factors
- purpose law
- comprehensiveness of perception
- quality of memory
- agility of memory
- persistence of memory
- accuracy of memory
- readiness of memory
- emotional memory
- action memory
- motion memory
- memory image
- eidetic image
- imaginative image
- individual image
- general image
- unintentional imagination
- involuntary imagination
- clarity
- intelligibility
- breadth and profundity of thinking
- independence (originality) and criticality of thinking
- flexibility and agility of thinking
- logic and preciseness of thinking

intuitive action thinking
concrete image thinking
representation thinking
visualization
integrity
operability
empirical thinking
theoretical thinking
convergent thinking
divergent thinking

re-creative thinking
creative thinking
connotation
denotation
abstraction
generalization
induce
discrimination
concept assimilation

## II. Material analysis

This figure is Ebbinghaus forgetting curve. Please briefly discuss laws of forgetting according to Ebbinghaus forgetting curve. (Refer to Appendix I)

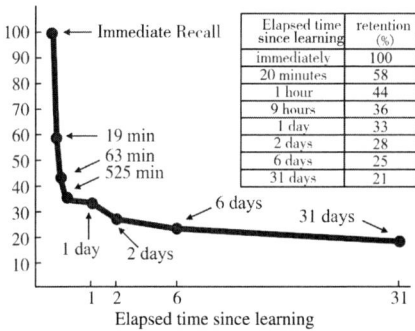

# Chapter 2　Cognitive Development of Primary School Children

*A remarkable story from history involves a young Thomas Edison. As a child, Edison was curious and full of questions. He often conducted small experiments, much to the annoyance of his teachers, who found him disruptive. One day, his mother, recognizing his potential, decided to homeschool him. She encouraged his inquisitive nature and allowed him to explore his interests freely. Edison transformed his home into a laboratory, experimenting with chemicals and electronics. His mother's support fostered his cognitive development, allowing him to learn through hands-on experiences rather than rote memorization. This environment nurtured his creativity and critical thinking skills.*

Edison's story illustrates the importance of supporting cognitive development in primary school children. When educators and parents encourage curiosity and provide opportunities for exploration, children are more likely to engage deeply with their learning. This approach not only enhances their understanding but also instills a lifelong love for discovery. Ultimately, fostering an environment where children can ask questions and experiment is crucial for developing independent thinkers who can innovate and adapt in an ever-changing world.

In this chapter, we will delve into the cognitive development of primary school children. The cognitive development focuses on thought processes and the behavior that reflects those processes. It encompasses both organismic and mechanistically influenced theories. It includes the cognitive-stage theory of Piaget and Vygotsky's sociocultural theory of cognitive development. From the perspectives of Piaget and Vygotsky, the cognitive development of school children in the concrete operation stage is discussed in this section.

## 2.1　Jean Piaget's cognitive-stage theory

The Swiss theoretician Jean Piaget's (1896-1980) cognitive-stage theory was the forerunner of today's "cognitive revolution" with its emphasis on mental processes. Piaget, a biologist and philosopher, viewed development as the product of children's efforts to understand and act on their world. From observations of children, Piaget created a comprehensive theory of cognitive development. Piaget suggested that cognitive development occurs through three interrelated processes: organization, adaptation, and equilibration.

Jean Piaget(1896-1980)

**Organization** is the tendency to create categories, such as birds, by observing the characteristics that individual members of a category, such as sparrows and cardinals, have in common. According to Piaget, people create increasingly complex cognitive structures called **schemes**, ways of organizing information about the world that govern the way the child thinks and behaves in a particular situation. As children acquire more information, their schemes become more and more complex.

**Adaptation** is Piaget's term for how children handle new information in light of what they already know. Adaptation occurs through two complementary processes: ① assimilation, taking in new information and incorporating it into existing cognitive structures, and ② accommodation, adjusting one's cognitive structures to fit the new information.

**Equilibration**, a constant striving for a stable balance or equilibrium, refers to the shift from assimilation to accommodation. When children cannot handle new experiences within their existing cognitive structures, they experience an uncomfortable motivational state known as disequilibrium. *For example, a child knows what birds are and sees a plane for the first time. The child labels the plane a "bird"(assimilation). Over time the child notes differences between planes and birds, which makes him somewhat uneasy (disequilibrium) and motivates him to change his understanding (accommodation) and provide a new label for the plane. He then is at equilibrium.* By organizing new mental and behavioral patterns that integrate the new experience, the child restores equilibrium. Thus assimilation and accommodation work together to produce equilibrium. Throughout life, the quest for equilibrium is the driving force behind cognitive development.

According to Piaget's theory, cognitive development occurs in four universal, qualitatively different stages: the sensorimotor stage (birth to 2 years), the pre-operational stage (2-7 years), the stage of concrete operations (7-11 years) and the stage of formal operations (11 years through adulthood) (refer to Table 2-2). Each stage emerges at a time of disequilibrium, to which the child's mind adapts by learning to think in a new or modified way. From infancy through adolescence, mental operations evolve from learning based on simple sensory and motor activity to logical, abstract thought.

Piaget's observations have yielded much information and some surprising insights. Piaget has shown us that children's minds are not miniature adult minds. Knowing how children think makes it easier for parents and teachers to understand and teach them. Piaget's theory has provided rough benchmarks for what to expect of children at various ages and has helped educators design curricula appropriate to varying levels of development.

## 2.2 Lev Vygotsky's sociocultural theory

The Russian psychologist Lev S. Vygotsky's (1978) sociocultural theory stresses children's active engagement with their environment; and he saw cognitive growth as a collaborative process. Vygotsky focused on the social and cultural processes that guide children's cognitive development. People learn through social interaction and acquire cognitive skills as part of their induction into a way of life. Shared activities help children internalize their society's modes of thinking and behaving and make those

Lev Vygotsky(1896-1934)

folkways their own. The special emphasis was on language, not merely as an expression of knowledge and thought but as an essential means to learning and thinking about the world. According to Vygotsky, adults or more advanced peers must help direct and organize a child's learning before the child can master and internalize it. This guidance is most effective in helping children cross the Zone of Proximal Development (ZPD). According to Vygotsky, children learn by internalizing the results of interactions with adults. This interactive learning is most effective in helping children cross the ZPD, the gap between what they are already able to do and what they are not quite ready to accomplish by themselves. Sensitive and effective instruction should be aimed at the ZPD and increase in complexity as the child's abilities improve. Responsibility for directing and monitoring learning gradually shifts to the child. The metaphor of scaffolds have been applied to this way of teaching.

Vygotsky's theory has important implications for education and for cognitive testing. **Scaffolding** is the temporary support from parents, teachers or advanced peers given to a child in doing a task until the child can do it alone. The ZPD, in combination with the related concept of scaffolding, also can help parents and teachers efficiently guide children's cognitive progress. The less able a child is to do a task, the more scaffolding, or support, an adult must give. As the child can do more and more, the adult helps less and less. When the child can do the job alone, the adult takes away the scaffold that is no longer needed. By enabling children to become aware of and monitor their own cognitive processes and to recognize when they need help, parents can help children take responsibility for learning.

## 2.3 Sensory development of primary school children

Sensation is the lower level of sensory perception, and the beginning of all human psychological activities. Of all the senses, the development of sight and hearing is particularly important.

### 2.3.1 Visual acuity

**Visual acuity** refers to the ability of the visual system to distinguish the smallest objects or details of objects, namely vision. The visual acuity of children before the age of 10 has been continuously improving. The normal visual acuity for children aged 5-7 should be 1.0. The visual development of children aged 8-9 is basically complete. The differential sensitivity of visual acuity in childhood increases more significantly than that of infants. However, the absolute sensitivity of visual acuity increases more slowly in childhood than in early childhood. When children enter primary school, various learning activities cannot be separated from their eyes, and scientific protection of their eyes and correction of vision are very important. In addition, the ability to distinguish colors also improves with age.

## 2.3.2 Hearing

Children's auditory abilities need to develop for many years. Children's ability to distinguish between high and low tones has significantly improved between the ages of 6 and 19. If the ability to distinguish tones is measured in units (unit 1) for 6-year-olds, it is 1.4 for 7-year-olds, 1.6 for 8-year-olds, 2.6 for 9-year-olds, 3.7 for 10-year-olds, and 5.2 for 19-year-olds (Zhu Zhixian, 1993). Children's auditory sensitivity increases before the age of 13, and their auditory ability gradually decreases as they reach adulthood (Peng Xiaohu et al., 2013).

## 2.3.3 Sensation integration

In the primary school education stage, we can see such phenomena: some children look very smart, but it is difficult for them to concentrate in class; some seem to be very sensible but hot-tempered, and they often cry and roll; some look cute, but they are timid and shy, and it is difficult for them to adapt to the new environment; some look clever, but their movements are uncoordinated, clumsy, and it is difficult for them to complete manual activities. These are all signs of sensory disintegration. According to the survey, 80% of young children and primary school children have inattention, hyperactivity, timidity, poor interpersonal relations, language development delay and other behavioral phenomena, which are caused by sensory integration disorders. It can be seen that most primary school students have varying degrees of disorder (Peng Xiaohu et al., 2013).

Sensory integration disorders are caused by an unsound central nervous system, such as developmental delays and mild brain dysfunction. In addition, sensory integration disorders are also related to environmental factors, such as premature birth or caesarean section; limited activity space resulting in insufficient crawling; overprotection or discipline; lack of peer groups; lack of exercise; early cognitive education; children's main toys of TVs and game consoles. Children who suffer from sensory integration disorders must be treated promptly. The best prevention period for sensory integration disorder is before 6 years old, and the best treatment period is 7-10 years old.

## 2.4 Perceptual development of primary school children

Along with the development of sensation, which lays a foundation for the development of perception, the perception also makes corresponding progress in terms of time, space, size, motor and shape.

### 2.4.1 The development of time perception

Time perception refers to the reflection of the duration, speed, and sequence of objective things in the mind. We usually perceive time through biological clocks, the rise and fall of the sun, the alternation of the four seasons, calendars, clocks, and other means. A 7-year-old child may initially be able to use a time ruler, but their level of use is not high. An 8-year-old child is generally able to actively use a time ruler, and the accuracy of time perception is close to that of adults. After children enter school, they begin to estimate the time they have experienced under the guidance of educational activities, such as a class, a day, a week, a month, one semester, one year, etc. Time perception is directly proportional to children's age and experience. As children age, their time perception gradually stabilizes, and the accuracy and initiative of their time perception will be greatly improved.

### 2.4.2 Development of spatial perception

Newly enrolled children are not yet proficient in perception of orientation, and often perceive direction according to their body position. It is easy for them to distinguish between front and back, up and down, but difficult to distinguish right and left. When learning to write, they often make mistakes about the orientation of Chinese Pinyin or numbers, *such as writing p as q, d as b, 2 as s, 8 as ∞ and so on.*

Their perception of spatial relationship develops rather significantly. Many 7-year-olds can find their way from house to school and from school to house, while most 4-year-olds cannot. Why? Because children in the stage of concrete operations can better understand spatial relationships. Both the ability to use maps and models and the ability to communicate spatial information improve with age (Gauvain, 1993). A child in the stage of concrete operations can use a map or model to help his/her search for a hidden object and can give someone else directions for finding the object. He/She can find his/her way to and from school, can estimate distances, and can judge how long it will take him/her to go from one place to another. He/She has a clearer idea of how far it is from one place to another and how long it will take him/her to get there, and he/she can more easily remember the route and the buildings along the way. His/Her experience plays a role in this development. A child who walks to school becomes more familiar with the neighborhood.

## 2.4.3 The development of size perception

After entering school, children mainly rely on intuition to compare the size of the shapes in first-grade mathematics, that is, through visual observation. *For example, children can judge the size of two circles at a glance.* As children grow older, primary school children's ability to distinguish the size of objects or shapes has transitioned from intuitive judgment to using reasoning to make judgments. *For example, in mathematics teaching, the size of the remaining area can be inferred by comparing it with the occupied area.* In terms of the ability to judge the size of the picture space, 7-8 year old children are in the transitional stage of the intersection of intuitive judgment and reasoning judgment, and more than 85% of primary school senior children have been able to use reasoning judgment to compare the size of space and area (Peng Xiaohu et al., 2013).

## 2.4.4 The development of shape perception

Elementary school children always associate shape perception with specific objects. *For example, they often refer to a square as handkerchief and a circle as ball.* Through planned mathematical learning, children will further develop their ability to perceive shapes, recognize shapes and master geometric concepts, and thus they can detach themselves from specific things and recognize the general characteristics of shapes.

## 2.4.5 The development of kinesthetic perception

Kinesthetic perception refers to the reflection of the human brain on the changes of position and speed of objects. When primary school children enter school, their basic movement skills, such as running, jumping, flipping, etc., can be completed freely, but the development of subtle movements is not sound, and the coordination of movements is not good, especially when learning to write, draw, and do manual work, which is very obvious. In the process of primary school teaching, attention should be paid to protecting and developing children's kinesthetic perception. Children should be required to write with a pencil first and then use a pen when the pencil is used freely, to practice the stroke order of new characters to enhance the accuracy of movement, and to practice writing with square-grid paper first, then with square paper, and finally with horizontal script paper to steadily develop their kinesthetic perception.

## 2.5 Memory development of primary school children

Primary school children's memory develops on the basis of early childhood, but after entering primary school, their memory and memory strategies undergo essential changes. As children move through the school years, and their knowledge expands, children become more aware of what kinds of information are important to pay attention to and remember. School-age children also understand more about how memory works, and this knowledge enables them to plan and use strategies, or deliberate techniques, to help them remember.

### 2.5.1 Development of memory

#### 1. The development of working memory

The efficiency of working memory increases greatly in middle childhood (i. e. primary school stage), laying the foundation for a wide range of cognitive skills. Because working memory is necessary to store information while other material is being mentally manipulated, the capacity of a child's working memory can directly affect his or her academic success (Alloway, 2006). Children with low working memory struggle with structured learning activities and have difficulty following lengthy instructions (Gathercole & Alloway, 2008). Individual differences in working memory capacity are linked to a child's ability to acquire knowledge and new skills (Alloway, 2006). The adoption of tools that assess working memory in the classroom can greatly influence achievement levels for children with low working memory.

## 2. Development of meaningful memory

Both the rote memory and meaningful memory abilities of primary school children are steadily increasing. Lower graders mainly use rote memory methods, *such as reciting multiplication tables*, while third and fourth graders' meaningful memory gradually surpasses rote memory, so middle and upper graders mostly adopt meaningful memory methods.

## 3. The development of intentional memory

Primary school students' ability of unintentional and intentional memory will increase with age, but the growth rate of intentional memory is more obvious. The development from predominance of unintentional memory in preschool to predominance of intentional memory is a significant feature of primary school students' memory development.

## 4. The development of image memory and semantic memory

Lower graders' image memory is obviously better than their semantic memory, and they are good at memorizing specific things, but they are not good at memorizing formulas, rules, laws, etc. With the continuous deepening of education, the growth of age and the further improvement of learning tasks, primary school children not only need remember some specific facts or images, but also remember some concepts, formulas, principles, and children's semantic memory has developed.

## 5. The development of metamemory

Between ages 5 and 7, the brain's frontal lobes undergo significant development and reorganization. These changes may make **metamemory**, which is knowledge about the processes of memory, improved possibly, (Janowsky & Carper, 1996). From kindergarten through fifth grade, children advance steadily in understanding memory (Kreutzer, Leonard, & Flavell, 1975). Kindergartners and first graders know that people remember better if they study longer, that people forget things with time, and that relearning something is easier than learning it for the first time. By third grade, children know that some people remember better than others and that some things are easier to remember than others.

## 2.5.2 Development of memory strategies

The memory of primary school children has been greatly developed not only because of the physical development and the clear purpose of learning, but also because of the gradual adoption of memory strategies(Table 2-1).

Table 2-1  Four common memory strategies

| Strategy | Definition | Development in middle childhood (i.e. stage of primary school) | Example |
| --- | --- | --- | --- |
| External memory aids | Prompting by something outside the person | 5- and 6-year-olds can do this, but 8-year-olds are more likely to think of it. | Dana makes a list of the things she has to do today. |
| Rehearsal | Conscious repetition | 6-year-olds can be taught to do this; 7-year-olds do it spontaneously. | Ian says the letters in his spelling words over and over until he knows them. |
| Organization | Grouping by categories | Most children do not do this until at least age 10, but younger children can be taught to do it. | Luis recalls the animals he saw in the zoo by thinking first of the mammals, then the reptiles, then the amphibians, then the fish, and then the birds. |
| Elaboration | Associating items to be remembered with something else such as a phrase, scene, or story. | Older children are more likely to do this spontaneously and remember better if they make up their own elaboration; younger children remember better if someone else makes it up. | Yolanda remembers the lines of the musical staff (E, G, B, D, F) by associating them with the phrase "Every Good Boy Does Fine." |

Sourse: Diane E. Papalia & Ruth D. Feldman, *Experience Human Development* (12th), Posts & Telecom Press, 2014, p.299.

**External memory aids** refer to prompts by something outside the person. *For example, writing down a telephone number, making a list, setting a timer, and putting a library book by the front door.* Saying a telephone number over and over after looking it up, so as not to forget it before dialing, is a form of **rehearsal**, or conscious repetition. It is not until primary school that children gradually learn and use this method effectively. Around the age of 7, children transition from not repeating to spontaneously repeating. *Sometimes mothers ask elementary school children to buy some daily necessities on their way home from school. To prevent accidents, children keep reciting in their minds several times.* **Organization** means mentally placing information into categories (such as animals, furniture, vehicles, and clothing) to make it easier to recall. Children will categorize and organize materials when extracting information. *When learning about animals, elementary school students will classify them according to "meat-eating animals" and "grass-eating animals".* In elaboration, children associate items with something else, such as an imagined scene or story. *To remember to buy lemons, ketchup, and napkins, for example, a child might visualize a ketchup bottle balanced on a lemon, with a pile of napkins handy to wipe up any spills.*

## 2.6　Thinking development of primary school children

Primary school children in the middle childhood have entered the stage of formal operations, and their thinking has changed a lot compared with early childhood.

### 2.6.1　Piaget's cognitive-stage theory

Our understanding of how children think owes a great deal to the work of the Swiss theoretician Jean Piaget. In asking why children answered questions the way that they did, Piaget realized that children of the same ages made similar types of errors in logic. From his observations of his own and other children, Piaget created a comprehensive theory of cognitive development. Piaget suggested that cognitive development begins with an inborn ability to adapt to the environment. By rooting for a nipple, feeling a pebble, or exploring the boundaries of a bed, young children develop a more accurate picture of their surroundings and greater competence in dealing with them. According to Piaget, children's cognitive development experience four stages (Table 2-2).

Table 2-2　Piaget's stages of cognitive development

| Stage | Characteristic | Example |
| --- | --- | --- |
| Sensorimotor stage (birth to 2 years) | Infants gradually become able to organize activities in relation to the environment through sensor and motor activity. The typical characteristic of this stage is that children's thinking and actions are closely linked. | *when babies see a toy on a table, they will try to reach for it.* |
| Preoperational stage (2 to 7 years) | Children develop a representational system and use symbols to represent people, places, and events. Language and imaginative play are important manifestations of this stage. Thinking is still not logical. The characteristic of this stage is that children are able to engage in internal thinking, rather than relying solely on their senses and movements. | *When children are playing games, they can use a wooden stick to represent a pet dog.* "妾发初覆额，折花门前剧。郎骑竹马来，绕床弄青梅。"（《长干行》李白） |

**Continued table**

| Stage | Characteristic | Example |
|---|---|---|
| Stage of concrete operations (7 to 11 years) | Children can solve problems logically if they are focused on the here and now but cannot think abstractly. The characteristic of this stage is that children begin to possess certain abstract thinking abilities and are able to solve real-life problems. | When children learn addition and subtraction, they can use specific objects or shapes to solve problems. |
| Stage of formal operations (11 years through adulthood) | People can think abstractly, deal with hypothetical situations, and think about possibilities. The characteristic of this stage is that children have the same logical thinking ability as adults and are able to engage in advanced thinking activities. | When children learn science, they can design experiments to verify their hypotheses. |

Source: Diane E. Papalia & Ruth D. Feldman, *Experience Human Development* (12th), Posts & Telecom Press, 2014, p. 30.

## 2.6.2 Achievement of thinking development in the stage of concrete operations

According to Piaget's cognitive-stage theory, children in the stage of concrete operations (7 to 11 years, i.e. stage of primary school) have a better development than children in preoperational stage of spatial concepts, causality, categorization, inductive and deductive reasoning, conservation, and number.

1. Development of seriation and transitive inference

Children show that they understand seriation when they can arrange objects in a series according to one or more dimensions, such as weight (lightest to heaviest) or color (lightest to darkest). By 7 or 8, children can grasp the relationships among a group of sticks on sight and arrange them in order of size (Piaget, 1952). *For example, Angelababy can arrange a group of sticks in order, from the shortest to the longest, and can insert an intermediate-size stick into the proper place. She knows that if one stick is longer than a second stick, and the second stick is longer than a third, then the first stick is longer than the third.* **Transitive inference** is the ability to infer a relationship between two objects from the relationship between each of them and a third object. *For example, if a//b and b//c, then a//c. For another, Lao Zi was earlier than Confucius, and Confucius was earlier than Mencius, so Lao Zi was earlier than Mencius.*

2. Development of cause and effect

Judgments about cause and effect also improve. A primary school child in the stage of concrete operations knows which physical attributes of objects on each side of a balance scale will affect the result. *For instance, number of objects matters but color does not.* He or she does not yet know which spatial factors, such as position and placement of the objects, make a difference. When 5- to 12-year-olds are asked to predict how levers and balance scales will perform under varying conditions, the older children give more correct answers. They understand the influence of physical attributes (the number of objects on each side of a scale) earlier than they recognize the influence of spatial factors (the distance of objects from the center of the scale) (Amsel, Goodman, Savoie, & Clark, 1996).

### 3. Development of categorization

**Categorization** refers to the ability to categorize that helps children think logically. Categorization includes such relatively sophisticated abilities as seriation, transitive inference, and class inclusion, which improve gradually between early and middle childhood. *For example, Clinton can sort objects into categories, such as shape, color, or both. He knows that a subclass (roses) has fewer members than the class (flowers) of which it is a part.*

### 4. The development of inductive and deductive reasoning

According to Piaget, children in the stage of concrete operations (7 to 11 years, i.e. stage of primary school) use only **inductive reasoning**. Starting with observations about particular members of a class of people, animals, objects, or events, they draw general conclusions about the class as a whole: "Our geese can't fly. Neither can Feng Chengcheng's geese and Zhou Xingxing's geese. So, it seems that all geese can't fly." **Deductive reasoning** starts with a general statement (premise) about a class and applies it to particular members of the class. If the premise is true of the whole class and the reasoning is sound, then the conclusion must be true: "All geese can't fly. Sima Bei is a goose, so Sima Bei can't fly." Researchers found second graders were able to answer both inductive and deductive problems correctly indicating that given age-appropriate tasks, these reasoning abilities developed early (Galotti, Komatsu, & Voelz, 1997).

### 5. The development of conservation

In solving various types of conservation problems, children in the stage of concrete operations (7 to 11 years, i.e. stage of primary school) can work out the answers in their heads; they do not have to measure or weigh the objects. If one of two identical clay balls is rolled or kneaded into a different shape—say, a long, thin sausage—Bob, who is in the stage of concrete operations, will say that the ball and the "sausage" still contain the same amount of clay. Lili, who is in the preoperational stage (2 to 7 years), is deceived by appearances. She says the long, thin roll contains more clay because it looks longer. Bob, unlike Lili, understands the principle of identity: he knows the clay is still the same clay, even though it has a different shape. He also understands the principle of *reversibility*: he knows he can change the sausage back into a ball. And he can *decenter*: he can focus on both length and width. He recognizes that although the ball is shorter than the sausage, it is also thicker. Lili centers on one dimension (length) while excluding the other (thickness) (Table 2-3).

Typically, children can solve problems involving conservation of substance, like this one, by about age 7 or 8. However, in tasks involving conservation of weight—*in which they are asked, for example, whether the ball and the "sausage" weigh the same*—children typically do not give correct answers until about age 9 or 10. In tasks involving conservation of volume—*in which children must judge whether the sausage and the ball displace an equal amount of liquid when placed in a glass of water*—correct answers are rare before age 12. Children's thinking at this stage is so concrete, so closely tied to a particular situation, that they cannot readily transfer what they have learned about one type of conservation to another type, even though the underlying principles are the same.

Table 2-3  The approximate age at which various types of conservation are achieved

| Conservation task | Conservation age | Equivalent objects | Change | Conservation question |
|---|---|---|---|---|
| Number conservation: Rearranging the spatial position of objects, but the numbers keep constant. | 6-8 years old | | | |
| | | Are there as many white circles as black ones, or… | | |
| Length conservation: a straight line becomes an irregular curve, but the length keeps constant. | 6-8 years old | | | |
| | | Does an ant walk the same distance on both roads? | | |
| Conservation of liquid: the size of the container changes, but the volume of liquid keeps constant. | 6.5-8.5 years old | | | |
| | | Is there the same amount of water in the two glasses, or… | | |
| Conservation of solid quantity: the shape of the mud block changes, but the quantity keeps constant. | 7-9 years old | | | |
| | | Are these two pieces of mud the same amount, or… | | |
| Conservation of area: the spatial positions of objects that occupy the same area are rearranged on the ground, but their area remains unchanged. | 8-10 years old | | | |
| | | Two houses were built on a grassland. | The location of the house has changed, is there as much grass around it as before, or… | |

**Continued table**

| Conservation task | Conservation age | Equivalent objects | Change | Conservation question |
|---|---|---|---|---|
| Conservation of weight: when the shape of a piece of mud on the balance changes, the balance remains in balance. | 9-10 years old | | ➡ | |
| | | Are these two pieces of mud still the same weight? | | |
| Volume conservation: The volume of water is easily affected by the volume of the object submerged in water, but not by its position, as well as its shape and weight. | 11-12 years old | | ➡ | |
| | | Is the water surface rising as high as before, or… | | |

Sourse: Holmas D. B. & Turner J. S., *Exploring Child Behaviour*, Brooks/Cole Publishing Company Monterey, 1986, p.350.

Bob, at age 7, knows that if a clay ball is rolled into a "sausage", it still contains the same amount of clay (conservation of substance). At age 9, he knows that the ball and the "sausage" weigh the same. Not until early adolescence will he understand that they displace the same amount of liquid if dropped in a glass of water.

### 6. Development of number and mathematics

By age 6 or 7, many children can count in their heads. They also learn to count on: $5+3=?$ They start counting at 5 and then go on to 6, 7, and 8, thus they solve the problem. It may take 2 or 3 more years for them to perform a comparable operation for subtraction, but by age 9 most children can either count up from the smaller number or down from the larger number to get the answer (Resnick, 1989). *For example, 7-year-old Lili can count in her head, can add by counting up from the smaller number, and can do simple story problems.*

Children also become more able to solve simple story problems, *such as "Lili went to the supermarket with ￥10 and spent ￥4 on candy. How much has she left?"* When the original amount is unknown—*"Lili went to the store, spent ￥3 and had ￥7 left. How much did Lili have* originally?"—the problem is harder because the operation to solve the problem (addition) is not as clearly indicated. Few children can solve this kind of problem before age 8 or 9 (Resnick, 1989).

The ability to estimate progresses with age. When asked to place 24 numbers along a line from 0 to 100, almost all kindergartners exaggerate the distances between low numbers and minimize the distances between high numbers. Most second graders produce number lines that are more evenly spaced (Siegler & Booth, 2004). Second, fourth, and sixth graders show a similar progression in producing number lines from 0 to 1,000 (Siegler & Opfer, 2003), most likely reflecting the experience older children gain in dealing with larger numbers.

School-age children also improve in three other types of estimation: computational estimation, such as estimating the sum in an addition problem; numerosity estimation, such as estimating the number of candies in a jar; and measurement estimation, such as estimating the length of a line (Booth & Siegler, 2006)

## 2.7 Imagination development of primary school children

Pupils can imagine according to the teacher's requirements, showing some voluntariness. *For example, they can read aloud with expression, can draw according to the teacher's description, and can construct and write essays around certain themes.* However, their imagination is often passive, and easy to be interfered by external factors to break away from the theme of imagination, and their imaginative content is often relatively simple.

## 2.8 Attention development of primary school children

The development of pupils' unintentional attention precedes that of their intentional attention, and the development transitions from unintentional attention to intentional attention, which is mainly manifested in the dominance of unintentional attention of primary school lower graders. However, with age and the maturity of the brain, intentional attention gradually forms and develops.

### 2.8.1 Unintentional attention prevails and intentional attention develops

Before the age of three, children's attention is largely unintentional. After the age of three, children enter kindergarten and begin to receive preschool education, and intentional attention gradually appears. After entering primary school, the unintentional attention of primary school lower graders has become rather mature and plays an important role in their cognitive activities. Concrete, vivid, interesting and intuitive things can easily attract their attention. As a result, intuitive teaching can better attract students' unintentional attention and achieve better teaching results.

As children age, they are increasingly able to control their attention, focus their attention on the target information of the task, and get rid of distracting stimuli (Miller & Weiss, 1981). Primary school children begin to be able to organize and control their attention independently, but their intentional attention still lacks self-awareness, and thus they often do not understand or forget the purpose of given tasks. The intentional attention of fifth graders has improved more than that of second graders. With continuous learning and improvement of knowledge, pupils' word-based second signal system and abstract logical thinking ability gradually develop, and their attention to materials with a certain level of abstraction gradually develops (Zhu Xiufang, 1986).

Pupils are easily attracted and excited by novel and interesting things, and their external manifestations of attention are obvious, often revealing various emotional colors. *For example, if students listen attentively in the classroom, they will show a solemn demeanor; if they listen happily, they will show a joyful smile, and even dance happily.*

### 2.8.2 Development of quality of attention

In class, some students listen attentively; some students look here and there; some students are careless and slow; others are not disturbed easily. In fact, these are the external manifestations of different attention qualities in primary school students. The quality of attention includes the span, stability, distribution and shifting of attention.

#### 1. Development of attention span

The attention span of primary school children is relatively narrow, and it gradually expands with the growth of age and rich experience. *For example, when children in lower grades are reading, they often read word by word with their fingers pointing to them. When calculating the addition of several numbers, they will forget the calculation they just did in the first step when starting the second step.* Due to the weak abstract thinking ability, primary school students are not good at finding the correlation between things, which affects pupils' attention span.

#### 2. Development of stability of attention

The stability of attention refers to the duration of attention on a certain thing or activity. The time of concentration gradually increases with age: 5- and

7-year-old children can concentrate for about 10 minutes; 5- and 7-year-olds for about 15 minutes or so; 7- and 10-year-olds for around 20 minutes; 10- and 12-year-olds for around 25 minutes; 13-year-olds and above for about 30 minutes (Peng Xiaohu, et al., 2013). Of course, the time of concentration is not absolute.

The stability of children's intentional attention from first grade to third grade begins to develop rapidly, but the friendship stability of girls has always been higher than that of boys (Ling Guangming, 2001).

### 3. Development of distribution of attention

Pupils' attention distribution ability is still relatively low in general, and it is difficult for them to take into account two things at the same time. Lower graders in primary school, especially the first grade children, can only focus their attention on an object at the same time, and they can not effectively distribute attention. Primary school children find it difficult to take notes while listening to class, especially lower grade children who often tend to care for one thing and lose the other.

### 4. Development of shifting of attention

As they age, primary school children are more and more able to actively shift their attention to constantly changing tasks of objectives according to task requirements. *For example, when reviewing English words, they focus more attention on unfamiliar English words.* They can actively and flexibly shift their attention from one object (one activity) to another object (another activity) based on a certain purpose (Fang Fuxi & Fang Ge, 2004). Primary school teachers, especially those in lower grades, should attach importance to organizing teaching and use intuitive teaching methods to attract students' unintentional attention, so as to realize the shifting of attention.

### 5. Development of selectivity of attention

School-age children can concentrate longer than younger children and can focus on the information they need and want while screening out irrelevant information. *For example, they can summon up from memory the appropriate meaning of a word and suppress other meanings that do not fit the context.* Fifth graders are better able than first graders to keep unwanted information from reentering working memory and vying with other material for attention (Harnishfeger & Pope, 1996). This growth of selective attention—the ability to deliberately direct one's attention and shut out distractions—may hinge on the executive skill of inhibitory control, the voluntary suppression of unwanted responses (Luna et al., 2004). Older children may make fewer mistakes in recall than younger children because they are better able to select what they want to remember and what they can forget (Lorsbach & Reimer, 1997).

## 2.9 Language development of primary school children

Language abilities continue to grow during middle childhood. School-age children are better able to understand and interpret oral and written communication and to make themselves understood. The development of children's language in middle childhood is specifically manifested in three aspects: vocabulary development, sentence development, and pragmatic ability development. Many children during this period start learning a second language on the basis of mastering their mother tongue.

### 2.9.1 Development of vocabulary

Children's vocabulary expands rapidly after entering school. A foreign study shows that children can master approximately 10000 words by the age of 6, and 40000 words by the time they graduate from primary school (Anglin, 1993). Chinese first and second graders know 1600 to 1800 Chinese characters, of which 800 to 1000 they can write. Third and fourth graders have accumulated 2500 commonly used Chinese characters, of which about 2000 they can write. Fifth and sixth graders have strong independent literacy skills, and have a cumulative knowledge of 3000 commonly used Chinese characters, of which about 2500 they can write (Peng Xiaohu, 2013).

The expansion of children's vocabulary is due to the enhancement of word formation ability and the acquisition of written language. *For example*, "公" *refers to male animals and* "母" *means female animals. Children who understand these meanings are naturally able to understand and construct new words, such as* "公牛", "公鸡", "公羊", "公猪", "母牛", "母鸡", "母羊", "母猪". Children can also construct vocabulary through association. *For example, they can associate* "yellow", "green", *and* "purple" *through the word* "red", *as well as* "red flag", "red car", *and* "red book".

As vocabulary grows during the school years, children use increasingly precise verbs. They learn that a word like *run* can have more than one meaning, and they can tell what meaning is intended from the context. Simile and metaphor, figures of speech in which a word or phrase that usually designates one thing is compared or applied to another, become increasingly common (Owens, 1996; Vosniadou, 1987).

### 2.9.2 Development of sentence

The development of sentences mainly involves syntactic development. After entering school, with the gradual acquisition of written language and the improvement of reading and writing ability, children become more and more proficient in mastering Chinese grammar rules, which is obviously reflected in the understanding of passive sentences (Fang Fuxi & Fang Ge, 2004).

Although grammar is quite complex by age 6, children during the early school years rarely use the passive voice (as in "The sidewalk is being shoveled") (Diane E. Papalia & Ruth D. Feldman, 2014). Kindergarteners have no difficulty understanding active sentences like "the dog stole meat", while they sometimes feel confused about the meaning of passive sentences like "the meat was stolen by the dog". 9-year-old children have the ability to convert active sentences into passive ones. By the age of 11, they can choose the correct answer for almost all forms of passive sentences.

Children's understanding of rules of syntax (how words are organized into phrases and sentences) becomes more sophisticated with age (Chomsky, 1969). Sentence structure continues to become more elaborate. Older children use more subordinate clauses ("The boy who delivers the newspapers rang the doorbell.").

Still, some constructions, such as clauses beginning with *however* and *although*, do not become common until early adolescence (Owens, 1996).

### 2.9.3 Development of pragmatic ability

The major area of linguistic growth during the school years is in **pragmatics**: the ability to effectively utilize language in communication. Pragmatics includes both conversational and narrative skills.

1. Development of oral language

On the basis of preschool oral language development, children's monologue language begins to rapidly develop. After entering primary school, due to learning requirements, monologue language gradually becomes the main form of oral language, such as answering teachers' questions and speaking at class meetings.

They can describe their ideas in more detail to help to make themselves understood accurately. *For example, preschool children usually give vague and unclear descriptions of the items they choose, such as "I want the red one", while the descriptions of the first graders have become more detailed and clear, such as "I want the red, round, and striped one".*

Elementary school children are already able to use more effective strategies in conversations with others. They quickly recognize a breakdown in communication and do something to repair it. *For example, five-year-old Kangkang cries and shouts when others fail to meet his demands. However, when the 8-year-old Mingming asked his mother to hand him a piece of watermelon, she ignored him as she noticed that the piece in his hand had not been eaten clean. So he said politely, "I'm sorry, I'm really thirsty. I'll eat up this piece first." Mom immediately handed him another piece. When facing with rejection, he was able to make his second request in a more gentle and polite way.*

When first graders tell stories, they often relate a personal experience. Most 6-year-olds can retell the plot of a short book, movie, or television show. They are beginning to describe motives and causal links. By second grade, children's stories become longer and more complex. Fictional tales often have conventional beginnings and endings ("Once upon a time ..." and "They lived happily ever after," or simply "The end"). Word use is more varied than before, but characters do not show growth or change and plots are not fully developed. Older children usually set the stage with introductory information about the setting and characters, and they clearly indicate changes of time and place during the story. They construct more complex episodes than younger children do, but with less unnecessary detail. They focus more on the characters' motives and thoughts, and they think through how to resolve problems in the plot (Diane E. Papalia & Ruth D. Feldman, 2014).

2. Development of written language

Learning to read and write—a major goal of the primary curriculum—frees children from the constraints of face-to-face communication, giving them access to the ideas and imagination of people in faraway lands and long-ago times. Once children can translate the symbols on a page into patterns of sound and meaning, they can develop increasingly sophisticated strategies to understand what they read; and they can use written words to express ideas, thoughts, and feelings.

The development of written language of primary school children is mainly reflected in their literacy, reading, writing, and mastery of grammar.

1) Literacy runs through the entire primary school stage and even in secondary school. First grade, third grade, and eighth grade are key age groups, and the difference between the most and least literacy is particularly obvious.

2) Reading is a complicated process. The acquisition of writing skills goes hand in hand with the development of reading. Through the internal language, children use their own words to understand and transform the original text, so as to turn the original thoughts into their own thoughts. To achieve this process, children must achieve a level of proficiency in writing. Children's first reading activity can only be reading aloud.

3) Writing is the advanced form and process of written language, which mainly involves transitioning from spoken words to written words. Writing is difficult for young children. At the beginning of school, children do not consciously engage in writing, are not good at consciously organizing their language activities, and cannot consider their writing content and methods based on the characteristics of the target audience. The development of writing ability in primary school goes through three stages: preparation stage (i. e. oral stage), transition stage (transition from oral to written, i. e. writing oral content in written form; transition from reading to writing, such as imitating writing, rewriting, and abbreviating), and independent writing stage (Writing requires the child to judge independently whether the communicative goal has been that. The child must keep in mind a variety of other constraints: spelling, pronunciation, grammar and capitalization).

## 2.9.4 Development of second-language learning

Most children in China start learning a second language (mainly English) in primary school. By the time they graduate from elementary school, they have been still just inexperienced bilinguals (persons who are fluent in two languages).

Some children's parents are proficient bilinguals. This kind of families use an **English-immersion approach** (sometimes called ESL, or English as a second language), in which children are immersed in English from the beginning, and they have grown up in bilingual environments. By the time they enter primary school, they have already been able to speak two languages fluently. Some schools use the English-immersion approach, in which language-minority children are immersed in English from the beginning, in special classes, and they have grown up in bilingual environments. Other schools have adopted programs of bilingual education, in which children are taught in two languages, first learning in their native language with others who speak it and then switching to regular classes in English when they become more proficient in it. These programs can encourage children to become bilingual and to feel pride in their cultural identity.

Advocates of early English immersion claim that the sooner children are exposed to English and the more time they spend speaking it, the better they learn it. The research has shown that proficient bilingual children score higher than monolingual children in tests of analytical reasoning, concept formation, and cognitive flexibility (Hakuta, et al., 1987). Statistical analyses of multiple studies conclude that children in bilingual programs typically outperform those in all-English programs on tests of English proficiency (Crawford, 2007; Krashen & McField, 2005). The learning of the second language enhances the child's language awareness and promotes the child's ability to analyze the language. Therefore, second language education should not only be strengthened, but also be advanced, and where possible, the earlier the better (Fang Fuxi & Fang Ge, 2004).

In conclusion, cognitive development in primary school children is a crucial aspect of their overall growth and learning. During these formative years, children transition from concrete thinking to more abstract reasoning, allowing them to tackle complex problems and engage in critical thinking. This development is influenced by various factors, including their environment, interactions with peers and adults, and educational practices. Encouraging curiosity and providing stimulating experiences can significantly enhance cognitive skills. Educators and parents play a vital role in fostering an environment that promotes exploration and creativity. It is essential to recognize that each child develops at their own pace, and tailored support can help them reach their full potential.

It is imperative to implement strategies that nurture these skills in primary school settings. We prepare children not only for academic success but also for lifelong learning and adaptability in an ever-changing world. As children progress through primary school, their expanding cognitive abilities pave the way for more complex learning and lifelong intellectual curiosity.

# Ⅰ. Review and reflection

| | |
|---|---|
| organization | metamemory |
| schemes | external memory aids |
| adaptation | rehearsal |
| assimilation | organization |
| accommodation | seriation |
| equilibration | transitive inference |
| zone of proximal development | categorization |
| ZPD | inductive reasoning |
| scaffolding | deductive reasoning |
| visual acuity | English-immersion approach |
| hearing | bilingual education |
| sensation integration | |

# Ⅱ. Material analysis

Please use Piaget's cognitive-stage theory to analyze the performance of the "妾" described in the poem. (Refer to Appendix Ⅰ)

**长干行**

*李白*

妾发初覆额,折花门前剧。
郎骑竹马来,绕床弄青梅。

# Chapter 3  Cognitive Development of Middle School Children

*Consider the case of a middle school student named Malala. Initially, Malala struggled with math and often felt discouraged. However, her teacher introduced project-based learning, allowing students to apply math concepts to real-life problems, like budgeting for a school event. As Malala engaged in this project, she began to see math not just as abstract numbers but as a tool for making decisions. She collaborated with classmates, shared ideas, and learned to approach problems from different angles. This hands-on experience sparked her curiosity and boosted her confidence. Over time, Malala's cognitive abilities flourished. She developed critical thinking skills, learned to analyze data, and became adept at problem-solving. By the end of the project, she not only excelled in math but also gained a deeper understanding of teamwork and communication.* Malala's story illustrates the significance of fostering cognitive development in middle school children. Providing opportunities for active learning and collaboration encourages students to think critically and creatively. This growth mindset not only enhances academic performance but also equips them with essential life skills for the future.

It is cognitive development that explains why children answer questions in this way and not in that way, according to Piaget's stages of cognitive development, including the sensorimotor stage (birth to 2 years), preoperational stage (2 to 7 years), concrete operational stage (7 to 11 years), and formal operational stage (11 years to adulthood). Elementary school children in the concrete operational stage are able to use mental operations, such as reasoning, to solve concrete (actual) problems, but their thinking is still limited to real situations in the here and now. Middle school students' thinking may start to become not confined to the here and now; they begin to imagine various possibilities with abstract thinking, see things as either black or white, and analyze and solve problems from various aspects. What makes middle and primary school students think so differently? We mainly discuss the characteristics of middle school students' cognitive development and the influencing factors in this chapter.

## 3.1 Development of middle school children's sensation, perception and observation

Compared with pupils, middle school children's observational ability has improved greatly, especially in the voluntariness, persistence, accuracy, and generality of their observations, with some perceptions even surpassing those of adults. They can observe not only the surface features of things but also the essential features.

### 3.1.1 Development of middle school children's sensation

Compared to elementary school children, middle school children develop better sensitivity and observation skills. With the continuous improvement of visual perception, the accuracy of distinguishing various colors and chromaticity is also increasing. Compared to first-grade elementary school children, middle school children have improved their accuracy in distinguishing various shades by over 60%. Around the age of 15, their visual and auditory sensitivity can even surpass that of adults. The ability of middle school children to distinguish pitch is also constantly improving, and they have a high level of accuracy in distinguishing scales.

### 3.1.2 Development of middle school children's perception

As their sensory abilities develop, adolescents' perceptual abilities have also improved greatly. Middle school children have significantly enhanced their perception of intention and purpose and are able to consciously perceive relevant things according to teaching requirements. The accuracy and generality of their perception are further developed, and logical perception appears. Due to their greater abstractness in spatial perception, they can proficiently grasp three-dimensional spatial relationships, leading to the gradual formation of long-distance spatial perception.

Middle school students are able to master various geographical spatial relationships and form spatial representations such as longitude and latitude, the Earth, and the universe. However, they still have difficulty dealing with more complex spatial relationships. In terms of time perception, junior middle school children can more accurately understand shorter time units, such as months, weeks, hours, and minutes; however, for larger historical time units such as "centuries" and "decades", although they can begin to understand them, they are often not very accurate, while senior middle school children can achieve this.

Middle school students can quickly separate the perceptual object from the background, allowing for a correct understanding of things, which indicates that their perceptual selectivity has developed significantly. All the factors that affect the development of adolescents' attention influence their choice of perceptual objects, such as the intuitiveness and novelty of perceptual things, as well as the children's own interests, needs, and motivations.

In terms of perceptual wholeness, middle school children have already developed characteristics of global perception. In teaching activities or daily life, they can address certain deficiencies in things. However, due to limitations in knowledge and life experience, they often ignore weak stimuli and pay too much attention to strong stimuli, resulting in incomplete or even incorrect responses.

Due to the limitations of the development level of logical thinking, the perceptual constancy of junior middle school children develops less than that of senior middle school children. Junior middle school children are easily troubled by partial and one-sided stimuli and cannot reflect objective things stably. Senior middle school children are more capable of grasping the essential characteristics of things, using a variety of concepts, theorems, or laws flexibly, and comprehending by analogy and drawing inferences about other cases from one instance.

In terms of perceptual organization, middle school children can combine, supplement, delete, or replace things according to their experience, forming a relatively complete understanding. However, junior middle school children naively and rawly use these processing methods, relying largely on their own subjective imagination, which sometimes makes their understanding of knowledge seem far-fetched.

### 3.1.3 Development of middle school children's observation

The core of perceptual ability is the ability to observe, which directly affects middle school children's learning and academic achievement. Therefore, the characteristics of the development of middle school children's observational ability represent the developed level of their perceptual ability to some extent.

Voluntariness, purposefulness, and consciousness in middle school children's behavior have constantly improved. Compared with primary school children's observation, junior middle school children's observation has greatly improved. Junior middle school children can consciously eliminate interference and focus on scheduled observational activities without teachers' supervision or guidance. However, their observational activities, which are carried out according to adult requests, have certain passivity, while senior middle school children's observational activities are comparatively more voluntary; they can consciously and actively determine their observational objects and purposes and independently complete more detailed observational tasks.

The continuous observational time without the necessity of larger efforts under certain teaching conditions is about 20 minutes for children aged 7-10, 25 minutes for children aged 10-12, and about 40 minutes for junior middle school children. When members of a model airplane team checked malfunctions of the model airplane, the second-grade junior middle school children were able to average one hour and 35 minutes of observation, while first-grade senior middle school children averaged three hours (Qiu Li, 2013).

The accuracy of observation among middle school children has constantly improved. Due to immature physiological development, primary school children's observations are often inaccurate, filled with randomness, arbitrariness, and one-sidedness. With physiological development, middle school children's observational accuracy has developed rapidly. Studies have shown that middle school children's visual perception has improved by more than 60% compared to first-graders in primary school, with some perceptions even surpassing those of adults, making them more accurate observers of things.

With the development of voluntariness, persistence, and accuracy in middle school children's observation, their observational generality has improved greatly. They can observe not only the surface features of things but also the essential features.

## 3.2 Development of middle school children's memory

The middle school stage is an important period of life development, and the memory of middle school children is also at a golden stage of life development. Not only is the development speed fast, but there are also many qualitative changes.

### 3.2.1 Characteristics of the memorization of middle school children

**1. Intentional memorization gradually dominates learning.**

Intentional memory has clear purposes, specific tasks, and flexible methods, accompanied by active thinking and volitional efforts, making it a proactive and self-conscious memorization activity. Systematic and complete scientific knowledge can be effectively obtained through intentional memorization, making it dominant in learning and working. Primary school is a stage of transition from aimless and unplanned unintentional memorization to purposeful and planned intentional memorization. In the middle and later periods of junior middle school, intentional memorization is basically dominant, but it remains passive, with its purposes and tasks primarily set by adults. Senior middle school children can consciously determine their purposes to control their memorization activities. Due to the improvement in the intentionality of adolescents' memorization, the effect of memorization also improves greatly. The amount of memory of first graders in senior middle school is twice that of first graders in junior middle school and four to five times that of first graders in primary school (Qiu Li, 2013).

**2. Meaningful memorization gradually becomes the main type of memory in learning.**

Primary school students are accustomed to using rote memory to learn materials. With age, especially in junior middle school, students gradually learn and master the methods and skills of meaningful memorization, and the use of rote memory is relatively reduced, replaced by the development of meaningful memorization.

Pupils' rote memory (simply repetitive memory) components dominate. For junior high school children, the component of meaningful memory (memory based on the internal relationships between things) gradually strengthens its advantage (see Figure 3-1).

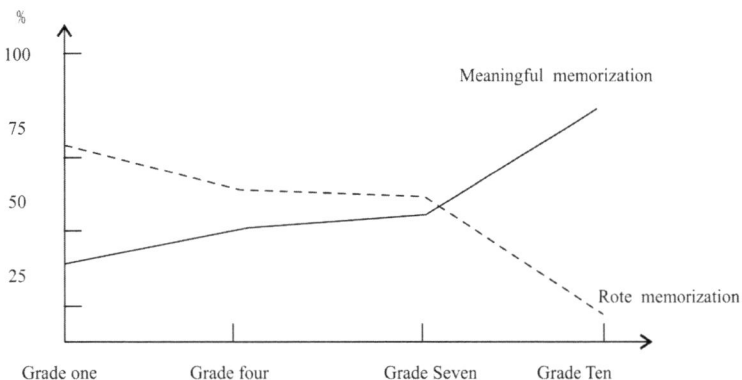

Figure 3-1 Component changes of rote memorization and meaningful memorization of primary and secondary school students

Source: 陈辉,《短时记忆容量的年龄特点及材料特点》,《天津师范大学学报》,1986(4):25—30.

Research has shown that the number of items that junior middle school students can correctly recall is, on average, 4.43 when memorization is easy to organize meaningfully, while the number of items that senior middle school students can correctly recall is, on average, 5.80. When materials for memorization are just suitable for rote memorization, the number of items that second-grade junior middle school students can correctly recall is, on average, 3.19, whereas that of second-grade senior middle school students is, on average, only 2.80 (Chen Hui, 1986). It can be seen that the level of meaningful memory of middle school students increases with age, while the level of rote memory decreases with age.

**3. Abstract memorization develops rapidly and plays a dominant role.**

Based on the content of memorization, the content of middle school students' memory gradually changes from concrete memory to abstract memory with the growth of age. The ability of abstract memorization of middle school students has been rapidly developed, and the practical ability of concrete image materials and abstract materials has been continuously improved. This is manifested in that they not only have to learn knowledge from intuitive and concrete materials but also have to master a large number of concepts, rules, and principles of various disciplines, and make judgments, reasoning, and proofs. Junior middle school students memorize materials mainly with the help of abstract memory. Senior middle school students' memory contents are basically abstract materials, but image memory still plays an important role in learning. Primary and secondary school students were asked to recall the memorized contents after the researchers read them such concrete words as "house", "cup", and so on. They were then asked to recall the memorized contents after the researchers read them such abstract words as "sports", "relation", and so on. If the amount that first-graders in primary school could reproduce was 100, the increments that students in other grades could reproduce are shown in Table 3-1.

Table 3-1  Comparison of increments of image memory and abstract memory

| Grade | The percentage of increase of the number of memory ||
| --- | --- | --- |
|  | Concrete memory | Abstract memory |
| Grade Two | 28 | 68 |
| Grade Four | 50 | 68 |
| Grade Seven | 84 | 192 |
| Grade Nine | 99 | 192 |
| Grade Eleven | 77 | 195 |

Source: 卢家楣,《心理学基础理论及其教学应用》,上海教育出版社,1998,第148—149页.

## 3.2.2  The characteristics of middle school children's retention of memory

**1. The retention time of memory increases with age, and students' interest in emotional experience materials gradually increases.**

Compared with elementary school children, the retention time of memory for middle school children extends with age, and their intellectual activities are more significantly accompanied by emotions. Therefore, in the process of accumulating knowledge and experience, they also remember the emotions they experienced at that time, and even if they forget the memory content in the future, they retain their emotions and emotional experiences. Students of different ages were asked to remember 10 words related to emotional experiences, such as pain, sadness, contempt, and happiness, and the results showed that the ability of middle school students to remember emotional materials had greatly improved.

**2. The amount of memory of middle school children continues to increase, and the scope of memory continues to expand.**

The memory range is expressed in terms of the amount of memory. The range of memory for the same material at the same time interval is expanding with the growth of students' learning abilities and age. The expansion of memory range is most obvious in junior middle school (Yin Keli, 2014). However, middle school students still lack memory experience and are not good at connecting what they have learned with what they already know, and their memory methods are often not reasonable enough.

### 3.2.3 Characteristics of middle school children's recall

**1. The effect of memory is significantly enhanced with age.**

Compared with elementary school children, middle school children's memory ability has greatly improved in both recognition and reproduction. The explicit memory, implicit memory, daily memory, and delayed memory of children aged between 6 and 14 develop rapidly with age and continue to steadily rise after the age of 14 (Cheng Zaohuo & Geng Ming, 1997).

**2. Middle school students have gradually mastered the skills and methods of recall.**

As middle school students grow older and gain more knowledge and experience, they have mastered certain skills and methods, and they gradually become proficient in using systematic search and recall to extract knowledge.

1) Organizing memorization materials. The most commonly used method for students to organize memorization materials is to write an outline, which means that while memorizing, they systematically write the subheadings of the materials according to their meanings. The process of organizing memorization materials can not only enhance students' enthusiasm for thinking activities but also form meaningful connections through organized and systematic materials. According to an experimental study, the forgetting rate of memorizing without writing an outline is

43.2%, while the forgetting rate of memorizing the same content and writing an outline is only 24.8% (Zhang Shifu, 1997).

2) Utilizing association. Objective things are interrelated, and our memory reflects and stores this interconnectedness. As long as one is good at utilizing various interconnected clues, they can easily recall one thing from another. The presence or absence of associations in learning has a significant impact on the effect of recall, and after the age of 16, associative learning develops rapidly and shows an almost linear upward trend (Sun Changhua et al., 1992).

3) Applying reasoning. Using reasoning to recall is based on the essential connections and laws between things. It may not be effective if most theorems, definitions, concepts, and formulas are recalled by rote in learning, but if reasoning is applied according to its essential connections, it can be recalled quickly and accurately. With the development of their thinking ability and the learning requirements set by teachers, middle school students gradually help themselves master some reasoning methods.

There are many factors that affect the memory effectiveness of middle school students, such as the purpose and task of memory, the attitude and emotional state during memory, the nature of activity tasks, the quantity and nature of materials, and the amount and method of memory, among others.

## 3.3 Development of middle school children's thinking

According to Piaget's Cognitive-Stage Theory, middle school students are in the stage of formal operations (age 11 to adulthood). Middle school students can think abstractly, deal with hypothetical situations, and consider possibilities. The development of middle school students' thinking has an important impact on their ideas and behavior.

### 3.3.1 Development of middle school children's thinking

1. **Action thinking and image thinking develop continuously and promote the development of logical thinking.**

Middle school students' action thinking and image thinking are still developing and integrating with abstract logical thinking and dialectical logical thinking. The development of action thinking promotes the technical abilities of middle school students, while the development of image thinking enhances their artistic abilities. Generating abstract relationships from available information and then comparing those abstract relationships to each other is a broadly applicable skill underlying many tasks in which adolescents' competence leaps forward. Piaget (1952) described a study in which students in the concrete operational stage were given a set of 10 proverbs and a set of statements with the same meanings as the proverbs. They were asked to match each proverb to the equivalent statement. Concrete operational children can understand the task and choose answers; however, their answers are often incorrect because they frequently do not understand that a proverb describes a general principle. For example, when asked to explain the proverb "Don't cry over spilled milk", the child might explain that once milk is spilled, there is no use crying, but they might not see that the proverb has a broader meaning. The child is likely to respond to the concrete situation of spilled milk rather than understanding that the proverb means "don't dwell on past events that can't be changed". Adolescents and adults have little difficulty with this type of task.

### 2. The overall structure of thinking has been basically formed.

The basic formation of the overall structure of thinking mainly refers to the development of abstract thinking and dialectical thinking based on the good development of middle school students' action thinking and image thinking. Middle school students' abstract logical thinking develops rapidly and begins to occupy a dominant position in the junior middle school stage. In the senior middle school stage, their abstract thinking not only occupies absolute superiority but also transitions from empirical thinking to theoretical thinking. Senior middle school students can use theories as a guide to analyze factual materials and expand their cognitive field. The development of abstract logical thinking provides the necessary conditions for adolescents to learn various theories. Because middle school students have a stronger ability for abstract logical thinking, they can apply advanced reasoning processes and logical thinking processes to social and ideological problems. They begin to think about abstract issues, including political issues, interpersonal issues, philosophical issues, and ethical issues. All these issues involve some abstract concepts, such as democracy, friendship, fairness, loyalty, and so on.

Middle school students' dialectical logical thinking is also developing rapidly and reaches a basic level of maturity in the senior middle school stage. Dialectical logical thinking is the highest form of human thinking. The maturity of dialectical logical thinking marks the formation of the overall structure of adolescents' thinking.

### 3. The profundity of thinking is improving day by day.

With the improvement of abstract logical thinking and the continuous enrichment of knowledge and experience, junior middle school students can make good use of various knowledge to enhance their understanding of abstract materials, which shows their thinking has a certain degree of profundity. However, junior high school students' thinking is also superficial and one-sided. For example, junior middle school students tend to be extreme, enjoy splitting hairs, are often confused by the external characteristics of things, and cannot grasp the essence of things during problem analysis.

Senior middle school students' thinking is basically close to adults' and at a mature level. They can get rid of the limitations of concrete things and better use theoretical assumptions for thinking activities. Their thinking has higher predictability, reflecting their deep understanding of the relationships between things. They can consciously use formal logic rules to think. Of course, although senior high school students' thinking is more profound than that of junior high school students, sometimes the profundity of their thinking still possesses some one-sidedness.

### 4. The creativity of thinking increases gradually.

Junior high school students show obvious thinking characteristics of creativity and criticality. They have a strong thirst for knowledge and a spirit of exploration, enjoy strange fantasies, and like to create new styles and be unconventional. They are not content to accept the teacher's explanations passively and try to prove their ability and talent. The development of their creative thinking is consistent with that of their critical thinking. Junior high school students do not easily accept others' opinions and often review them; sometimes, they even take an overly skeptical and critical attitude. Senior middle school students' creative thinking has developed more than that of junior middle school students. Senior middle school students can study creatively and analyze and solve problems independently.

However, middle school students' creative thinking is immature. They do not possess strong discrimination abilities. They are susceptible to the influence of incorrect thinking and can easily waver in the face of difficulties.

### 5. The self-monitoring ability of thinking has been significantly enhanced.

The self-monitoring ability of thinking is the ability for individuals to monitor and control their own thinking processes, which is an important component of metacognitive ability. The concrete operational child, when told that A is bigger than B and B is bigger than C, understands that A is bigger than C. However, if the problem has been phrased in the following way, only an older child who has entered the formal operational stage will be able to solve it: "B is smaller than A, and B is bigger than C; who is the biggest of the three?" Here, the younger concrete operational child might get lost in the combinations of greater-than and less-than relationships. Adolescents in the formal operational stage may also get confused by the relationships in this problem, but they can imagine several different relationships among the sizes of B, A, and C and can determine each size accurately until they arrive at the correct one. This example illustrates another ability of pre-adolescents and adolescents who have reached the formal operational stage: They can monitor or think about their own thinking.

The self-monitoring ability of junior middle school students' thinking begins to develop, and they can make certain adjustments to simple thinking activities based on the results of these activities, but this adjustment is only preliminary. On the one hand, the planning of thinking is not perfect enough, and they cannot determine the program of thinking activities according to strict logical rules, which is involuntary. On the other hand, they regulate thinking activities mainly by the feedback information from the results of thinking activities and are not good at controlling thinking activities during the process of thinking. As senior middle school students become more proficient in thinking methods and corresponding logical rules, their self-monitoring ability of thinking has been significantly improved. Senior middle school students can determine the way to solve problems according to their needs and monitor their thinking activities in the process to ensure the correctness and efficiency of their thinking activities.

**6. Middle school students develop their ability for hypothetical deductive reasoning and can return to reality step by step by testing various possibilities.**

Adolescents are already able to perform hypothetical deductive reasoning, the ability believed by Piaget to accompany the stage of formal operations, to develop, consider, and test hypotheses. That is to say, they can develop a hypothesis and design an experiment to test it. When they face problem situations, they can first apply "general theories" to think about all possible factors that may affect the results. Then, through deductive reasoning, hypotheses are formed, predicting under what conditions certain results will be produced. Finally, through experiments and the use of systematic scientific analysis methods, all hypotheses are tested one by one to verify their authenticity and draw conclusions.

Elementary school children in the concrete operational stage approach the pendulum problem differently from middle school children in the formal operational stage. The children and adolescents were given a pendulum consisting of a string with a weight at the end. They could change the length of the string, the amount of weight, the height from which the pendulum was released, and the force with which the pendulum was pushed. They were asked which of these factors influenced the frequency (the number of swings per minute). Only the length of the string makes any difference in the frequency of the pendulum: The shorter the string, the more swings per minute. This experiment is illustrated in Figure 3-2.

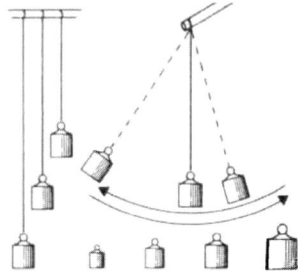

Figure 3-2  Piaget's Pendulum experiment: Participants are required to determine which factor or combination of factors can increase the speed of oscillation

Source: Robert E. Slavin, *Educational Psychology Theory and Practice* (10th), Posts & Telecom Press, 2017, p. 37.

The adolescent who has reached the stage of formal operations is likely to proceed quite systematically, varying one factor at a time (e. g. , leaving the string the same length and trying different weights). For example, in the Inhelder & Piaget experiment, one 15-year-old selected 100 grams with a long string and a medium-length string, then 20 grams with a long string and a short string, and finally 200 grams with a long string and a short string and concluded, "It's the length of the string that makes weight go faster and slower; the weight doesn't play any role" (Inhelder & Piaget, 1958). In contrast, 10-year-olds (who can be assumed to be in the concrete operational stage) proceeded in a chaotic fashion, varying many factors at the same time and hanging on to their preconceptions. One boy varied simultaneously the weight and the push; then the weight, the push, and length; then the push, the weight, and the elevation; and so on. He first concluded, "It's by changing the weight and push, certainly not the string." When asked how he knew that the string had nothing to do with it, he answered, "Because it's the same string." He had not varied its length in the last several trials; previously, he had varied it simultaneously with the push, thus complicating the findings of the experiment (Inhelder & Piaget, 1958).

From this perspective, adolescents in the formal operational stage already possess the ability of hypothetical deductive reasoning. They can propose hypotheses, conduct systematic scientific experiments, explore, and solve various scientific problems like scientists.

7. **The ability of hypothetical conditional reasoning has developed maturely.**

The ability of young adolescents is an aptitude for reasoning about situations and conditions that have not been experienced. The preadolescent begins to be able to think abstractly and to see possibilities beyond the here and now. These abilities continue to develop in adulthood. The ability to deal with potential or hypothetical situations comes with the formal operational stage; the form is now separate from the content.

The adolescent can accept, for the sake of argument or discussion, conditions that are arbitrary, that are not known to exist, even those that are known to be contrary to fact. Adolescents are not bound to their own experiences of reality, so they can apply logic to any given conditions. One illustration of the ability to reason about hypothetical situations is found in formal debate, in which participants must be prepared to defend the other side of an issue, regardless of their personal feelings or experience, with their success judged on documentation and logical consistency. *If you require fourth- and ninth-graders to suspend their own opinions to support the proposition that "schools should have classes for six days per week and 48 weeks per year," comparing their responses can dramatically illustrate the differences in the ability of children and adolescents to set aside their own views. The adolescents are far more likely to be able to set aside their own opinions and think of reasons why more days of school might be beneficial.* The abilities that make up formal operational thought—thinking abstractly, testing hypotheses, and forming concepts that are independent of physical reality—are critical to acquiring higher-order skills. *For example, learning algebra or abstract geometry requires the use of formal operational thought, as does understanding complex concepts in science, social studies, and other subjects* (Robert E. Slavin, 2017).

### 3.3.2 Impact of the development of abstract logical thinking on adolescents

Due to the development of abstract logical thinking, adolescents' views on themselves and the surrounding environment have undergone great changes, and their behavior has also undergone various changes, which are highlighted in the following aspects.

**1. Middle school children like to argue.**

Once adolescents acquire the new way of thinking of formal operations, they always want to use it to practice, consolidate, and improve it. A child who used to be very obedient now likes to argue and talk back to his parents after entering middle school because, at this time, he realizes that his parents' opinions are not always right. Even if they are right, things might have been better done using other methods (he thinks of other possibilities and can collect various facts to prove his hypothesis).

The reason why he doesn't argue with parents is that he just doesn't want to argue, and the sly smile on the corner of his mouth has already explained everything. In short, as he thinks deeper, he discovers the essence behind the phenomenon that he did not see in the past. Wise parents who know that their child's tendency to argue is a sign of maturity will accept this kind of disobedience happily. Whenever an argument arises, they focus on the principal aspect of the problem rather than escalating into meaningless arguments. If the child's opinion is correct, parents should sincerely accept it. If it's not right, through equal discussion, parents should let children have a deeper understanding of the complexity and diversity of things, as well as the reasons behind the parents' claims. If children cannot understand for a while, parents should be patient and give them enough time to think and make judgments.

**2. Middle school children attach importance to self-attention.**

Due to adolescents' ability to reflect on the consequences of their actions and the physical and psychological changes that come with puberty, they have begun to pay more attention to themselves, focusing on their appearance, clothing, and speech and behavior. After entering middle school, boy students think that they should have strong and developed chest and arm muscles, and they begin to pay attention to physical exercise. *For example, Zhang Shuo comes to school early every morning to run, plays parallel bars, plays basketball, and so on, and he also often looks at himself in front of the mirror, bends his arms, and checks if his muscles are bulging.* Girls think they should be more beautiful, and they begin to pay more attention to their appearance, clothing, hairstyles, and so on. *For example, the mother complained about her daughter Wen Yabing, who has just entered senior high school, that she combed her hair in front of the mirror and washed her face in the bathroom for at least more than one hour every morning.*

Piaget believed that adolescents have developed a new egocentrism with the emergence of formal operations, which manifests their inability to distinguish their own abstract viewpoints from others'. For a period of time, adolescents always think about how important their thoughts, appearance, and behavior are because they believe that others must also see them in the same way. As a result, there are two cognitive distortions in their relationships with others.

The first type is a *hypothetical audience*. Adolescents always believe that they are standing in the center of the stage and that they are the object of attention for others. This phenomenon is called the "spotlight effect" in psychology. Therefore, adolescents spend a lot of time dressing up and carefully checking their clothes and appearance, and they are also very sensitive to public comments, even a bit neurotic. Due to the existence of hypothetical audiences, adolescents have added many unnecessary troubles. *For example, Mei Suyue hates herself for being too fat. One time, several boys were laughing and discussing together, "Eating potatoes can make you as fat as big bread soaked in water." She listened and burst into tears, but in fact, no one said anything about her.*

The second type is called *personal fiction*. Because adolescents always think that others are staring at and thinking about them, they are hot-headed and think how important they are. They are unique and different. Others riding through the red light may be hurt, but they will not, and others will be caught cheating in exams, but they won't. Due to this thinking, they are also prone to various extreme behaviors to show how brave and special they are.

These two cognitive distortions are particularly evident in the middle school stage when formal operations gradually form. With age and cognitive maturity, these distortions gradually decrease and disappear. Some developmental psychologists believe that these two phenomena indicate an increased ability to pick up social opinions, which makes them more concerned about how others think of them and enjoy showing themselves in front of others to impress them. In fact, from another perspective, having such thoughts is not bad. If guided correctly, they can pay more attention to self-improvement, construct an independent self-image, and develop a more mature parent-child relationship and peer relationship.

3. Middle school children are idealistic.

Adolescence is a romantic era full of ideals and passion. Since the thinking mode in the stage of formal operational thinking starts from hypothetical possibilities, it enables teenagers to break away from the constraints of reality and open the door to the kingdom of ideals. They can imagine a more ideal family, a better social system, a better way of life, and better interpersonal relationships, and explore the possibility of realizing their ideals. Therefore, young people from ancient to modern times, both at home and abroad, are the most active and least conservative social force. They are willing to take on social obligations and responsibilities, constantly test their beliefs and values, and correct the direction of life through their own practice.

Due to the idealism of adolescents, they cannot tolerate the various shortcomings and drawbacks of real life. They aspire to reform, abandon the old for the new, and dare to criticize current shortcomings. Many young people with lofty ideals have emerged in the long history of China, and the Chinese people will remember them forever. *For example, Zhou Enlai studied for the rise of China, Kang Youwei and*

*Liang Qichao initiated the Gongche Shangshu Movement, Zu Di practiced swordsmanship upon hearing the cock, Chen Tang swore that those who offended our China would be punished no matter how far away, Huo Qubing built altars to offer sacrifices to heaven in Langjuxu Mountain, and so on.*

On the other hand, due to the idealism and criticism, adolescents may also have difficulties in interpersonal relationships. Because adult parents have rich life experience and deal with problems more realistically, there is a gap between the two generations, which is often called the generation gap. Adults often cannot tolerate the immaturity of adolescents and prefer to intervene in their behavior. However, their real-life parents are far from the ideal parents, and they become picky about their parents. However, idealism and love for criticism are precious "edges" in adolescents. As they grow older and mature in cognition, once they discover that others have both advantages and disadvantages, it is beneficial for them to establish long-term and lasting interpersonal relationships with others and discover more appropriate ways to transform and build the real world.

4. Middle school children are better at planning but immature.

With the development of abstract thinking ability, adolescents are better at analyzing and handling problems than elementary school children. Their self-regulation ability of behavior has been enhanced, and they excel in planning and managing their time, so their learning ability is also stronger. Because adolescents consider various possibilities and, after careful consideration, discover that there are many options to choose from, they tend to hesitate when making decisions. Parents and teachers should provide them with timely assistance and be good advisors, but should not make decisions on their behalf.

Adolescents' abstract thinking ability grows too fast, and they also need to have a "toddling process" when using this new way of thinking. Therefore, teachers and parents should understand many typical behaviors of adolescents, such as liking to argue, enjoying criticizing and making comments, self-attention, hesitation, etc., and from a positive perspective, they should not react negatively. The various immature behaviors of adolescents are caused by unfamiliarity with newly developed and powerful ways of thinking. Parents and teachers should not only share the joy of their growth but also provide reasonable and active guidance to help adolescents handle their growing pains correctly and promote their healthy physical and mental growth (Fang Fuxi & Fang Ge, 2004).

## 3.4 Development of middle school children's imagination

1. Middle school children's imagination possesses strong voluntariness.

The voluntariness of imagination is mainly manifested as the ability to consciously determine the purpose and task of imagination and the ability to imagine around the purpose. Junior middle school children can better imagine around the topic of imagination and exclude the interference of other factors, but their imagination still possesses passivity, so they are not good at actively putting forward the task of imagination. Senior middle school children can not only quickly complete complex tasks of imagination but also take the initiative to propose tasks of imagination. The development of the voluntariness of their imagination impels them to carry out activities of small inventions and creations independently and promotes them to form personal ideals with social significance. *For example, the fastest first-grade students in senior middle school were able to write an 800-word essay in 17 minutes in one experiment.*

2. The creativity of middle school students' imagination gradually prevails.

In middle school, with the profundity and abundance of image contents, and with the improvement of cognitive operational ability of imagination, the creativity of adolescents' imagination has developed greatly and is gradually becoming dominant. *For example, the number of middle school children who successfully create and invent is significantly higher than that of primary school children.* When the creativity of middle school students' imagination has generally improved, the level of their creativity also shows a significant trend of differentiation. The creativity of some middle school students' imagination develops faster and reaches a higher level; vice versa.

3. Middle school children's imagination is more realistic.

Due to the significant improvement of their perceptual ability, middle school children's ability of representation has greatly developed. The concrete representation more accurately reflects the details of the object; the comprehensive representation better reflects the whole and structure of the object. At the same time, their ability to understand words has been greatly improved. Therefore, middle school students' imagination can more accurately and completely reflect objective reality and possesses higher realism. Middle school students can actively suppress imagination that does not conform to reality, and the fictional elements in their imagination gradually reduce. With the accumulation of life experience, especially the accumulation of scientific knowledge, adolescents are better able to distinguish between what is real and what is fictive, which is evident in their reading interests. Middle school students' interest in fairy tales is greatly reduced, and they prefer literary and artistic works full of reality, such as works describing life. However, their unrealistic imagination still occurs from time to time in middle school. Some students still have wild ideas, the main reason for which is that their willpower is so weak that it is difficult for them to suppress unrealistic imagination. These wild ideas not only seriously interfere with their learning but can also lead them astray on the road of life.

## 3.5 Development of middle school children's attention

1. Attention transitions from unintentional attention to intentional attention.

Individual attention begins with unintentional attention, which mainly depends on the role of external stimuli. The unintentional attention gradually develops and deepens with the development of individuals' own interests and hobbies. Junior middle school children's intentional attention gradually develops and replaces the dominant position of unintentional attention, and their learning purpose, planning, and self-consciousness have made great progress. Eighth-graders' unintentional attention develops to its peak and then gradually declines. They can consciously monitor and regulate their attention so that their attention can focus on school learning tasks. With the development of middle school students' intentional attention, the school can get rid of the restriction of students' interest when arranging students' learning content, encouraging them to accept a large amount of knowledge efficiently and widely. In addition to the dominance of intentional attention, middle school students are better able to alternate between intentional and unintentional attention, thus observing specific objects for longer periods of time. Middle school students' attention gradually develops and deepens into a higher form.

2. The quality of attention continuously improves.

Firstly, the stability of attention has increased rapidly. For example, under good teaching conditions, the stability of attention of junior middle school students can be maintained for about 40 minutes. Secondly, the attention range has been correspondingly expanded and improved. Studies have found that the attention span of children at the age of 13 is close to that of adults. Thirdly, the ability of attention distribution has developed accordingly. Junior middle school students begin to be able to both listen and take notes at the same time. Finally, the ability of attention transfer has been greatly improved. In general, the period of rapid growth of students' ability to transfer attention is from Grade 2 in primary school to Grade 2 in junior middle school; the period of stagnation is from Grade 2 in junior middle school to Grade 2 in senior high school; and the period of slow growth is from Grade 2 in senior high school to Grade 2 in college. *For example, junior middle school students can shift their attention to classroom learning more quickly than primary school students from recess to class.*

3. Middle school students' attention obviously develops into several different types.

The middle school students' attention can be divided into: the emotional type in which unintentional attention dominates; the volitional type with the predominance of intentional attention; and the conscious volitional type with the predominance of post-conscious attention.

## 3.6 Development of middle school children's speech

Due to the fact that abstract propositions are expressed through language, the development of speech plays an important role in promoting the improvement of abstract thinking ability in adolescents. The development of speech and thinking reinforces each other. The emergence of formal operational ability enables adolescents to understand and use various abstract or profound words more and more, further expanding their vocabulary and deepening their understanding of word meanings. Correspondingly, their mastery of syntax and pragmatic ability is also further improved.

After children enter middle school, they become very interested in literary works. They begin to extensively explore ancient and modern literary works at home and abroad, including novels, poems, essays, etc. Reading literary works not only has a beneficial impact on their studies but also enriches their spiritual life, deepens their understanding of life and society, and improves their language comprehension and expression abilities. The excellent performance in language has also driven the improvement of grades in other subjects.

Many middle school students like to keep diaries and have an excerpt notebook of famous quotes. They allow everyone to read the excerpt notebook of famous quotes, but others cannot read their diaries because they are their personal "privacy". They sometimes also criticize their parents for speaking "illogically" and "not dividing problems into two". Middle school children now use more irony in their speech. *For* example, when they feel stuffy and hot, they will deliberately shout, "This room is so cool, so cool." This means reminding their mother to turn on the air conditioning quickly. Sometimes, they also use satire, even if it is well-meaning. This speech style has never been used by them when they were pupils.

The development of adolescent speech is clearly reflected in the improvement of their written speech ability, as they write longer sentences and can use complex sentence structures to express their meaning. Before writing an article, they can carefully review the topic and prepare a draft, taking into account the structure and expression of the article. As high school students, their writing ability has reached a mature level comparable to that of adults. Due to learning grammar, middle school students begin to consciously apply grammar knowledge to analyze compositions and various language phenomena. *For example, one day when Macron was eating breakfast very slowly, his mother urged him to say, "Eat quickly." He deliberately pretended not to hear and continued to have breakfast slowly. After a while, his mother said again, "I told you to eat quickly; why are you still eating so slowly?" He replied, "Who did you say just now? There was no subject when you spoke."*

The improvement of middle school students' speech ability is also evident in their ability to change their speech style according to different situations. *For example, during speech competitions, the debate between the two sides heats up, and everyone speaks at a faster pace with a more rigorous sentence structure and argumentation at this time. When performing a play, they need to memorize lines and adjust their speaking speed and sentence expression according to the requirements of the character. At a birthday party, they can use passionate language to bless their friends. Once they speak on behalf of the class at a school rally, they have written a speech draft beforehand, consulted with the class teacher's opinions, and repeatedly revised it.*

The development of language ability among middle school students not only results from environmental requirements but also reflects their improvement in reflection and self-regulation of speech abilities (Fang Fuxi & Fang Ge, 2004).

In conclusion, cognitive development during middle school is a pivotal stage that shapes a child's ability to think critically, solve problems, and understand complex concepts. As adolescents transition into more abstract thinking, they become better equipped to analyze information and make informed decisions. This period is marked by increased independence and social interaction, which significantly influence their cognitive growth.

Educators and parents play a crucial role in providing supportive environments that foster curiosity and intellectual engagement. By encouraging exploration and critical thinking, we can help middle school children develop essential skills for future academic and personal success. Recognizing the unique challenges and opportunities of this developmental stage will enable us to nurture their cognitive abilities effectively, preparing them for the complexities of high school and beyond.

# I. Review and reflection

| | |
|---|---|
| visual acuity | transitive inference |
| hearing | categorization |
| sensation integration | inductive reasoning |
| external memory aids | deductive reasoning |
| rehearsal | English-immersion approach |
| organization | bilingual education |
| seriation | |

    development of middle school children's sensation, perception, observation, memory, thinking, imagination, attention and speech

    characteristics of middle school children's memorization

    characteristics of school children's retention of memory

    characteristics of middle school children's recall

    impact of the development of abstract logical thinking on adolescents

# II. Material analysis

*Zhang Shuo's mother has complained recently that her son, a new first-year high school student, especially likes to talk back to his parents and he loves to argue with them a bit regardless of whether his parents are right or wrong. Her mother sought the help of a psychologist for counseling.*

Please analyze objectively Zhang Shuo's situation according to the cognitive development law of middle school students and give some advice to his parents about how to deal with this situation. (Refer to Appendix I )

# Chapter 4　Theories of Learning

The evolution of learning theories illustrates a profound shift in our understanding of how knowledge is acquired and processed. Initially, behaviorism dominated the landscape, focusing on observable behaviors and the influence of external stimuli. Pioneers like B. F. Skinner emphasized reinforcement and conditioning, suggesting that learning is a response to environmental factors.

However, as researchers sought to understand the complexities of human thought, cognitive theories emerged. Jean Piaget's work highlighted the active role of learners in constructing knowledge through experiences, emphasizing developmental stages in children. His insights shifted the focus from mere behavior to the mental processes underlying learning.

Lev Vygotsky further enriched this discourse by introducing social constructivism, positing that cognitive development is deeply influenced by social interactions and cultural contexts. His concept of the "Zone of Proximal Development" illustrated the importance of collaborative learning and guidance.

In recent decades, the integration of cognitive psychology and neuroscience has provided a more nuanced understanding of learning processes, exploring how memory, attention, and problem-solving interact. Today, learning theories recognize the dynamic interplay between individual cognition and social environments, shaping educational practices and fostering a deeper comprehension of how we learn. This journey reflects an ongoing quest to unravel the complexities of human learning.

Psychology has been studying the problem of learning for more than a hundred years. In the developmental history of psychology, most early psychologists focused on the nature of learning and the process of learning, while later psychologists focused on the study of learning conditions, motivation, strategies, and other basic factors affecting learning. Although researchers have different perspectives, views, horizons, and methods, and different learning theories, all of them are of great help in understanding the phenomenon of learning.

## 4.1　Learning

Many psychologists and educators have proposed various definitions of learning from different perspectives based on different theoretical foundations or research achievements. Although definitions vary, consensus has been reached in the following three areas. Firstly, learning is a common phenomenon shared by humans and animals, and it runs through the entire lives of both lower and higher animals, as well as humans. Secondly, learning is an ongoing process of acquiring experience. Thirdly, learning manifests as a relatively stable change in individual behavior due to experience.

In a broad sense, learning is a relatively persistent process of behavioral and internal psychological changes that an organism undergoes through practice or experience throughout its life. In a narrow sense, learning is the process of consciously and actively acquiring social and individual experience in the context of social life practices, facilitated by social transmission and mediated by language.

To sum up, students' learning is a purposeful, planned, and organized process of mastering systematic scientific knowledge and skills, developing various abilities, and forming a specific worldview and moral qualities under the guidance of teachers.

## 4.1.1 Connotation of learning

Learning is the relatively persistent change in behavior or behavioral potential that an individual experiences or practices in a specific context. John Dollard and George A. Miller believed that learning is composed of four elements: drive, cue, response, and reward.

The connotation of learning can be understood from the following aspects: ① Learning is essentially an adaptive activity. ② Learning is a common phenomenon in both humans and animals. ③ Learning is caused by repeated experiences; some viewpoints directly emphasize that the occurrence of learning is due to experience. ④ Learning is the process by which an organism acquires experience. ⑤ The process of learning can be intentional or unintentional. ⑥ Learning leads to relatively persistent changes in behavior or behavioral potential. However, it is worth noting that not all behavioral changes are generated by learning, and factors such as physiological maturity, fatigue, and medication can also cause behavioral changes.

We can judge whether an activity is learning or not from the following two aspects: one is to judge directly according to the definition of learning; the second is to use the "five 'non' principles" of learning, that is, non-instinct, non-maturity, non-fatigue, non-medicine, and non-disease.

### 4.1.2 Role of learning

The role of learning is manifested in (1) learning as a condition for individuals and the environment to achieve balance; (2) learning can influence maturity; (3) learning can stimulate the potential of human brain intelligence, thereby promoting the development of individual psychology.

## 4.2 Learning classification

The learning phenomenon is very complex, and the learning principle often depends on the specific situation. In other words, we should distinguish different learning phenomena and then discuss their laws respectively. Cognition is not easy to acquire. Early psychologists were influenced by Darwinian theory of evolution in their study of learning, believing that human and animal learning could be explained by common laws. Therefore, they tended to take animals such as cats, dogs, and mice as research objects to explore these common laws. After World War II, many psychologists thought deeply about this phenomenon and finally realized that human learning was very complex, making it difficult to explain learning with principles derived from animal studies. It was necessary to study human learning in different categories and discuss the rules of learning separately. In 1962, Melton hosted a conference about human learning, focusing on the discussion of problems related to the classification of human learning types, and the types of human learning were also published after the conference. Since then, psychological researchers have divided learning into various types from different perspectives according to different learning theories.

### 4.2.1 Classification of learning subjects

According to different learning subjects, learning can be divided into animal learning, human learning, and machine learning.

1. Animal learning

Animal learning is limited to passively adapting to environmental changes to meet physiological needs. It mainly relies on direct ways to obtain individual experience and is limited to the first signal system.

2. Human learning

There are essential differences between human learning and animal learning in the following three aspects: the sociality of human learning, the use of language as the medium, and proactivity.

Human learning and animal learning have some things in common, but their differences are fundamental. Using animal learning to explain human learning will certainly erase the sociality of human learning. Human learning is a process of consciously and actively mastering social and individual experience, with language as the intermediary in social life practice.

**3. Machine learning**

Machine learning mainly refers to computer learning and is a research field of artificial intelligence.

## 4.2.2 Classification of learning results

In 1977, R. M. Gagne, an American psychologist, proposed a classification of learning results. He summed up the learning results that students acquire in one word—capability. Capability is an implicit psychological state and quality acquired by the learner, and its existence is inferred from the learner's external performance. Gagne divided the capability acquired by students into five categories (Table 4-1).

Table 4-1 Classification of learning results

| Fields | Learning results | Concepts | Examples |
| --- | --- | --- | --- |
| Cognitive field | Intellectual skills | Intellectual skills refer to the capability to use symbols or concepts to interact with the environment. | *Identifying the diagonal of a rectangle; demonstrating the use of the object form of a personal pronoun after a preposition* |
| | Cognitive strategy | Cognitive strategies are the means used by individuals to control their own learning, memory, and thinking activities. | *Using images as an intermediary to learn foreign words; solving problems by backward induction; learning the new word like this: merchant—摸钱的—商人* |
| | Speech skills | Speech skills are the ability to use language to present information. | *Stating Newton's first law; narrating the historical significance of the May Fourth Movement* |
| Motor skill | Motor skills | Motor skill is the ability to operate motor steadily and smoothly, accurately and timely. | *Practicing calligraphy; measuring the acceleration of gravity with an experimental instrument* |
| Emotional field | Attitude | Attitude is an internal state that affects an individual's behavioral choices for people, events and things. | *Choosing to read science fiction; choosing running as a form of exercise* |

### 4.2.3 Classification of learning hierarchy

According to the sequence of learning situations from simple to complex and the learning hierarchy from low to high, Gagne divided learning into eight categories and constructed a complete learning hierarchy.

**1. Signal learning**

Signal learning, the simplest form of learning, refers to the process of making a response to a signal, and its process is: stimulus — reinforcement — response. For example, Pavlov's classical conditioning: stopping when seeing a red light.

**2. Stimulus-response learning**

Stimulus-response learning refers to the learning of the response to a stimulus in a certain situation to obtain a specific result. *For example, Thorndike's and Skinner's operational conditioning, which, unlike classical conditioning, belongs to stimulus-response learning.* The process of operational conditioning is situation — response — reinforcement. That is, an organism is first in a situation, then responds, and finally, the response receives reinforcement. *For example, primary school students do their homework to receive the teacher's praise.*

**3. Chained learning**

Chained learning refers to the learning of connecting two or more stimulus-response behaviors to form a series of connected stimulus-response behaviors. Any kind of motor skill cannot be formed without chained learning. *For example, learning a series of catching and dodging actions in basketball or opening a door by holding, pressing, pushing, and other actions.*

**4. Associative learning of speech**

Associative learning of speech is a kind of chained learning that forms a series of language units. *For example, making formal sentences with words.*

**5. Discrimination learning**

Stimulus discrimination occurs when two stimuli are sufficiently distinct from each other, such that one evokes a conditioned response while the other does not. Stimulus discrimination provides the ability to differentiate between stimuli. *For example, Dog Cleo comes running into the kitchen when she hears the sound of the electric can opener, which she has learned is used to open her dog food when her dinner is about to be served. She does not bound into the kitchen at the sound of the food processor, although it sounds similar. In other words, she discriminates between the stimuli of the can opener and the food processor*. Discrimination learning refers to the learning of distinguishing the similarities and differences of various stimuli and making different responses to them. Discrimination learning is essentially a kind of perceptual learning, that is, perceptual differentiation. Discrimination encompasses single discrimination (responding respectively to objects according to their shape, size, or color) and multiple discrimination (putting easily confusing words together for students to recognize). *For example, choose the word with a different pronunciation from the others*:

　　A. *book*　B. *food*　C. *tooth*　D. *good*

### 6. Concept learning

Concept learning refers to the learning of making the same response to the same kind of stimuli when classifying stimuli, that is, responding to the abstract characteristics of similar things. In other words, concept learning refers to the learning of the common nature of a kind of thing and responding to the abstract characteristics of similar things. For example, learning the concept of a square in mathematics or learning the concept of speed in physics.

### 7. Rule learning

Rule learning, also known as principle learning or law learning, refers to the learning of the relationship between two or more concepts. Example-rule method and rule-example method are two basic ways of rule learning. The example-rule method refers to the method of summarizing the principles from a series of examples presented in teaching. The rule-example method refers to the method of presenting the rules to be learned first, and then illustrating the rules with examples.

### 8. Problem-solving learning

Problem-solving learning, also known as advanced-rule learning, refers to the learning of using the learned principles or rules to solve problems in various situations.

In 1971, Gagne revised the classification of learning, merging the first four categories into one and expanding concept learning into two categories: specific concept learning and definitional concept learning, that is, ① chained learning; ② discrimination learning; ③ specific concept learning; ④ definitional concept learning; ⑤ rule learning; ⑥ problem-solving learning.

## 4.2.4 Ausubel's classification of learning style

Ausubel distinguished learning from two dimensions: learning is divided into reception learning and discovery learning based on the way students learn; learning is divided into meaningful learning and rote learning based on the relationship between learning content and the learners' cognitive structure(Figure 4-1).

**1. Rote learning and meaningful learning**

Rote learning refers to the acquisition of arbitrary and literal connections, which occurs when the learner fails to establish non-artificial and substantive connections between learning materials and the learner's original cognitive structures. Meaningful learning refers to the process in which the learning material is connected to the learner's existing knowledge in a non-artificial and substantive way.

**2. Reception learning and discovery learning**

Reception learning refers to learning in which the content is taught to the learner in a conclusive manner, requiring no independent discovery. In contrast, discovery learning involves the learner discovering the content themselves before they can assimilate it into their cognitive structure. Discovery learning is a method where students are provided with relevant materials, allowing them to uncover knowledge and understand concepts and principles through exploration, experimentation, and critical thinking. Discovery learning differs from reception learning in that its process is more complex, as it includes an additional stage—problem-solving. Furthermore, reception learning and discovery learning serve different roles in intellectual development and cognitive functioning.

Ausubel pointed out that the two dimensions are independent of each other, but the two extremes of these dimensions are not absolute, and there are transitional forms between them. Some learning exhibits both the nature of rote learning and meaningful learning, or the nature of discovery learning and reception learning. See Figure 3-1 for specific combinations.

According to the level of consciousness during learning, American psychologist Arthur S. Reber divided learning into *implicit learning and explicit learning*. According to the content of learning, Chinese scholar Feng Zhongliang categorized learning into *knowledge learning, skill learning, and the learning of behavioral norms*.

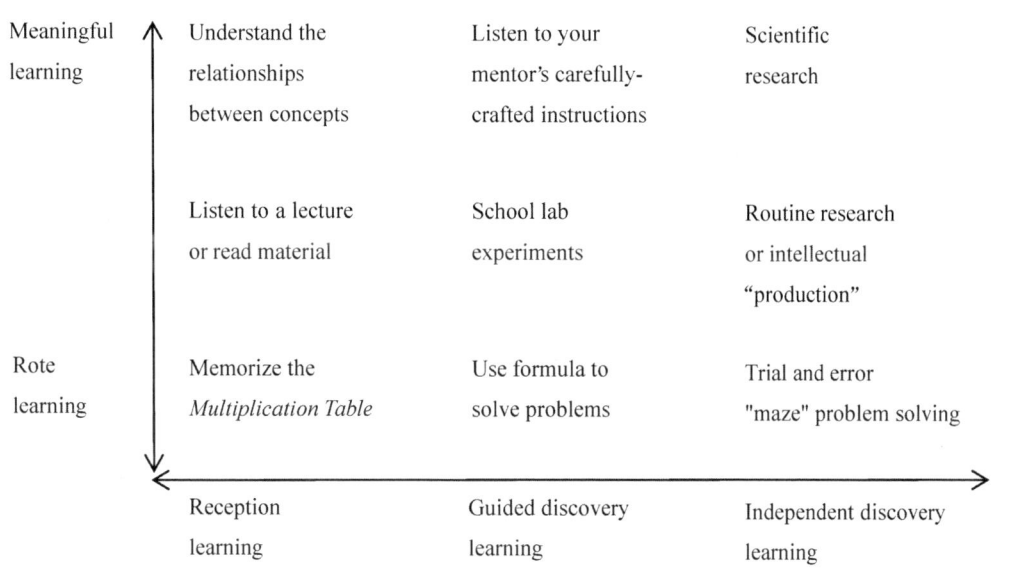

Figure 4-1  Ausubel's classification of learning style

Source: 施良方,《学习论(第 2 版)》,人民教育出版社,2001,第 223 页.

## 4.3  Behaviorism learning theory

Pavlov(1849 – 1936)

Behaviorism is one of the main schools of modern American psychology and has a great influence on western psychology. Its most fundamental point is to deny consciousness and take the individual explicit behaviors as the research object of psychological angle. The behaviorism theories of learning introduced in this section are mainly about the ones by the behaviorism representatives such as Thorndike, Pavlov, Skinner and Bandura.

### 4.3.1  Pavlov's classical conditioning theory

Ivan Pavlov (1849-1936) was a famous Russian psychologist. His classical conditioning theory of learning was developed based on his research work.

#### 1. Pavlov's classical experiment

Pavlov's classical conditioning experiments comprised three stages: before conditioning, during conditioning, and after conditioning. At the beginning of the experiment, the dogs were presented with the stimulus of a bell, and the food was offered half a minute after the bell rang, allowing the dog's salivary response to be observed and recorded. When the bell was repeatedly paired with the food many times, the dog also exhibited a salivary response when the bell was presented without the food.

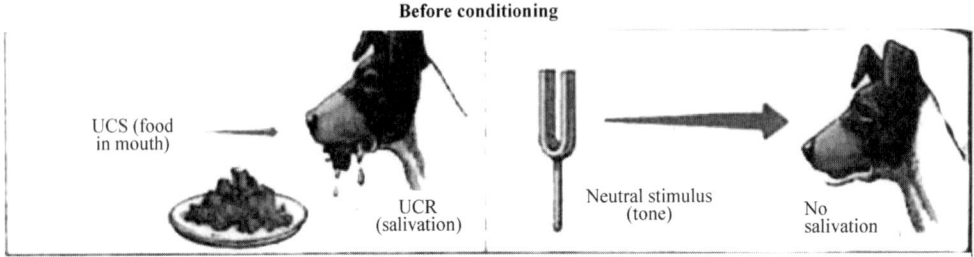

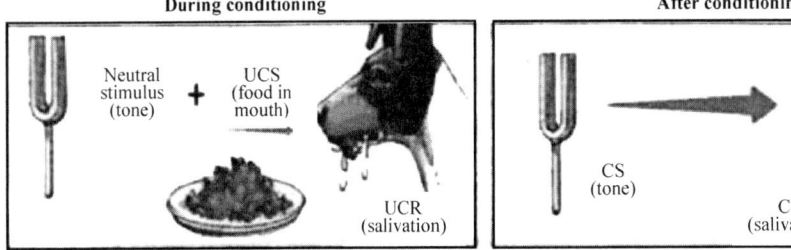

Figure 4-2 The basic process of classical conditioning

Before conditioning, the food can elicit the dog's salivary response, while the bell cannot elicit the dog's saliva. The food is called the unconditioned stimulus (UCS), the bell is called a neutral stimulus (NS), and the salivary response induced by food is called the unconditioned response (UCR). During conditioning, after the bell is repeatedly paired with the food, the bell and the food elicit the dog's saliva together. The dog's salivation still belongs to the unconditioned response (UCR). After conditioning, when the bell is presented alone without food, the dog will salivate. Thus, the bell (NS) has acquired the ability to elicit the salivary response that was previously restricted only to the food and becomes the conditioned stimulus (CS). The salivary response that can be elicited by presenting the conditioned stimulus alone is called the conditioned response (CR) (Figure 4-2).

Although the subjects of Pavlov's experiment were dogs, conditioned reflexes are also present in humans. Some people may be conditioned to fear neutral stimuli that are not harmful. *For example*, *"Once bitten, twice shy"; school weariness and exam anxiety.*

2. Learning laws of classical conditioning

1) Law of acquisition

The connection between the conditioned stimulus and the unconditioned stimulus is presented multiple times to obtain and strengthen the conditioned response. The process of establishing the conditioned response is known as acquisition. *For example, when presented with a connection between sound stimulation and feeding, the dog exhibits a salivary response to the sound.*

2) Law of extinction

Extinction is a basic phenomenon of learning that occurs when the frequency of a previously conditioned response decreases and eventually disappears. *For example, after the formation of classical conditioning, if a dog that has become conditioned to salivate at the ringing of a bell never receives food again when the bell is rung, the frequency of the salivation (CR) gradually weakens or even disappears.*

3) Law of recovery

Pavlov discovered this phenomenon: when he returned to his dog a few days after the conditioned behavior had seemingly been extinguished, if he rang the bell, the dog once again salivated. This phenomenon is known as spontaneous recovery, which refers to the reemergence of an extinguished conditioned response after a period of time without further conditioning. *For example, spontaneous recovery helps explain why it is so hard to overcome drug addiction, give up smoking, and stop playing computer games.*

4) Law of generalization

Pavlov noticed that his dogs often salivated not only at the ringing of the bell used during their original conditioning but also at the sound of a buzzer. Such behavior is the result of stimulus generalization. Stimulus generalization is a process in which, after a stimulus has been conditioned to produce a particular response, stimuli that are similar to the original stimulus also produce the same response. Once any animal has learned to respond conditionally to a particular conditioned stimulus, other stimuli similar to the conditioned stimulus can also induce a conditioned response. *For example, "once bitten, twice shy."*

5) Law of discrimination

Stimulus discrimination occurs when two stimuli are sufficiently distinct from each other such that one evokes a conditioned response, but the other does not. Stimulus discrimination fosters the ability to differentiate between stimuli. In the process of stimulus discrimination, the conditioned stimulus and a stimulus similar to the conditioned stimulus are presented to the organism respectively. The conditioned stimulus is enhanced, while the unrelated stimulus is not strengthened, allowing the organism to distinguish the different effects of the two stimuli. *In Pavlov's experiments, for example, dogs established a conditioned response to a bell and* produced a generalized response to an electric buzzer. If the response to the bell is repeatedly enhanced (food is given) and the response to the electric buzzer is not enhanced (no food is given), the dog will eventually learn to respond only to the bell (salivation).

6) Law of higher-order conditioning

After a conditioned reflex is formed, the conditioned stimulus can induce a response in the organism similar to that of an unconditioned stimulus. The process in which a conditioned stimulus conditions another neutral stimulus is called higher-order conditioning. By that analogy, the second conditioning can be established based on the first conditioning, and the third conditioning can be established based on the second conditioning.

In real life, the process of students' conditioned tension or anxiety caused by exam failure undergoes a process of higher-order conditioning. Exam failure begins as a neutral event, but when it is connected to criticism from parents and teachers or ridicule from classmates, which directly leads to anxiety, exam failure becomes the conditioned stimulus. Criticism or ridicule itself is an unconditioned stimulus for students' unconditioned anxiety, and over time, failure in exams will cause conditioned anxiety. Additionally, cues related to the test situation may also become conditioned stimuli. *For example, students may feel anxious when they walk into an examination room.*

7) Two signal systems

Any physical conditioned stimulus that can cause a conditioned response is called a stimulus of the first signal system. A conditioned stimulus that is mediated by a language sign and can cause a conditioned response is called a stimulus of the second signal system. "谈虎变色" and "望梅止渴" belong to the conditioning of the second signal system. The essential difference between human learning and animal learning lies in the second signal system dominated by language.

Classical conditioning effectively explains how an organism learns to connect two stimuli so that one replaces the other and forms a connection with the conditioned response. However, classical conditioning cannot explain the learning phenomenon where the organism, in order to achieve a certain result, takes the initiative to make some voluntary response. *For example, a child takes the initiative to do household chores in order to receive their mother's praise; a student studies hard to gain the teacher's praise and classmates' approval or to secure a good job in the future; workers take the initiative to work overtime to earn additional pay or to seek a promotion in the future. To explain these phenomena requires the aid of operant conditioning.*

## 4.3.2 Thorndike's connection and trial-and-error learning

Edward L. Thorndike, a famous American psychologist, is the founder of connectionist theory of learning, a pioneer of scientific educational psychology, and the father of modern educational psychology. He moved educational psychological research towards a scientific approach. Thorndike defined the learning process of animals and humans as the connection between stimulus and response. He believed that knowledge and skills must be acquired through the process of "trial-error-retrial", which is based on animal experiments with cats in a "puzzle box". Thorndike's theory of connection is the first relatively complete theory of learning in the history of educational psychology, systematically answering some of the most basic questions about learning and laying a foundation for educational psychology to become an independent discipline.

Edward Lee Thorndike (1874–1949)

### 1. Thorndike's puzzle box experiment

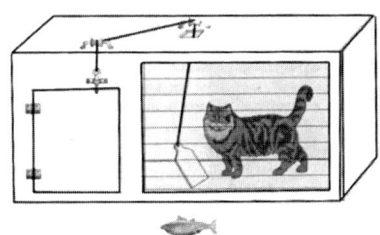

Figure 4-3　Thorndike's puzzle box

In this experiment, a hungry cat was placed in a box equipped with a device to open the latch, and a small fish that the cat could see was placed outside the box. The cat could only get food out of the box when it stepped on the device to open the door with its front paw. After a series of blind attempts, the cat finally stepped on the device, opened the door, escaped from the box, and ate the fish. The cat was put back into the box multiple times. After several attempts, the cat escaped from the box faster and faster, making fewer and fewer mistakes. After repeated attempts, the cat learned to make a successful response and abandoned the unsuccessful responses, automatically forming the connection between the stimulus of the box situation and the response of stepping on the device (Figure 4-3). *For example, children's willfulness is closely related to operant conditioning. In fact, children's willfulness is shaped by operant conditioning. Some children often make unreasonable demands of their parents, forcing them to comply. In order to avoid public awkwardness, the parents eventually promise their children what they want. If this occurs frequently, children develop a habit of willfulness and bad behavior, especially in public. The process of forming willfulness is a process of establishing operant conditioning. Operant conditioning is pervasive in our daily life.*

### 2. The essence of learning

The essence of learning is to form the connection between stimulus and response, represented by the formula S-R. He believed that the connection between the stimulus and the response is direct and does not require an intermediary. The learning process involves forming the connection between stimulus and response, established through trial and error. In other words, learning is the connection and is based on trial and error. The connection formed between situational stimulation and the motor impulse response is the basis of learning and also the fundamental unit of psychological behavior.

### 3. The process of learning

The learning process is a gradual process of blind and erroneous trials. Throughout this process, as the number of incorrect responses gradually decreases and the number of correct responses gradually increases, a strong connection is formed between stimulus and response. This theory is also known as the trial-and-error theory.

### 4. The principles of learning

1) Law of readiness

The law of readiness means that the strengthening or weakening of the connection depends on the learner's psychological readiness and adjustment. Readiness does not refer to the readiness of knowledge or maturity before learning, but rather to the preparatory set of learners at the beginning of the learning process. This set refers to a state of readiness in mental activity, which affects the tendency to solve problems. In other words, whether the learner will respond to a stimulus is related to their readiness to learn. Learners feel satisfied when they prepare and engage in activities, annoyed when they prepare but do not engage, and also annoyed when they are forced to engage without preparation. *For example, the cat must be hungry before being placed in the box to ensure that learning takes place. If the cat is well-fed and placed in the box, it will most likely not exhibit any behavior of learning to escape but will instead curl up and sleep.*

2) Law of exercise

The law of exercise means that the connection between the stimulus and the response will be strengthened by repetition or practice; the strength of the connection will weaken without repetition or practice. If practiced and applied regularly, the strength of the connection will gradually increase. The more repetitions of a stimulus, the stronger the stimulus-response connection. The closer the practice, the greater the strength of the connection. If not used, the strength of the connection gradually diminishes, and the longer it goes unused, the more easily it diminishes. The law of exercise is divided into two sub-laws: the law of use and the law of disuse.

3) Law of effect

The law of effect refers to the idea that the connection between the stimulus and the response can be strengthened by leading to satisfactory results or weakened by leading to unsatisfactory results. That is, if an action is followed by a satisfactory change in a situation, the likelihood of the action being repeated in similar situations will increase. However, if an unsatisfactory change follows, the likelihood of the behavior being repeated will decrease. In this way, we can see that the consequences of a person's current behavior play a key role in determining their future behavior. *For example, in Thorndike's experiments, in addition to the requirement that the cat be hungry, food is also an important condition for learning to occur.*

### 5. The educational significance of connection and trial-and-error theory

Although Thorndike's connection and trial-and-error theory derives from animal experiments, it still holds great relevance for human learning, especially for students' learning. According to students' learning characteristics, this theory emphasizes "learning by doing," that is, learning concepts, principles, skills, and strategies through actual operational processes. Specifically, it has the following guiding significance for education:

1) In the learning process, teachers should allow students to make mistakes and encourage them to try more and learn from those mistakes, so that the knowledge gained will be more solid.

2) Any learning should take place under conditions where students are well-prepared, and "surprise attacks" should not be carried out frequently. (Law of readiness)

3) In the learning process, we should strengthen reasonable practice and pay attention to practice from time to time after learning. (Law of exercise)

4) In practical education, teachers should strive to help students achieve positive self-satisfaction in their learning and prevent the acquisition of negative consequences. (Law of effect)

### 4.3.3 Skinner's operant conditioning theory

Edward L. Thorndike laid the foundation for operant conditioning theory, while Skinner systematically developed this theory and made it exert great influence on the educational practice.

**1. Skinner's classical experiment and behavior classification**

1) Skinner's classical experiment—operant conditioning

Skinner was famous for developing and using the Skinner box (Figure 4-4), a learning device that contains a simple apparatus for studying the behavior of animals, usually rats and pigeons. A Skinner box for rats consists of a lever that is easy for the rat to press, a food dispenser that can deliver a food pellet, and a water dispenser. The rat cannot see anything outside of the box, so all stimuli are controlled by the experimenter. In the experiment, while running around in the box, the rat happened to step on the lever, and a food pellet was delivered. After a few attempts, the rat would press the lever until it had eaten enough. The food reward conditioned the rat's behavior, strengthening the pressing of the lever and weakening other behaviors (such as wandering around the box). The rat learned the response of pressing the lever to obtain food in this experiment, connecting the reinforcer (food) with the operant response (pressing a lever) to form operant conditioning. Pressing the lever becomes a means or tool to get food, so operant conditioning is also called instrumental conditioning.

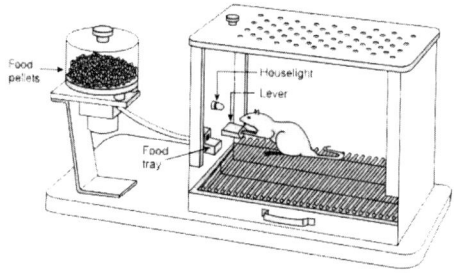

**Figure 4-4 Skinner box**

2) Classical conditioning and operant conditioning

It is easy to find the difference between them by comparing Pavlov's classical conditioning with Skinner's operant conditioning (Table 4-2).

Table 4-2  Comparison of classical conditioning and operant conditioning

|  | Classical conditioning | Operant conditioning |
|---|---|---|
| Representative | Pavlov | Skinner |
| Common characteristics | Reinforcement ||
|  | Individuals' behaviors are passively reinforced by conditioned stimuli. | Individuals' behaviors are reinforced by the outcomes of their own active operational behaviors. |
| Nature of behaviors | Non-spontaneous (An individual cannot control his behavior) Emotional Physiological | Spontaneous (An individual can control his behavior) |
| Order of events | The behavior appears after the stimulus. | The behavior appears before the stimulus (consequence). |
| Occurrence of learning | Neutral stimulus is connected with unconditioned stimulus. | The consequence of the behavior affects the subsequent behavior. |
| Examples | *After a doctor in white gives a child a series of painful injection (an unconditioned stimulus), the child will be afraid of any person in white.* | *A student who fails (punishment) after drinking out the night before a test is less likely to drink out the night before the next test.* |

3) Classification of behaviors

Through extensive experimental research, Skinner believed that there were two types of human and animal behaviors: respondent behavior and operant behavior. Classical conditioning theory can explain the generation of respondent behavior, while operant conditioning theory can explain the generation of operant behavior. **Respondent behavior** is caused by a specific stimulus and is an involuntary reflex response, such as a dog's salivating response to food or a breeder's footsteps; the response does not occur if the stimulus is not present. **Operant behavior**, which is not connected with any specific stimulus, is the organism's spontaneous and voluntary behavior. The rat in the Skinner box pressed the lever; the Skinner box was just a situational condition, and the lever in the box had the nature of a stimulus only after the rat operated it.

Skinner believed that most human behaviors are operant behaviors in daily life, such as reading, writing, swimming, cycling, etc. , which represent human active adaptation to the environment. The behavior itself is influenced by the consequences or by the law of reinforcement.

2. Laws of operant conditioning

1) Reinforcement

Reinforcement is the process of increasing the frequency, intensity, and speed of an organism's response to appropriate reinforcers, such as the process that leads the rat to continually press the lever. Skinner believed that reinforcement is an effective and important condition for shaping behavior; the process of reinforcement is the process of learning. Reinforcement can affect the speed of behavior acquisition and response, as well as the speed of behavior extinction. Reinforcement comprises positive reinforcement and negative reinforcement. **Positive reinforcement**, also known as active reinforcement, increases the response frequency by presenting a desired and pleasant stimulus. **Negative reinforcement**, also known as passive reinforcement, increases the frequency of response by eliminating or terminating an aversive or unpleasant stimulus. The comparison of positive reinforcement and negative reinforcement is shown in the table below (Table 4-3).

Table 4-3   Comparison of positive reinforcement and negative reinforcement

|  | Positive reinforcement | Negative reinforcement |
| --- | --- | --- |
| Reinforcer | Positive reinforcer | Negative reinforcer |
| Basic condition for the distinction | The stimulus that meets the individual's needs. | The stimulus that the individual hates and tries to avoid. |
| Condition after the response | The stimulus appears after the response and reinforcement of the response. | The stimulus disappears after the response and reinforcement of the response. |
| Example | *When a student answers questions, the teacher praises him, which may lead to the increase of the students' active behavior of speaking.* | *When we get into a car and hear an annoying ringing bell that doesn't stop until we put on the seat belt, we form a good habit of buckling up as soon as we get in the car through negative reinforcement.* |

2) Schedule of reinforcement

A schedule of reinforcement is a variety of arrangements of reinforcement made according to the appropriate combination of the number of desired responses and the time interval between reinforcements. When we refer to the frequency and timing of reinforcement that follows desired behavior, we are talking about schedules of reinforcement. Behaviors that are reinforced every time they occur are said to be on a **continuous reinforcement schedule**; only some behaviors, but not all, that are reinforced are on a **partial (intermittent) reinforcement schedule**. Intermittent reinforcement schedules can be divided into two categories: schedules that consider the *number of responses* made before reinforcement is given, called fixed-ratio and variable-ratio schedules, and those that consider the *amount of time* that elapses before reinforcement is provided, called fixed-interval and variable-interval schedules, which can combine into four kinds of reinforcement schedules (Table 4-4). In general, the effect of intermittent reinforcement is better than that of continuous reinforcement; the effects of variable-interval and variable-ratio reinforcement schedules are better than those of fixed-interval and fixed-ratio reinforcement schedules.

Table 4-4 Classification of schedules of reinforcement

| Classification | Concepts | Characteristics | Examples |
| --- | --- | --- | --- |
| Fixed-ratio reinforcement | A reinforcement will be given after a certain number of desired behaviors. | Predictable | *Piece-rate wage; one chance to speak raising hand every three times.* |
| Fixed-interval reinforcement | A reinforcement will be given after a certain time interval. | Predictable | *Hourly wage; final exam of each semester.* |
| Variable-ratio reinforcement | A reinforcement will be given after an indefinite number of desired behaviors | Unpredictable | *Fishing; buying a lottery; playing mahjiang* |
| Variable-interval reinforcement | A reinforcement will be given after an indefinite time interval. | Unpredictable | *Surprise quiz* |

Source: Robert E. Slavin, *Educational Psychology Theory and Practice* (10th), Posts & Telecom Press, 2017, p. 130.

3) Reinforcer

A stimulus or event that increases the frequency of a behavior is called a **reinforcer**. According to the time of its occurrence and whether it is desirable or unpleasant, reinforcers can be divided into positive reinforcers and negative reinforcers. **A positive reinforcer** is a stimulus that follows a response and increases the rate of occurrence of that response. *If food is provided to the monkey after it turns a somersault, it is more likely that the monkey will turn a somersault again in the future.* The paychecks that workers receive at the end of the month, for instance, increase the likelihood that they will return to their jobs the following month. **A negative reinforcer** refers to an unpleasant stimulus whose removal increases the probability that a prior response will be repeated in the future. A mother might say to her son, "*If you get an A in tomorrow's test, you won't have to do homework for the rest of the week.*" The homework is the negative reinforcer. An alarm is a negative reinforcer for the student who has to get up early to go to school. The stimulus that meets the individual's needs is the positive reinforcer; the stimulus that the individual dislikes and tries to avoid is the negative reinforcer. The stimulus that disappears after the response and reinforcement of the response is also considered a negative reinforcer.

According to the source, reinforcers can be divided into primary reinforcers and secondary reinforcers. **Primary reinforcers**, also known as original reinforcers or physiological reinforcers, include all stimuli that reinforce without any learning taking place. Some examples are food, water, security, love, warmth, and sex, which satisfy basic physiological needs. Secondary reinforcers include those stimuli that do not initially play a reinforcing role but later do as a result of being paired with primary reinforcers or other reinforcers. For human beings, secondary reinforcers include many stimuli (such as money, grades, praise, toys, games, fun activities, privileges, social status, power, wealth, reputation, etc.) that reinforce a large number of behaviors, most of which are determined by social culture, and constitute extremely powerful secondary reinforcers that influence human behavior. Teachers can sometimes use primary reinforcers (such as candy) to reinforce students' correct behaviors, but they should use secondary reinforcers (such as grades, appreciation, encouragement, and praise) more often.

4) Premack Principle

When choosing reinforcers, one can follow the **Premack Principle**, also known as **Grandma's Rule**, which refers to the use of high-frequency behaviors as effective reinforcers for low-frequency behaviors. The grandmother, who is doing needlework, asks her grandson to bring her presbyopic glasses and says, "Fetch my glasses, and I'll give you some candy." Because candy is what the grandson prefers, he is willing to fetch the glasses for his granny. Otherwise, the grandson is not willing to fetch the glasses for his grandmother. In daily life, people use rewards to positively reinforce others' behaviors, consciously or unconsciously. *For example, teachers praise students who maintain discipline in class; parents reward children who perform well in exams, and bosses increase salaries for employees who work hard.*

5) Practical reinforcer

Anything that children like can be an effective reinforcer, but there are obvious practical limitations on what should be used in the classroom. One general principle of positive reinforcement is that it is best to use the least elaborate or tangible reinforcer that will work. In other words, if praise or self-reinforcement will work, don't use certificates. If certificates will work, don't use small toys. If small toys will work, don't use food. One way to find out what reinforcers to use is to ask the students themselves, who are more likely to work for a reinforcer they have selected. However, do not hesitate to use whatever practical reinforcer is necessary to motivate children to do important tasks. In particular, try all possible strategies for reinforcement before even considering punishment. A few categories of reinforcers and examples of each appear here. These are arranged from least to most tangible.

① Self-reinforcement. Students may be taught to praise themselves, give themselves a mental pat on the back, check off progress on a form, take a short break, or otherwise reinforce themselves for completing an assignment or staying on task.

② Praise. Phrases such as "Good job", "Way to go", "I knew you could do it", and other verbal praise can be effective, but the same message can often be delivered with a smile, a wink, a thumbs-up signal, or a pat on the back. In cooperative learning and peer tutoring, students can be encouraged to praise each other for appropriate behavior.

③ Attention. The attention of a valued adult or peer can be a very effective reinforcer for many children. Listening, nodding, or moving closer may provide a child with the positive attention he or she is seeking. For outstanding performance or for meeting goals over a longer time period, students might be allowed a special time to visit with the custodian, help in the office, or take a walk with the principal.

④ Grades and Recognition. Good marks and other honors (e. g. , certificates of accomplishment) can be effective both in providing students with positive feedback on their efforts and in communicating progress to families, who are likely to reinforce good reports themselves. Public displays of good work, notes from the principal, and other commendations can have the same effect. Quiz scores, behavior ratings, and other feedback given frequently can be more effective than report card grades covering months of work.

⑤ Call Home. Calling or sending a note to a child's caregivers to recognize success can be a powerful reinforcer.

⑥ Home-based Reinforcement. Families can be effective partners in a reinforcement system. Teachers can work out an arrangement with families in which children receive special privileges at home if they meet well-specified standards of behavior or performance.

⑦ Privileges. Children can earn free time, access to special equipment (e. g. , soccer balls or games), or special roles (such as running errands or distributing papers). Children or groups who have behaved well can simply be allowed to line up first for recess or dismissal or have other small privileges.

⑧ Activity Reinforcers. After achieving preestablished standards, students can earn videos, games, or access to other fun activities. Activity reinforcers lend themselves particularly well to group contingencies, in which a whole class can earn free time or special activities if students collectively achieve a standard.

⑨ Tangible Reinforcers. Children may earn points for achievement or good behavior that they can exchange for small toys, erasers, pencils, marbles, comic books, stickers, and so on. Tangible reinforcers usually work better if children have a choice among several options.

⑩ Food. Raisins, apples, carrots, yogurt, or other healthy snacks can be used as reinforcers (Robert E. Slavin, 2017).

2. Escape conditioning and avoidance conditioning

When the aversive stimulus or unpleasant situation occurs, the organism makes a response to escape the aversive stimulus or unpleasant situation, and the probability of the response increases for similar situations in the future. This kind of conditioning is escape conditioning, which reveals how organisms learn to eliminate pain. *For instance, taking a detour after seeing garbage on the road; leaving the house temporarily when it becomes too noisy; or falling into a pit teaches you to be cautious.*

When the stimulus signal indicating the imminent emergence of an aversive stimulus presents itself, the organism can spontaneously make a response, thus avoiding the emergence of the aversive stimulus, and the probability of the response occurring in similar situations in the future increases. This kind of conditioning is **avoidance conditioning.** Avoidance conditioning is based on escape conditioning. After experiencing the pain of aversive stimuli or unpleasant situations, individuals learn to respond to signals that predict aversive stimuli or unpleasant situations, thus avoiding pain, such as quickly moving away from a car horn when crossing the street.

Escape conditioning and avoidance conditioning are types of negative reinforcement, but they are obviously different. In escape conditioning, the aversive stimulus or unpleasant situation has occurred before the individual responds, and the individual actually experiences the pain caused by the aversive stimulus. In avoidance conditioning, aversive stimuli or unpleasant situations are avoided by the organism's prior response, and the organism is not actually subjected to the aversive stimuli. As a result, avoidance conditioning is more active in maintaining behavior than escape conditioning, which is also the theoretical basis for educators to emphasize "nipping in the bud" in moral education. Although avoidance conditioning is based on escape conditioning, it is unnecessary for students to experience some pain; thus, educators should instruct students to learn from others who have faced dangers to form avoidance conditioning. *For example, schools warn students not to play with fire, not to swim in rivers, not to play excessive video games, and so on before winter and summer vacations every year. People who take the driver's license exam must watch videos of tragic traffic accidents.*

3. Punishment and extinction

1) Punishment

Punishment refers to the negative result or consequence an organism suffers to eliminate or inhibit the response after exhibiting behavior that doesn't align with expectations. Punishment comprises positive punishment and negative punishment. In both cases, "positive" means adding something and "negative" means removing something.

**Positive punishment** refers to reducing the occurrence of undesirable behaviors by presenting individuals with unpleasant or unwanted stimuli. Positive punishment weakens a response through the application of an unpleasant stimulus. *For instance, criticizing a student for not wearing a uniform to school; spanking a child for misbehaving; or spending 10 years in jail for committing a crime.*

**Negative punishment** refers to reducing the occurrence of undesirable behaviors by removing something that the individual likes or desires. For example, punishing a child for failing an exam by confiscating his iPad. When a teenager is told he will no longer be able to play games because of his poor grades, or when an employee is informed that he has been demoted with a pay cut due to a poor job evaluation, negative punishment is being administered.

In real life, people often confuse negative reinforcement with punishment. The difference between a reinforcer and a punisher is that a reinforcer, whether positive or negative, increases the frequency of a response after its appearance, while a punisher decreases the frequency of a response.

Unlike reinforcement, which produces an increase in behavior, punishment reduces the likelihood of a prior response. The differences between reinforcement and punishment are shown in Table 4-5.

Table 4-5  Differences between reinforcement and punishment

| Difference | Reinforcement | | Punishment | |
|---|---|---|---|---|
| Classification | Positive reinforcement | Negative reinforcement | Positive punishment | Negative punishment (Removing rewards) |
| Characteristics | Present pleasant stimulus | Remove aversive stimulus | Present aversive stimulus | Remove pleasant stimulus |
| Purpose | Increase the frequency of response | | Decrease the frequency of response | |
| Examples | Praise. | Be exempt from doing the housework. | Spank the child for running around. | Don't go out to play until you finish your homework. |

According to operant conditioning, teachers should use positive reinforcement to shape students' good behavior and use negative reinforcement to eliminate or correct bad behavior in the educational process. Teachers should be careful when using punishment, as it can only inform students what not to do, but not what to do or how to do it.

2) Extinction

Extinction is a basic phenomenon of learning that occurs when a previously conditioned response decreases in frequency and eventually disappears. Behavior intensifies when the reinforcer is first withdrawn and then rapidly weakens until the behavior disappears. When reinforcers are withdrawn, individuals often increase their rate of behavior for a while. *For example, think of a door that you've used as a shortcut to a place you go frequently. Imagine that one day the door will not open. You may push even harder for a while, shake the door, turn the handle both ways, and perhaps even kick the door. You are likely to feel frustrated and angry. However, after a short time, you will realize that the door is locked and go away. If the door is permanently locked (without your knowing it), you may try it a few times over the next few days and then perhaps once after a month; only eventually will you give up on it.* Your behavior when confronted by the locked door is a classic extinction pattern. Still, the behavior may return after much time has passed. *For example, you could try the door again a year later to see whether it is still locked. If it is, you will probably leave it alone for a longer time, but perhaps not forever.*

The characteristic **extinction burst** — the increase in levels of a behavior in the early stages of extinction — has important consequences for classroom management. *For example, imagine that you have decided to extinguish a child's inappropriate calling out of answers (instead of raising his hand to be recognized) by ignoring him until he raises his hand quietly. At first, ignoring the child is likely to increase his calling-out behavior, a classic extinction burst. You might then mistakenly conclude that ignoring isn't working when, in fact, continuing to ignore inappropriate call-outs is exactly the right strategy if you keep it up.* Worse, you might finally decide to give in and recognize the child after the third or fourth call-out. This would teach the worst possible message: that calling out works eventually if you keep doing it. This will probably result in an increase in the very behavior you are trying to reduce, as the child learns that "if at first you don't succeed, try, try again."

Extinction of a previously learned behavior can be hastened when some stimulus or cue informs the individual that behaviors that were once encouraged will no longer be reinforced. *In the case of the locked door, a sign saying, "Door permanently locked. Please use other entrance" would have greatly reduced the number of times you tried the door before giving up on it. Call-outs will be reduced much more quickly if the teacher tells his class, "I will no longer respond to children unless they are silent and raising their hand," and then ignores all other attempts to get his attention* (Robert E. Slavin, 2017).

4. Programmed instruction

1) Connotation and basic theory of programmed instruction

Skinner applied the principles of operant conditioning to teaching activities and put forward the theory of programmed instruction and its instructional model.

Programmed instruction is a form of individualized instruction. Skinner decomposed large problems to be learned into a series of small problems, arranged and presented to students according to certain procedures, and required students to learn and answer questions. After answering the questions, students received timely feedback.

The basic theory of programmed instruction is to adopt the successive approximation method and continuously strengthen the designed program to help students form the behavior patterns that educators hope for. In teaching, the knowledge of each subject should first be decomposed into small knowledge items with internal logical connections, and then the knowledge items should be arranged into a coherent and progressively deepening sequence. Students should then learn in order, with feedback and reinforcement provided during the learning process, so that they can ultimately master the knowledge.

2) Principles of programmed instruction

① The principle of small steps. The teaching materials or programmed instruction machines used by students should divide the learning content into many small units. The small units are interconnected and layered in depth. The difficulty gap between neighboring small units is small, making it easy for learners to succeed.

② The principle of positive response. To ensure that students remain in a positive state during the learning process, teachers should reinforce them in a timely manner to support continuous learning activities.

③ The principle of self-pacing. Students can choose the most appropriate learning pace according to their ability to comprehend, allowing them to succeed easily and maintain strong learning motivation.

④ The principle of timely feedback. Timely feedback means that students can immediately know whether their answers are correct. Correct answers can help students build confidence, maintain learning behavior, and progress to the next stage of learning.

⑤ The principle of low-error rate. Ensure that learners reduce their error rate to a minimum during learning to achieve the effect of reinforcement.

3) Behavior modification

Behavior modification, or behavior therapy, is a deliberate form of operant conditioning used to eliminate undesirable behavior, such as temper tantrums, or to instill desirable behavior, such as putting away toys after playing. *For example, every time a child puts away toys, he or she receives a reward, such as praise, a treat, or a new toy.*

4) Behavioral shaping

**Shaping** is the teaching of a new skill or behavior by means of reinforcement for small steps toward the desired goal. Skinner believed that "education is to shape behavior". He used the method **of successive approximation** to continuously reinforce responses that tend to be shaped until the new behavior required is introduced. *For example, parents training their children's social skills can reinforce a child's behavior of opening doors for guests for the first time; then, when they greet the guests, parents give them reinforcement; after that, when they actively communicate with the guests, they will be reinforced. In this way, parents can teach their children to communicate effectively with others. Thus, the new behavior has been shaped.*

In classroom teaching, shaping is an important tool. When shaping behaviors, teachers should pay attention to the principle that students must be reinforced within their capabilities, and these behaviors must be able to extend to new behaviors. *For example, if students can solve 10 math problems within 15 minutes, and then they can solve 10 math problems within 12 minutes, this should be reinforced. But they should never be required to solve 10 math problems within 8 minutes before reinforcing.* However, a student who can solve 20 questions must finish all 20 questions before reinforcement is given, and reinforcement cannot be provided for solving fewer than 20 questions. Most students need reinforcement along the way. Should a kindergarten teacher withhold reinforcement until a child knows the sounds of all 26 letters? Certainly not. It would be better to praise children for recognizing one letter, then for recognizing several, and finally for learning the sounds of all 26 letters.

## 4.3.4 Bandura's observational learning theory

Behaviorists see the environment acting on the person as the chief impetus for development. However, the American psychologist Albert Bandura argued that this may be true for animal learning, but not for human learning, because people acquire a lot of knowledge, skills, social norms, and more from indirect experiences. People can learn indirectly by observing others' actions and their consequences, which Bandura called observational (social) learning.

**Albert Bandura**
(1925 – 1921)

1. Bandura's classical experiments and discoveries

The classic experiment in social learning theory was a study conducted by

Bandura in 1965. Sixty-six four-year-olds were chosen and randomly divided into three groups. Different groups of children watched the consequences of different treatments for the same aggressive behavior in a movie. The first group observed a model being rewarded for aggressive behavior. The second group observed a model being punished for aggressive behavior. The third group viewed a model who was neither rewarded nor punished for aggressive behavior. Then, the children were left alone in the same experimental situation as that in the movie and played for 10 minutes while the experimenters observed their behavior. They found that, compared with the other two groups, almost no one in the second group mimicked aggressive behavior; they acquired *vicarious punishment (you do not learn from shortcomings when you, as a bystander, see others being punished)*, while most members of the first group mimicked aggressive behavior, acquiring vicarious reinforcement.

The findings of the experiment indicate that the consequences of the aggressive behavior of the model are the decisive factors in whether children spontaneously imitate such behavior. Among these factors, vicarious punishment reduces the imitation of aggressive behavior.

2. The essence of learning—observational learning

According to Bandura, learning is a process in which individuals obtain new behavioral responses or modify existing responses by observing the behaviors of others and their reinforcement results. Classic observational learning theory maintains that people learn appropriate social behaviors chiefly by observing and imitating models—that is, by watching other people, such as parents, teachers, or sports heroes. This process is called **observational learning** or *modeling*. People tend to choose models who are prestigious, who control resources, or who are rewarded for what they do—those whose behavior is perceived as valuable in their culture. Imitation of models is the most important element of how children learn a language, deal with aggression, develop a moral sense, and learn gender-appropriate behaviors. Observational learning can occur even if a person does not imitate the observed behavior.

Observational learning has several obvious characteristics: ① Observational learning does not depend on direct reinforcement. ② Observational learning does not necessarily result in explicit behavioral responses. People can learn how to behave before they perform the behaviors by observing others' exemplary actions, thereby avoiding many unnecessary mistakes and dangerous outcomes. ③ Observational learning is cognitive.

### 3. Process of observational learning

Bandura's analysis of observational learning involves four processes: attention, retention, reproduction, and motivational processes (Figure 4-5).

1) Attention process

This determines which model behaviors an individual will choose to observe among numerous model behaviors. This process is influenced by various factors, such as the characteristics of the model behaviors. If model behaviors are unique, significant, or novel, they are more likely to attract the observer's attention. The observer's own interests, needs, and cognitive levels are also crucial. Observers with a strong interest in or specific need for a certain field will be more inclined to pay attention to model behaviors related to that field. Additionally, observers with higher cognitive levels may be better at capturing the key elements in model behaviors.

2) Retention process

In the retention phase, the observer remembers the behaviors learned from the model situation and represents, encodes, and stores them in memory in the form of images and language. That is, the model behavior is first converted into memory images, and then the memory images are converted into verbal codes. Both images and verbal codes are stored in the mind, which plays a guiding role in learners' future behavior.

3) Reproduction process

In reproduction, the observer converts the images and symbolic concepts of the model situation into explicit behaviors.

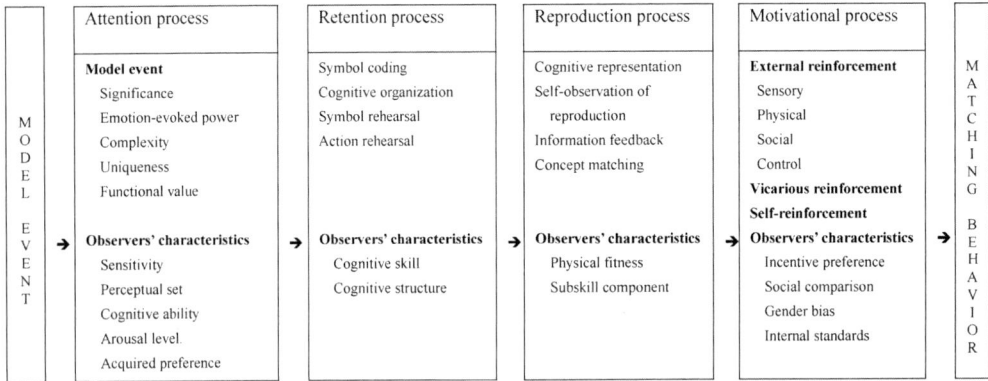

Figure 4-5 Four processes of observational (social) learning

Source: Bandura A., *Social Foundation of Thought and Action: A Social Cognitive Theory*, Prentice Hall, 1986, p. 52.

4) Motivational process

This process determines whether the observer will actually implement the observed model behaviors. Bandura also believed that not all learned behaviors are manifested, and whether learners display learned behaviors is influenced by reinforcement, which includes external reinforcement, vicarious reinforcement, and self-reinforcement. External reinforcement, such as rewards and punishments from the outside, has a direct impact on the observer's motivation. *For example, receiving praise enhances the motivation to implement model behaviors. Conversely, if you work hard to help the company make a profit and your boss gives you a bonus, you will be motivated to work even harder.* Vicarious reinforcement refers to the incentive or warning effect on oneself by observing the consequences of model behaviors. It is believed that everyone has the experience of seeking a reference point when facing an uncertain situation, deciding whether to take action by observing the behavior of others. *For example, if you are unsure of the consequences of slacking off at work, you might first observe your colleagues. After seeing that their salaries have been deducted, you decide to abandon the idea of slacking off and work diligently.* "杀鸡儆猴" *is a typical form of vicarious reinforcement.* Self-reinforcement is the process by which observers reward themselves for performing behaviors that meet or exceed their standards. People tend to engage in self-satisfying behaviors and reject those they dislike, which is a form of self-reinforcement. *For example, if you find yourself dozing off during your studies or work, you might slap yourself in the face to wake up, or follow a weekly plan and reward yourself with a big meal.* "头悬梁,锥刺股" *is a typical form of self-reinforcement.*

In the practical work of moral education, teachers should provide students with good models to learn from and maintain the model behavior, create opportunities for students to reproduce the model behavior, give timely praise and encouragement for positive behaviors, and modify and eliminate undesirable behaviors.

## 4.4 Cognitive learning theory

The cognitive learning theory holds that the process of an organism acquiring experience is the formation of a new cognitive structure through active internal information processing. Representatives of cognitive learning theory include the Gestalt School, Bruner, Ausubel, and Gagne.

### 4.4.1 Gestalt-insight learning theory of Gestalt school

Gestalt psychology is a school of psychology founded at the University of Berlin in Germany in 1912. The founders of Gestalt psychology are Max Wertheimer (1880-

1943), Wolfgang Köhler (1887-1967), and Kurt Koffka (1886-1941). Köhler conducted extensive experimental research on the learning of chimpanzees and proposed the Gestalt learning theory.

### 1. Köhler's classic experiments

In the series of box experiments(Figure 4-6), Köhler (1925) placed chimpanzees in a cage with boxes and bananas hanging from the top. The simple problem situation is that chimpanzees only need one box to reach the bananas, while the complex problem situation requires the chimpanzees to stack several boxes to reach the bananas.

In the experiments with the complex problem situation, two boxes were available. When Chimpanzee One saw the bananas hanging from the top of the cage, his initial reaction was to reach for them. However, he could not get them and had to sit on Box One to rest, but he had no intention of using the boxes. Later, when Chimpanzee Two walked away from Box Two, which he had been lying on originally, Chimpanzee One saw Box Two, moved it under the bananas, and stood on the box to stretch out his hand to get the bananas. However, the box was still not high enough for him to reach the bananas, and he had to sit down on Box Two to rest. All of a sudden, Chimpanzee One leaped, carried Box One that he had been sitting on, stacked it on Box Two, and then quickly climbed up onto the boxes to obtain the bananas. Three days later, Köhler slightly changed the experimental situation, but the chimpanzees were still able to use their previous experience to solve new problems.

**Figure 4-6  Köhler's box experiment**

### 2. The essence of learning—formation of new gestalt

From the results of learning, it is clear that learning is not the formation of a stimulus-response connection, but the formation of a new gestalt. Gestalt is a type of psychological structure, a whole that is functionally interrelated and interactive, reflecting the cognition of the relationships between things in the environment.

### 3. The process of learning

Gestalt has the functions of self-organization and self-improvement. When something is presented before us, a gestalt that corresponds to it exists in our mind. When the internal gestalt is not consistent with objective reality, defects in the gestalt will appear. Gestalt shows a tendency to compensate for its own defects, and the results of these activities make the gestalt itself more complete or form a better "gestalt". Based on this view, gestalt psychologists believe that the learning process involves forming a gestalt through positive organization in the mind in response to the current problem situation.

From the perspective of the learning process, learning is achieved through insight. Thus, learning is not a blind attempt but a successful outcome due to an understanding of the situation. Insight involves understanding one's own actions and circumstances, especially the relationship with the target object.

### 4. Thorndike's theory of connection and trial-and-error learning and the theory of gestalt-insight learning

The Gestalt school has made an important contribution to the development of learning theory by affirming the active role of the learner, viewing learning as a process of actively constructing a gestalt, emphasizing the role of cognitive functions such as observation, insight, and understanding in learning, and criticizing Thorndike's connectionism and trial-and-error learning theory.

However, Köhler's gestalt-insight learning and Thorndike's connectionism and trial-and-error learning are not mutually exclusive or absolutely opposed. Connectionism and trial-and-error are often the preludes to insight, which is, to some extent, the result of practice. Both connectionism and trial-and-error, as well as insight, are common in human learning. They represent two types of learning that occur in different ways, at different stages, or at different levels. In general, simple problem-solving that the learner has experience with often does not require repeated trial and error, while for complex and creative problem-solving, the learner typically cannot achieve insight until they have mostly gone through the process of connectionism and trial-and-error.

## 4.4.2 Tolman's theory of cognitive learning

Tolman was a representative of new behaviorism and the founder of teleological behaviorism. He introduced the concepts of overall behavior patterns and intermediary variables, constructed a new symbolic gestalt theory, and became a pioneer of cognitive

E. C. Tolman
(1886 – 1959)

psychology.

## 1. The basic point of view

Tolman was a behaviorist influenced by the Gestalt school. His cognitive learning theory and internal reinforcement theory have contributed to the development of modern cognitive learning theory. His main ideas about learning include:

1) Learning is purposeful and involves the acquisition of expectations. The purpose of learning is the main distinction that separates human learning from animal learning. Expectation, which is the core concept in Tolman's learning theory, refers to an internal state of readiness established by individuals based on their previous experiences, as well as the cognitive concepts about goals formed through learning.

2) Learning involves the cognition of gestalt and the process of forming a cognitive map, rather than merely learning a series of stimuli and responses. Thus, Tolman advocated changing the S-R formula into the S-O-R formula. S represents the stimulus, R represents the response, and O represents the organism. O, as a mediating variable, represents changes in the psychological state of the organism. Tolman believed that the internal state and process of the organism (O) play an important mediating role between the stimulus and the response. His viewpoint emphasizes that after an individual receives a stimulus, he does not simply make a direct response; rather, he determines the final response through internal cognitive processing and learning processes. This theory is significant for understanding the complexity of human behavior and the learning process. *For example, when you see a food advertisement (stimulus S), you (organism O) may consider whether you are hungry, whether you have money, and whether you want to eat this food, and then decide whether to go buy it (response R).* Tolman's views are supported by experiments on place learning and latent learning.

## 2. Place learning

The experiment was designed by Tolman and Honzik (1932) and carried out in the channels shown in Figure 4-7. The subject was a rat. By the time it was first trained, the rat had already become familiar with all three channels and had developed a tendency to choose them in the order of Channels 1, 2, and 3. In the experiment, Channel 1 was blocked at A, and the rat chose Channel 2 to run to the food box. When Channel 1 was blocked at B, the rat did not choose Channel 2 first and then Channel 3 as it had previously developed the habit; instead, it avoided trying Channel 2 and immediately chose Channel 3. Based on this, Tolman suggested that when the rat ran through the channels, it formed a cognitive map of the channels in its mind, or a gestalt, and was able to take action according to the cognitive map rather than relying on blind behavioral habits.

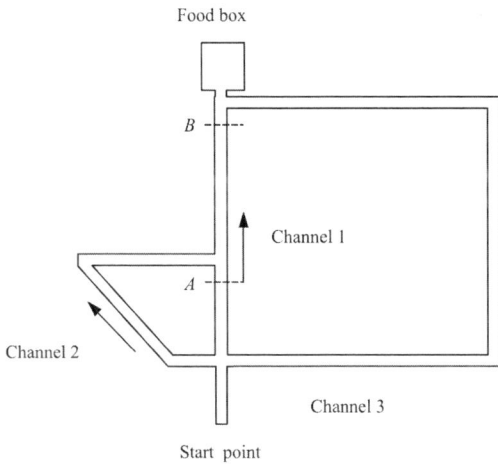

Figure 4-7　Tolman's maze experiment

Source：陈琦、刘儒德,《当代教育心理学(第 2 版)》,北京师范大学出版社,2007,第 158 页.

### 3. Latent learning

**Latent learning** refers to learning that occurs even without reinforcement, but the result of learning is not immediately obvious; it is "latent". Once the learning is reinforced and the organism has the operational motivation, the result of learning becomes apparent through action. According to Tolman, learning requires not only knowledge but also goals; if there are no goals, learning may not manifest itself, and its consequences may not necessarily be evident in explicit actions.

## 4.4.3　Bruner's cognition-discovery learning theory

Jerome S. Bruner (1915-2016) was a prominent psychologist in the field of cognitive education in the United States. He objected to procedural instruction based on reinforcement, believing that guiding students to learn step by step can lead only to rote learning and does not guarantee that students will apply knowledge in different situations. Bruner argued that the purpose of learning is to transform the basic structure of a subject into the cognitive structure of the student's mind through discovery learning. Therefore, his theory is often referred to as cognitive-discovery learning theory or cognitive-structure teaching theory.

**Jerome S. Bruner
(1915 – 2016)**

### 1. Cognitive learning view

The essence of learning is the active formation of cognitive structures, rather than the passive formation of stimulus-response connections. Learners do not passively accept knowledge; instead, they actively acquire knowledge and construct their knowledge systems by connecting newly acquired information with existing cognitive structures. Cognitive structure refers to an internal cognitive system that reflects the stable connections or relationships between concepts, as well as the overall content and organization of a learner's thoughts.

Learning includes three processes: acquisition of new knowledge, transformation of knowledge, and evaluation. Learning activities begin with the acquisition of new knowledge, which may refine existing knowledge or contradict it. The transformation of knowledge involves going beyond the given information and using various methods to change it into other forms to adapt to new tasks and acquire more knowledge. Evaluation of knowledge is an examination of knowledge transformation, through which we can determine whether our approach to handling knowledge is suitable for the new task and whether we are using it correctly.

### 2. Structural teaching view

Bruner argued that learning theory is descriptive rather than prescriptive, as it explains what the real situation is. Teaching theory, on the other hand, is conventional and serves as a normative theory that clarifies the rules for the best ways to acquire knowledge and skills.

1) The purpose of teaching lies in understanding the basic structure of a subject. **The basic structure of a subject** refers to its fundamental concepts, principles, attitudes, and methods. Because Bruner emphasized initiative in learning and the importance of cognitive structure, he advocated that the ultimate goal of teaching is to promote students' general understanding of subject structures. He believed that when students grasp the basic structure of a subject, they can easily understand the specific content, memorize it more effectively, facilitate learning transfer, increase their interest in learning, and promote the development of children's intelligence and creativity.

2) Teachers should master the teaching principles related to the basic structure of a subject.

① Principle of motivation: All students have an intrinsic desire to learn, and intrinsic motivation is the fundamental driver of sustained learning. Students possess three basic intrinsic motivations: the curiosity drive (the desire to learn), the competence drive (the desire to succeed), and the reciprocity drive (the need to interact positively with others). If teachers effectively promote and regulate students' inquiry activities, they can stimulate these intrinsic motivations and successfully achieve predetermined learning goals.

② Principle of structure: Any knowledge can be represented in three forms: enactive representation, iconic representation, and symbolic representation. Enactive representation involves learning through actions without the help of language. Iconic representation uses images based on perceptual materials to aid learning. Symbolic representation involves learning through language, allowing for logical deduction once experiences are transformed into linguistic forms. The choice of representational method should depend on the student's knowledge background and the nature of the subject.

③ Principle of procedure: Each subject generally has various procedures, and no single procedure is applicable to all learners. Specific procedures should be adopted based on the learner's prior knowledge, stage of intellectual development, the nature of the material, and individual differences.

④ Principle of reinforcement: To improve learning effectiveness, learners need feedback on their results. Therefore, the timing and methods of reinforcement in teaching are crucial for learning success. Feedback should be provided at the moment when the student is evaluating their work. Providing results too early can cause panic and interfere with exploration activities, while feedback too late may result in missed opportunities for assistance and potentially incorrect information.

### 3. Discovery learning

According to Bruner, discovery is the main means of educating children. The best way for students to grasp the basic structure of a subject is through discovery learning. Discovery learning refers to a teaching method where students are provided with relevant learning materials, allowing them to discover knowledge and understand concepts and principles independently through exploration, operation, and thinking. Bruner believed that teaching should not only enable students to firmly grasp scientific knowledge but also help them become autonomous and independent thinkers who can progress on their own after formal schooling.

1) Functions of discovery learning

Discovery learning can enhance intellectual potential. It facilitates the transformation from extrinsic motivation to intrinsic motivation. It helps students learn methods of discovery and exploration, and it promotes the retention of learned materials. However, discovery learning is also constrained by factors such as students' prior knowledge, intelligence levels, the nature of learning materials, teachers' guidance, and available teaching time.

2) The principles of discovery learning

Bruner proposed that four principles should be followed in the implementation of discovery learning:

① Teachers should explain the learning situation and the nature of teaching materials to students.

② Teachers should appropriately organize teaching materials according to students' experiences.

③ Teachers should arrange the complexity of teaching materials and their logical order according to students' psychological development levels.

④ Teachers should ensure that the difficulty of the materials is moderate to maintain students' internal learning motivation.

3) Characteristics of discovery learning

① Emphasize the learning process: Bruner asserted that students should be active explorers during the teaching process, with the teacher's role being to create situations that allow for independent exploration. The main purpose of students' learning is not to memorize what the teacher says or the content in textbooks, but rather to participate in establishing the knowledge system of the subject.

② Emphasize intuitive thinking: The discovery learning method particularly highlights the importance of intuitive thinking in students' learning. Intuitive thinking relies on images rather than verbal information. Therefore, teachers should avoid providing verbal information prematurely during students' exploration activities and instead encourage rich imaginative activities.

③ Emphasize intrinsic motivation: Bruner stressed the importance of fostering students' intrinsic motivation and suggested that teachers should encourage this motivation or transform extrinsic motivation into intrinsic motivation. He believed that the discovery activity form of learning stimulates students' curiosity, driving them to explore unknown outcomes and easily develop intrinsic motivation in learning activities.

④ Emphasize information extraction: Bruner maintained that the primary challenge of human memory is to extract information rather than simply store it. The key to effective information extraction lies in how information is organized, knowing where it is stored, and how to retrieve it. According to Bruner, when students are personally involved in discovering things, they tend to process and organize information effectively, which enhances memory retention.

4) Steps of discovery learning

① Propose problems that interest students.

② Allow students to experience uncertainty about the problem to stimulate their desire to explore.

③ Provide a variety of hypotheses for problem-solving.
④ Assist students in collecting and organizing information to draw conclusions.
⑤ Organize students to review relevant materials and reach conclusions.
⑥ Guide students to use analytical thinking to verify conclusions and ultimately solve problems.

Bruner's learning theory emphasizes students' initiative in learning, their existing cognitive structures, and independent thinking, as well as the importance of cultivating intrinsic motivation and thinking abilities. Bruner applied cognitive learning theory to teaching practice, providing a theoretical basis for educational reform and prompting educators to rethink their approaches to teaching and textbook development. The discovery learning he advocated has not only become a recognized learning method but has also been widely studied and applied as a teaching method.

However, Bruner's learning theory overlooks the particularities of students' learning, overemphasizes discovery learning, places too much emphasis on students' subjective initiative, neglects the characteristics of school education, and diminishes the teacher's guiding role. The practical application of the discovery teaching method is limited and is primarily suitable for certain subjects and for primary or lower-grade secondary school students.

### 4.4.4 Ausubel's meaningful reception learning theory

Ausubel was a famous educational psychologist in the United States who was contemporaneous with Bruner. According to the way of learning, he distinguished between reception learning and discovery learning; and based on the relationship between learning materials and the original knowledge structure, he categorized learning as rote learning and meaningful learning. In his view, if students' learning is valuable, it should be as meaningful as possible, and students' learning primarily involves meaningful reception learning.

Ausubel(1918—2008)

#### 1. Reception learning

Ausubel believed that students' learning is primarily reception learning, which is different from discovery learning. The process of discovery learning is more complicated than that of reception learning because there is an additional stage— problem-solving—in discovery learning. At the same time, reception learning and discovery learning play different roles in intellectual development and cognitive function. A large amount of material is acquired through reception learning, while various problems are solved through discovery learning. In children's development, however, reception learning appears later than discovery learning. The emergence of reception learning indicates that children have reached a higher level of cognitive maturity.

Additionally, it is necessary to distinguish reception learning from passive learning. Passive learning is the opposite of active learning. Reception learning may be active or passive, but it is not necessarily related to being passive or active. It is incorrect to equate reception learning with passive learning.

According to Ausubel, both reception learning and discovery learning can be either rote or meaningful. It is a misconception that reception learning is necessarily rote and that discovery learning is necessarily meaningful. Proper teaching does not necessarily lead to students' rote reception learning. Meaningful learning and rote learning are not absolutes, but rather exist at opposite ends of a continuum.

Reception learning is not exclusively rote learning; it can and should be meaningful learning. Similarly, discovery learning is not necessarily meaningful learning; it can also be rote learning. Schools should focus on meaningful reception learning.

### 2. Meaningful learning (Meaningful speech learning)

Ausubel's theory of meaningful learning mainly explains students' learning in the classroom. **Meaningful learning** is a method in which learners establish a genuine and substantial connection between the new knowledge represented by symbols and the existing appropriate concepts in the learner's cognitive structure. Ausubel believed that students learn systematic knowledge represented by language symbols in school mainly through meaningful learning rather than rote learning. Students' meaningful learning in school should encompass meaningful reception learning and meaningful discovery learning, but meaningful reception learning is emphasized more because it allows students to acquire a significant amount of systematic knowledge in a short period of time.

The essence of meaningful learning is the process of establishing genuine and substantive connections between new concepts represented by symbols and the existing appropriate concepts in the learner's cognitive structure. It is the process of assimilating new concepts into existing ones. The non-artificial connection refers to the internal connection rather than an arbitrary association, which is established on a reasonable logical basis between new knowledge and relevant concepts in the original cognitive structure. The substantive connection refers to words or expressions that, although different, are equivalent, meaning that this connection is non-literal.

### 3. Conditions of meaningful learning

Ausubel believed that meaningful learning can take place only when certain conditions are met. He divided the conditions for meaningful learning into objective conditions and subjective conditions.

1) Objective conditions refer to the influence of the nature of the learning materials themselves. Materials for meaningful learning must conform to genuine and substantial standards, meaning that they are logically meaningful. For example, textbooks generally meet this requirement.

2) Subjective conditions refer to the influence of learners' own factors. The main manifestations are as follows:

① Learners must have the mental set for meaningful learning. This mental set means that learners must have the tendency to actively connect the new knowledge represented by symbols with the appropriate knowledge existing in their cognitive structure.

② Learners' cognitive structure must contain an appropriate framework that can assimilate new knowledge.

③ Learners must actively make the new knowledge with potential significance interact with the related old knowledge in their cognitive structure so that the old knowledge can be reformed and the new knowledge can obtain practical meaning, that is, psychological meaning.

### 4. Learning models

At present, although the modes of learning and teaching in the school context are very different, they can be incorporated into the following dimensional system.

The first dimension is divided according to the degree of meaning of the learning materials. The second dimension is divided according to the way or mode of learning. The two dimensions can generate more models through cross-combination, which can cover all common learning models (Figure 4-8).

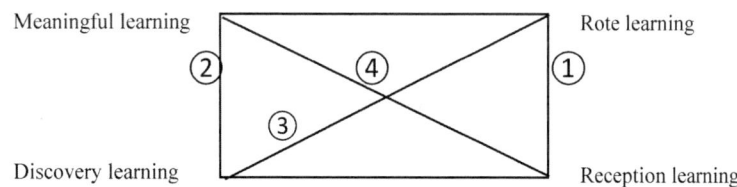

**Figure 4-8 Modes of learning**

Source: 山香教师招聘考试命题研究中心,《河南省教师招聘考试专用教材教育理论基础》,首都师范大学出版社,2015,第383页.

Model One is rote reception learning. Most traditional classroom teaching models today should be classified into this category. Model Two is meaningful discovery learning. Model Three is rote discovery learning. Model Four is meaningful reception learning.

In classroom teaching, teachers should choose different teaching methods according to the various learning contents, allowing reception learning and discovery learning, as well as meaningful learning and rote learning, to blend with each other and jointly promote development.

### 5. Principles and strategies of organizational learning

1) Principle of gradual differentiation

According to the principle of gradual differentiation, the most general and inclusive concepts should be taught first, followed by a gradual differentiation based on specific details. This approach provides ideal fixed points for teaching each knowledge unit, meaning that prior knowledge plays a foundational role in understanding new knowledge.

2) Principle of integrative reconciliation

The principle of integrative reconciliation requires students to recombine the existing elements in their cognitive structure.

3) Strategies for organizing learning—advanced organizer

To implement the principles of integrative reconciliation and gradual differentiation, Ausubel proposed the concept of the advanced organizer.

**An advanced organizer** is a guiding instructional material presented before the actual learning task. The levels of abstraction, generalization, and synthesis of the advanced organizer are higher than those of the learning task, and it is clearly connected with the existing concepts in the cognitive structure and the new learning task. *For instance, introducing the concept of a parallelogram before learning about rectangles, rhomboids, and squares. It is necessary to learn about triangles first before studying isosceles triangles, equilateral triangles, and right triangles.*

The main function of the advanced organizer is to build a bridge between old and new knowledge, making the connections between them clear, and to provide a cognitive framework or fixed point for learning new knowledge before students can meaningfully receive the new content.

Ausubel believed that advanced organizers not only help learners acquire new knowledge but also aid in knowledge retention. Advanced organizers can focus students' attention on the key aspects of the new knowledge to be learned; highlight the relationship between new knowledge and existing knowledge; and provide a framework (fixed point) for new knowledge. They can also assist students in recalling existing knowledge related to the new knowledge, thereby facilitating better connections.

### 4.4.5 Gagné's theory of information-processing learning theory

Gagné was one of the most influential educational psychologists in the 20th century. Gagné deeply studied learning, instructional design, intelligent skills, etc., put forward the theory of cumulative learning, gave an eclectic explanation of the nature of human learning and made a systematic theory of educational psychology.

Robert Mills Gagné (1916－2002)

Gagné believed that learning is a process with a beginning and an end, which can be divided into several stages, each requiring different information processing. The events that occur at each stage of information processing are called learning events. Accordingly, the teaching process should not only consider students' internal processing but also influence this process. Therefore, the teaching stage and the learning stage are completely corresponding. Teaching is shaped by teachers' arrangement and control of these external conditions; the art of teaching lies in whether the learning phase aligns completely with the teaching phase.

#### 1. Information processing model of learning

Gagné (1965) regarded the learning process as one of information processing. He believed that the learning model is used to explain the structure and process of learning, which is of great practical significance for understanding teaching and the teaching process, as well as how to arrange teaching events. He described a typical learning structure model (Figure 4-6), which is divided into two parts.

The first part of the structure on the right, called operational memory, represents an information flow. The stimulus from the environment acts on the learners' receptors and then arrives at the sensory register, where the information is initially selected and processed. The information stays for 0.25 to 2 seconds before entering short-term memory. It remains here for 2.5 to 20 seconds before entering long-term memory. Later, when recall is required, the information is extracted from long-term memory and returns to short-term memory, where it arrives at the response generator. Here, the information is processed and converted into behavior, acting on the environment, so that learning occurs.

The second part of the structure on the left includes executive control and expectancy. Expectancy refers to the goals that students expect to achieve, which is their learning motivation. Expectancy plays an orientational role, guiding learning activities in a certain direction. It is because students have specific expectations of

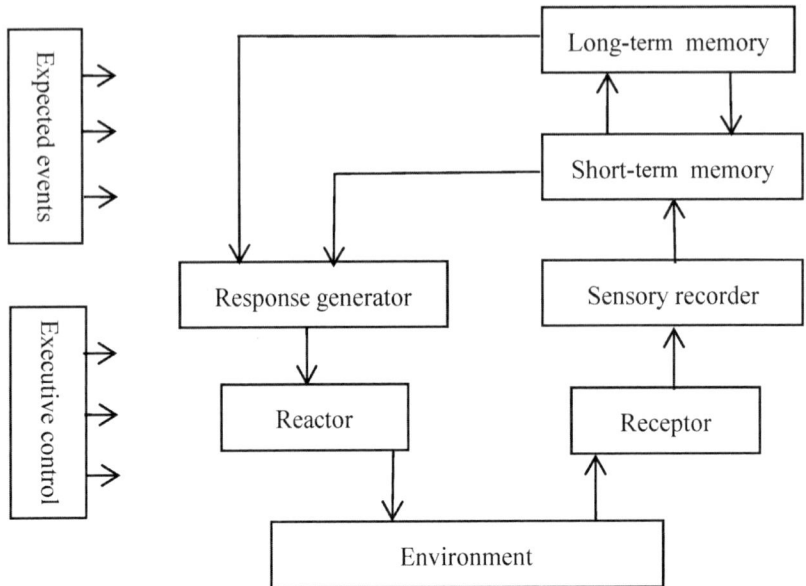

**Figure 4-9 Information processing model of learning**
Source: 莫雷,《教育心理学》.广东高等教育出版社,2002,第 150 页.

learning that feedback from teachers has a reinforcing effect. Executive control plays a regulating and controlling role in enabling learning activities to be realized. The function of the second part is to enable learners to initiate learning, change learning, strengthen learning, and promote learning, while also intensifying, weakening, or changing the direction of information flow.

From the information processing model of learning, learning is the result of the interaction between students and the environment.

2. Learning process and teaching events

Gagné believed that the external and internal conditions of learning should be distinguished. The internal activity that occurs in the learner's mind (central nervous system) is the learning process, which occurs under the influence of the outside world. Learning consists of a series of events. The events that occur at each stage of information processing are called learning events, which are the processes of students' internal processing. Teaching events are the external conditions of learning, which completely correspond to and are unified with the learning stages. Teaching is composed of these external conditions controlled by teachers. In teaching, the learning stage and the teaching stage are completely consistent. Teaching is a set of external conditions designed to launch, stimulate, maintain, and improve learners' learning purposefully and systematically. On this basis, Gagné put forward the hypothesis of eight stages of the learning process and the corresponding psychological processes (Figure 4-10).

1) Motivation stage—Stimulating learners' learning motivation

This is the preparatory stage of the entire learning process. Students' motivation or expectancy has an important influence on the whole learning process. The primary task in the teaching process is to help students establish motivation. In the teaching situation, therefore, the first thing that teachers should consider is stimulating the motivation for students' learning activities, that is, the motivation to try to achieve a certain goal.

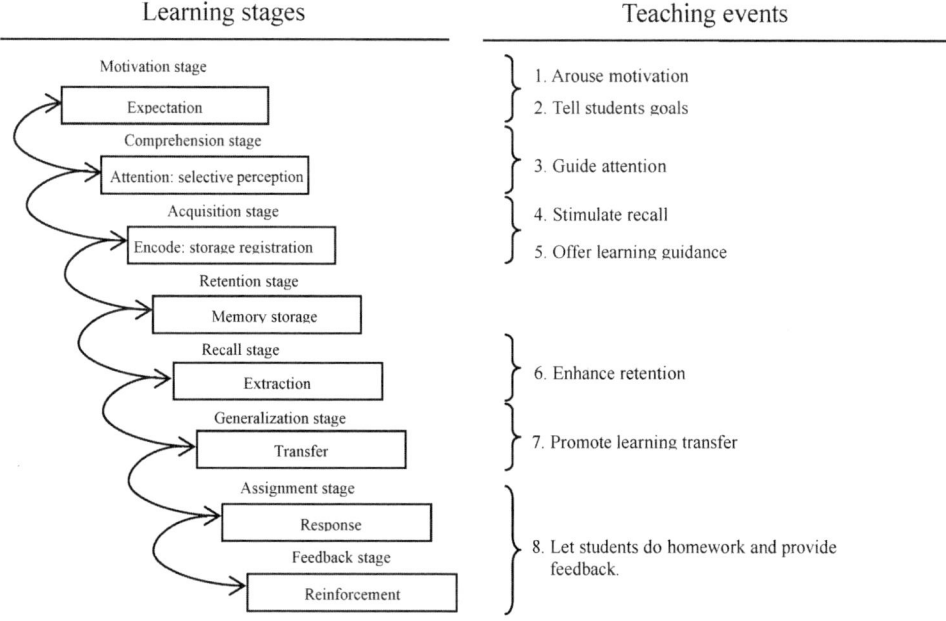

Figure 4-10  Learning stages and teaching events

Source: 冯忠良、伍新春,《教育心理学(第 2 版)》,人民教育出版社,2010,第 128 页.

2) Comprehension stage—Attention and selective perception

Students who are motivated to learn must pay attention to the stimuli related to the learning content and neglect other stimuli. For example, when students are listening to a class, they must focus on the content of the teacher's speech, not the intonation of the teacher's voice. Therefore, only through selective perception of the characteristics of external stimuli can students progress to other learning stages.

3) Acquisition stage — Learned information enters short-term memory, is encoded, and stored

The acquisition stage involves further encoding and processing the information stored in short-term memory and transferring it to long-term memory.

4) Retention stage—Encoded information is stored in long-term memory

After rehearsal and reinforcement, the acquired information is stored in long-term memory in the form of semantic coding.

5) Recall stage—Information retrieval is carried out

The information acquired by students should be presented in the form of homework, and information extraction is a necessary part of it. Teachers can provide various clues to help students find information for extraction. However, it is more important for students to master the strategies for information extraction to become independent learners.

6) Generalization stage—The transfer of learning is realized

According to Gagné, generalization is what we usually refer to as the transfer of learning. Teachers should guide students to summarize and master the rules and principles to help them apply what they have learned in different situations.

7) Assignment stage—Response generation stage

Students demonstrate their operational activities through assignments. Students can determine whether they have grasped the material by completing homework.

8) Feedback stage—Expectancy has been confirmed and reinforcement has been received

The feedback here is similar to reinforcement. Gagné pointed out that students' expectancy formed in the motivation stage can be affirmed through feedback, thereby strengthening their learning motivation.

The corresponding learning stage links these internal processes with the external events that constitute teaching.

## 4.5  Constructivist learning theory

Constructivist learning theory is a further development of cognitive learning theory, which has a profound influence on current educational reform. It is not a specific theory of learning but a collective term for many theoretical viewpoints. The founder of constructivism is Piaget, who made a systematic and classic exposition of the theory. Dewey's experiential learning theory and Vygotsky's cultural-historical theory also have an important influence on contemporary constructivism.

The core view of constructivist theory is that learners must discover and transform complex information by themselves in order to achieve success. According to constructivist theory, learners constantly use new information to test old experiences and modify them when they are no longer applicable. Because constructivism emphasizes that students are active learners, constructivist teaching strategies are often called student-centered teaching. In the student-centered classroom, the teacher is an assistant rather than a master, helping students find meaning rather than "one person alone having the say" or controlling all classroom activities (Robert Slevin, 2004).

## 4.5.1 The main content of constructivist learning theory

### 1. Views of knowledge

To some extent, constructivism questions the objectivity and certainty of knowledge and emphasizes the dynamic nature of knowledge. Constructivism believes that knowledge is not the final answer to a problem but a new hypothesis and explanation that is constantly corrected with human progress. Knowledge cannot accurately summarize the laws of the world but needs to be recreated based on specific situations. In addition, knowledge cannot exist outside the individual in the form of an entity. Although we give knowledge a certain external form through language symbols, learners still understand and construct their own knowledge based on their own experiential background.

### 2. Views of learning

Contemporary constructivists maintain that the world exists objectively, but it is up to each person to make sense of the world and give it meaning. Individuals construct, or at least explain, reality on the basis of their own experiences. Each person's empirical world is created with their own mind. As individuals have different experiences and different beliefs about those experiences, they have different understandings of the external world. Therefore, learning is not a process in which teachers simply pass knowledge to students, but a process in which students construct knowledge themselves. Students do not simply and passively receive information; they actively construct the meaning of knowledge, which cannot be replaced by others.

The learning process involves two aspects of construction: the construction of the meaning of new information and the transformation and reorganization of original experiences. The learning and understanding of any subject always involve the learners' original cognitive structures, and learners always understand and construct new knowledge and information based on their own experiences. That is to say, learning is not about passively receiving stimuli of information but actively constructing meaning and actively selecting, processing, and dealing with external information according to one's own experiential background, so as to obtain one's own meaning. The acquisition of meaning in learning is that each learner, on the basis of their original knowledge and experience, recognizes and encodes new information and constructs their own understanding. *For example, there are a thousand Hamlets in a thousand readers' eyes*. In this process, the learners' original knowledge and experiences are adjusted and changed with the introduction of new knowledge and experiences. Therefore, constructivists focus on how to construct knowledge based on original experiences, psychological structures, and beliefs.

Constructivist learning theory believes that situation, cooperation, conversation, and meaning construction are the four elements or attributes in the learning environment. Because learning is carried out in a certain situation—social and cultural background—the situation is the basic condition for meaning construction. The cooperation and conversation between teachers and students, as well as among students, are the specific processes of meaning construction, and meaning construction is the ultimate goal of constructivist learning. Views of constructivist learning emphasize three characteristics of learners' knowledge construction: *active constructivity of learning, social interactivity of learning, and situationality of learning*.

**Active constructivity of learning** means that students can synthesize, restructure, and transform their existing knowledge and experiences actively in order to interpret new information and ultimately construct the knowledge content of their own.

**Social interactivity of learning** refers to the process of internalizing relevant knowledge and skills and mastering relevant tools through participation in a certain social culture, which often needs to be completed through cooperation and interaction in a learning community. Learning is always carried out by learners in a certain social and cultural environment. Even though learners seem to be learning by themselves, the learning materials, tools, and environments they use all belong to society and are the accumulation of collective experiences.

**Situationality of learning** mainly refers to the situationality of learning, knowledge, and wisdom. Knowledge does not exist in isolation from the situation of activities, and only through practical application can knowledge be truly understood. Therefore, people's learning should be connected with contextualized social practice activities, and they can gradually master relevant social rules and form corresponding knowledge through participation in certain social events. The view of situational cognition has great implications for teaching. The viewpoint of situational learning shows that knowledge does not exist in books in isolation but is embedded in practice. Thus, we should pay attention to the problem situations and life situations associated with book knowledge in teaching activities. Teaching should focus on presenting knowledge in real situations to stimulate students' cognitive needs. *For example*, *you can hardly swallow 15g of salt on its own. However, if the 15g of salt is put into a bowl of delicious soup, you will fully absorb the 15g of salt while enjoying the tasty food. Context is to knowledge as soup is to salt. Just as salt needs to dissolve into the soup to be absorbed, knowledge needs to integrate into the context to demonstrate vitality and aesthetics. For another example, the positive role of situational teaching in promoting students' learning is self-evident. Language should be used in daily life, and situational teaching happens to be the best simulation and reproduction of life. Only by incorporating the salt of language skills into the soup of situations can language truly come to life and demonstrate vitality and beauty.*

3. Views of teaching

In teaching, constructivists propose the respect for students' views and experiences and attach importance to the problems related to students, which should be the focus of students and capable of capturing their interest. Constructivists advocate that teaching should be carried out according to the students' viewpoints and that teachers should adhere to the principle of "less but better" in teaching. "Less" means that teachers mainly teach basic scientific concepts, rules, theories, and models. "Better" means that students are required to learn deeply and meticulously and to understand the essence of science so that they will benefit throughout their lives. In the presentation of course content, the course content is transmitted from part to whole in traditional classrooms, emphasizing the mastery of basic skills; in constructivist classes, the course content is transmitted from whole to part, emphasizing the mastery of core concepts.

4. Views of students

Constructionism stresses that students don't walk into a classroom with empty heads. Constructivism attaches great importance to learners' existing experiences and holds that learners can often form explanations of problems based on relevant experiences and cognitive abilities when learning new information and solving new problems. These explanations are not random speculation but logical hypotheses derived from their empirical backgrounds. Therefore, teaching cannot ignore students' experiences. Teaching should take children's existing knowledge and experiences as the starting point for new knowledge and guide them to develop new knowledge and experiences from their original ones. As a result of differences in background experiences, students' understanding of problems is often varied. In the community of students, these differences themselves constitute a valuable learning resource.

### 5. Views of teachers

The cognitivism of information processing regards teachers as the instructors and designers of students' learning. However, constructivism prefers to view teachers as helpers and collaborators in students' learning. Constructivism believes that teaching is not simply about teachers transferring and conveying knowledge to students, but rather that teachers guide students to develop new knowledge and experiences from their original knowledge and experiences by providing help and support in the collaborative activities of teachers and students. In order to become effective helpers in students' meaning construction, teachers are required to play a leading role in teaching from the following three aspects:

1) Stimulate students' interest in learning and help them form intrinsic motivation.

2) Help students construct the meaning of current knowledge by creating situations that align with the teaching content and providing clues that indicate the connection between new and old knowledge.

3) To make meaning construction more effective, teachers should organize cooperative learning (discussion and communication) as much as possible and guide the process of cooperative learning to develop in a direction conducive to construction. The methods of guidance include posing appropriate questions to stimulate students' thinking and discussion; progressively leading questions step by step to deepen students' understanding of what they have learned in the discussion; inspiring and guiding students to discover rules by themselves, correct and supplement their own misconceptions, and avoid directly imparting information to students.

In summary, the core ideas of constructivism can be summarized as "student-centered, emphasizing students' active exploration, active discovery of knowledge, and active construction of the meaning of knowledge".

## 4.5.2 Models of classroom instruction based on constructivism

### 1. Scaffolding instruction

Scaffolding instruction, also known as instructional scaffolding, originated from the work of Lev Vygotsky (1978) in the field of educational psychology. The term "scaffolding" refers to the temporary support provided by a teacher or more capable peer to assist learners in reaching higher levels of understanding. Scaffolding is used to support learners as they acquire new knowledge and skills, gradually withdrawing support as they become more proficient. Through scaffolding (the teacher's help), the task of learning management is gradually transferred from teachers to the students themselves, and finally, the scaffolding is removed. Scaffolding instruction typically involves four main steps.

1) Assessment of learners' abilities

The first step is to assess the learners' current knowledge, skills, and understanding of the topic or task at hand. This assessment helps the instructor understand where the learners stand and identifies areas where support may be needed.

2) Providing supportive structures

In the second step, the instructor provides supportive structures or guidance tailored to the learners' needs. This support may include breaking down tasks into smaller, manageable steps, providing relevant resources, or offering explicit instructions to aid comprehension.

3) Gradual release of responsibility

The third step involves gradually releasing responsibility to the learners as they gain proficiency. The instructor begins by providing more support and guidance and then gradually reduces assistance as the learners become more independent.

4) Promoting independent learning

The final step focuses on promoting independent learning. The learners are encouraged to apply their newly acquired skills and knowledge autonomously, with the instructor providing feedback and guidance as needed.

In summary, scaffolding instruction begins with assessing the learners' current level, providing structured support tailored to their needs, and gradually withdrawing support as they become more competent and self-directed learners.

2. Anchored instruction

Anchored instruction, developed by John Bransford (1990) and his team, also known as situated learning, focuses on integrating authentic, real-world contexts into learning experiences. Anchored instruction utilizes multimedia "anchors," such as videos or simulations, to immerse learners in complex problem-solving scenarios. "Anchors" refer to real-world contexts or scenarios used to stimulate learners' interest and thinking. This method primarily involves guiding learning through real-life situations or cases to tackle complex problems. Its purpose is to enhance learners' problem-solving and interdisciplinary thinking skills. In practice, teachers design authentic scenarios for learners to explore, discuss, and collaborate to solve problems. The theoretical basis of anchored instruction is constructivism. Anchored instruction typically involves several steps.

1) Introduction of the anchor

In the first step, learners are presented with an anchor, which is a real-world problem or scenario serving as the focal point for learning. This anchor captures learners' interest and provides context for the subsequent learning activities.

2) Exploration and inquiry

The second step involves learners exploring the anchor and engaging in inquiry-based activities to analyze the problem, gather relevant information, and identify potential solutions. Learners may utilize multimedia materials, simulations, or case studies to deepen their understanding.

3) Guided problem-solving

In the third step, learners are guided through the problem-solving process by the instructor or facilitator. They receive support and scaffolding as they work towards solving the anchor problem, applying relevant knowledge and skills acquired through exploration.

4) Reflection and discussion

After attempting to solve the anchor problem, learners engage in reflection and discussion. They reflect on their learning experiences, discuss different approaches and strategies, and evaluate the effectiveness of their solutions.

5) Transfer and application

The final step focuses on transferring learning from the anchor problem to similar or related contexts. Learners apply their knowledge and problem-solving skills to new situations, demonstrating their ability to transfer learning beyond the initial anchor scenario.

In summary, anchored instruction involves introducing a real-world anchor, engaging in exploration and inquiry, guided problem-solving, reflection and discussion, and finally, transfer and application of learning. This approach aims to promote deep understanding, critical thinking, and the transferability of knowledge and skills.

### 3. Random entry instruction

Random entry instruction, also known as random entry teaching, originated from the work of Frederick Mayer (1992) and others in the field of educational psychology. It means that learners can randomly enter the study of the same teaching content through different approaches and methods to obtain a multi-faceted recognition and understanding of the same thing or problem. The term "random entry" refers to a teaching strategy where learners explore information through a random entry point rather than a structured, linear approach. Its main content involves presenting learners with various entry points into a topic or concept, encouraging exploration and discovery. Random entry instruction aims to foster creativity, critical thinking, and problem-solving skills by allowing learners to engage with content in non-linear ways. The process involves providing learners with diverse resources and stimuli, encouraging them to choose their starting point, facilitating exploration and inquiry, and promoting reflection on connections and patterns. Random entry instruction consists of the following steps: ① presenting a situation; ② accessing learning randomly; ③ training divergent thinking; ④ learning collaboratively; ⑤ evaluating the effect. Random entry instruction has a positive impact on learning outcomes by promoting engagement, autonomy, and a deeper understanding of complex concepts.

### 4. Cognitive apprenticeship

Cognitive apprenticeship originated from the work of Allan Collins, John Seely Brown, and Ann Holum (1989) in the late 1980s. Cognitive apprenticeship refers to the mode of supporting students' learning in a certain field by allowing them to acquire, develop, and utilize the activity tools in the real world. This model emphasizes the importance of experiential activities in learning and gives special weight to connecting learning with practice. This theory highlights learning through apprenticeship-style experiences, where novices work alongside experts to develop cognitive skills. Learners observe, imitate, and collaborate with experts on authentic tasks, gradually assuming more responsibility. Cognitive apprenticeship aims to make thinking processes visible and explicit. It's particularly beneficial for complex, real-world tasks where explicit instruction alone may fall short. Learners from various domains, including education, industry, and the arts, can benefit. The process involves modeling, coaching, scaffolding, and fading support as learners gain competence. Key elements include problem-solving, reflection, and meta-cognitive strategies. Cognitive apprenticeship has influenced educational practices by emphasizing the importance of authentic, context-rich learning experiences. Cognitive apprenticeship involves four main steps.

1) Modeling

In the first step, learners observe experts performing tasks while paying attention to their thought processes, strategies, and problem-solving approaches. Through modeling, learners develop an understanding of the task and its underlying cognitive skills.

2) Scaffolding

The second step involves providing structured support to learners as they engage in the task. Scaffolding may include prompts, hints, or guidance tailored to the learners' needs, gradually fading as they gain competence.

3) Coaching

In the third step, learners receive direct feedback and guidance from the expert or a more experienced peer. Coaches help learners refine their skills, troubleshoot challenges, and reflect on their learning process.

4) Articulation and reflection

The final step entails encouraging learners to articulate their thought processes, explain their reasoning, and reflect on their learning experiences. This self-reflection promotes meta-cognitive awareness and a deeper understanding of the task.

In summary, cognitive apprenticeship progresses from modeling to scaffolding, coaching, and finally, articulation and reflection, fostering the development of expertise through guided practice and reflection.

5. Top-down instruction

Top-down instruction is an approach where learners begin by grasping the broader context or main idea of a topic before delving into specifics. This involves presenting learners with overarching concepts or principles before exploring specific details. "Top-down" refers to starting with the big picture and then moving to the smaller components. This method allows learners to gain a holistic perspective before diving into the finer details, promoting better comprehension and organization of knowledge. Top-down instruction encourages learners to approach learning by first understanding the big picture, helping them contextualize and prioritize information effectively. Top-down instruction typically involves three main steps.

1) Global understanding

In the first step, learners are introduced to the overall concept or main idea of the topic being taught. This step aims to provide learners with a broad understanding of the subject matter before delving into specific details.

2) Identification of key components

In the second step, learners identify and focus on the key components or main elements that contribute to the understanding of the topic. This involves breaking down the topic into manageable chunks to facilitate deeper understanding.

3) Detailed exploration

The third step involves a more detailed exploration of each key component identified in the previous step. Learners delve into the specifics, analyze relationships, and explore connections between different elements to gain a comprehensive understanding of the topic.

In summary, top-down instruction starts with a broad overview, moves on to identifying key components, and then proceeds to detailed exploration to promote thorough comprehension of the subject matter.

### 4.5.3 Enlightenment of constructivist learning theory on current educational practice

Under the background of new curriculum reform, teachers should respect students' existing knowledge and experience in classroom teaching and continuously enhance students' active consciousness, helping them realize that the learning process is not merely passive, such as listening and remembering, nor just a process of information accumulation, but a two-way interaction between old and new experiences and an active process of progress and development.

1) From the constructivist view of knowledge, constructivism emphasizes that knowledge is an individual's understanding and interpretation of reality, which is influenced by specific experiences and culture. Therefore, different people have different understandings of knowledge construction. In the process of education and teaching, teachers should pay more attention to students' personalized characteristics and teach students according to their aptitude. They should not teach all students exactly the same knowledge of principles but enable each student to construct new knowledge based on their own experiences.

2) From the perspective of teaching, constructivism believes that learning is a process in which the subject of learning actively explores and constantly changes the object of learning to construct an understanding of its meaning. Therefore, we should pay attention to students' meaningful construction in teaching and inspire them to construct cognitive structures independently through appropriate teaching strategies. *For example, cooperative learning is an effective teaching strategy. Under teachers' guidance and assistance, students can form a learning group and discuss the learning content. By analyzing and debating various theories, opinions, and hypotheses together in the group, students can ultimately reach a consensus conclusion that is accepted by all.* Cooperative learning helps stimulate students' enthusiasm for participation, enhances their understanding of their own and others' ideas, promotes a deeper understanding of knowledge construction, establishes a more complete knowledge representation, and cultivates students' spirit of cooperation.

3) From the perspective of the learner, constructivism posits that students are active constructors of meaning, rather than passive recipients of external stimulation and instilled knowledge. Therefore, in addition to traditional knowledge teaching,

teachers should fully leverage students' roles as subjects, emphasizing their autonomy and initiative, so that students can take the initiative to find, analyze, and solve problems during the learning process. Students have shifted from passive receivers of knowledge to active gatherers of information, and teachers have transformed from indoctrinators of knowledge to guides who lead students in constructing knowledge meaning. Teachers are no longer the unquestioned authority in the eyes of students but rather assistants in their learning. Teachers and students have become collaborative learning partners.

## 4.6 Humanistic learning theory

Humanistic psychology, one of the main schools of contemporary psychology in the United States, arose in the 1950s and 1960s. It has formed the third ideological trend of psychology after behaviorism and psychoanalysis. Humanistic psychology not only opposes behaviorism, which regards people as animals or machines, but also criticizes cognitive psychology, which ignores the impact of human emotions, attitudes, values, etc., on learning, despite its emphasis on human cognitive structure. Humanistic psychology believes that psychology should explore the whole person (fully

**Carl Ransom Rogers**
(1902 – 1987)

functioning person), highlights the value of individuals, and emphasizes that human beings have both the potential for development and an internal tendency to realize that potential, namely, the tendency for self-actualization. Humanistic psychology advocates viewing people in real society as the object of psychological research, emphasizes the study of human practical experience, values, and significance, and cares about human nature, creative potential, freedom, and choice. Humanism places importance on the teaching process rather than the teaching content, and on the teaching method rather than the teaching result.

### 4.6.1 Rogers' learning theory

Humanistic learning theory is based on the basic theoretical framework of humanistic psychology, and its representative, Rogers, has made a special discussion on learning problems.

**1. View of meaningful free learning**

According to Rogers, students have two main types of learning: cognitive learning and experiential learning. They also have two main ways of learning: meaningless learning and meaningful learning.

**Meaningless learning** refers to most learning materials without personal significance, which, similar to the meaningless syllables in psychology, does not involve emotion or personal significance, but only engages the mind, that is, the accumulation of experience and the growth of knowledge. Meaningless learning has nothing to do with the *whole person* (emotional and rational), making it difficult to learn and easy to forget.

Meaningful learning is not just a form of learning that increases knowledge; it is a type of learning that is integrated with all parts of each person's experience and leads to significant changes in an individual's behavior, attitude, personality, and future course of action. It is a kind of learning that is connected to learners' various experiences and encourages them to engage wholeheartedly. *For example, by asking a student to take a glass of ice water, they can learn the meaning of the word "cold" and understand that ice melts when heated, as well as that water droplets form on the outside of the glass in the summer. Another example is when "one day, Sullivan took Helen to a well and let the water flow over her hand while spelling the word 'w-a-t-e-r' into her palm. This tactile experience allowed Helen to make a connection between the word and the substance. By repeatedly exposing Helen to the sensation of water and associating it with the word, Sullivan helped her develop a sense of language and understanding. This was a breakthrough moment in Helen's education, as it showed her the power of language and began her journey toward literacy."*

Meaningful learning consists of four elements:

1) Learning involves personal involvement, meaning the *whole person* (emotion and cognition) is engaged in learning activities, including cognitive and emotional participation;

2) Learning is self-initiated by learners, with intrinsic motivation playing a major role;

3) Learning enables students to achieve comprehensive development in their behavior, attitude, personality, and more;

4) The results of learning are evaluated by the learners themselves, who understand what they want to learn and what they have learned.

Rogers' concept of "meaningful learning" focuses on the relationship between learning content and individuals, while Ausubel's "meaningful learning" emphasizes the connection between new and old knowledge, which deals only with the mind, not with personal meaning. Therefore, from Rogers' viewpoint, Ausubel's "meaningful learning" is merely a form of "learning that occurs above the neck".

Rogers summarized his previous experiences and research, explaining the principles of free learning based on freedom.

1) Human nature is inherently good, and everyone has the potential to learn.

2) Meaningful learning occurs only when the teaching materials are significant and align with the students' purposes.

3) Effective learning can only take place in less stressful educational situations.

4) Active, spontaneous, and wholehearted learning produces the best results.

5) Self-assessment of learning outcomes can cultivate students' independent thinking abilities and creativity.

6) Importance is placed on the learning of life skills beyond knowledge to adapt to a changing society.

7) The position of learners is emphasized in teaching.

8) Learning that involves changing self-cognition can be threatening and is often resisted.

9) Stress is laid on learning by doing.

Humanism creates meaningful free learning, and meaningful learning emphasizes the relationship between learning content and individuals. It is not only about understanding meaning but also about autonomous and conscious learning initiated by learners. Learners are encouraged to choose learning materials and arrange their own learning situations within a considerable range.

### 2. Student-centered teaching view

Rogers believed that the educational goal is to promote change and learning, and to cultivate individuals who can adapt to change and know how to learn.

1) View of teaching

Rogers rejected behaviorists and psychoanalysts who view students as animals or machines, or as "larger rats" or "slower computers", or even more as selfish, sociopathic beings. He stressed the importance of treating students as human beings and believing in their potential. The process of education and instruction is to promote the development of students' personalities, develop their potential, and cultivate their enthusiasm and initiative in learning. Learning is a process of self-realization of human inherent energy, which underlines human dignity and value, and emphasizes the important role of unconditional positive regard in the process of individual growth. The purpose of education and the result of learning should be to make students highly adaptable and intrinsically free individuals.

Rogers advocated abolishing the role of a teacher and replacing it with a facilitator of learning. The core of the teaching principle advocated by Rogers is to allow students to learn freely. As long as facilitators trust students' learning potential and are willing to let them learn freely, they will find the best way to adapt to their own style and promote learning through communication with students. The key to promoting students' learning lies in specific factors of psychological climate that exist in the interpersonal relationships between facilitators and learners. The factors of psychological climate that promote learning include: ① Truthfulness or sincerity. The learning facilitator expresses their true self, without any pretense, hypocrisy, or defense; ② Unconditional positive regard. The facilitator respects the emotions and opinions of learners, cares about all aspects of learners, and accepts the values and emotional expressions of learners as individuals; ③ Empathetic understanding. The learning facilitators can understand learners' internal reactions and their learning processes.

2) Mode of teaching

① Non-directive instruction. Student-centered instruction is also called non-directive instruction. In this mode, the most meaningful role of the teacher is not as an authority but as a "midwife" and "catalyst." A teacher is only a "person who provides convenient conditions for learning" and a "facilitator of learning." In this mode, Rogers emphasized ⅰ) being student-oriented; ⅱ) allowing students to learn spontaneously; ⅲ) eliminating threats to learners; ⅳ) providing students with a sense of security. Humanistic theory advocates self-motivated and self-regulated learning, emotional education, authentic assessment, cooperative learning, open classrooms, and open schools. ② Implementation stage of non-directive instruction. The process of non-directive instruction includes five stages: ⅰ) Determination of the help situation, meaning teachers should encourage students to express their feelings freely; ⅱ) Exploration of the problem, where teachers encourage students to define the problem themselves. Teachers should accept students' feelings and clarify them when necessary; ⅲ) Formation of insight. Teachers allow students to discuss problems and express their views freely and provide help as needed; ⅳ) Planning and decision-making, where students plan preliminary decisions, and teachers help clarify these decisions; ⅴ) Integration, where students gain profound insights and take more positive actions, which teachers should support.

3) Strategies for implementation of non-directive Instruction

Carl Rogers advocated for a process-oriented philosophical view and opposed anything fixed, rigid, or immutable. Although he never explicitly and systematically described a structured approach to non-directive teaching, we can still discern implementation strategies for non-directive instruction from his fundamental theoretical assumptions. ① Teachers should have unwavering confidence in themselves and full trust in students' independent thinking and self-learning abilities. ② Teachers should share the responsibility of teaching activities with others. Curriculum planning, teaching management, budgeting, and policy formulation should be the joint responsibility of the group. ③ Teachers should provide students with learning materials. ④ Students should explore the problems they are interested in. In the process of exploration, they make choices about their own learning methods and take responsibility for the results of these choices, forming their own learning plans. ⑤ An atmosphere conducive to learning should be provided, one that is full of genuineness, care, and understanding. ⑥ Students should focus on their own experiences in the learning process. Although the learning content is important, it comes second. ⑦ Self-training is emphasized, and students should regard training as their responsibility. ⑧ The importance of self-evaluation is highlighted. Feedback from group members or teachers will also affect students' self-evaluation. In addition, the modes of humanistic instruction also include: the mode of topic-centered classroom discussion, the mode of open classrooms, and the teaching mode of free learning.

### 4.6.2 Maslow's learning theory

American psychologist Maslow is widely recognized as one of the leading figures in humanistic psychology.

**1. Self-actualization personality view**

Humanistic psychologists believe that human growth stems from the self-actualization need, which is the drive for personality formation, development, expansion, and maturity. Maslow believed that the self-actualization need is "a person's desire for self-actualization and self-improvement, which is a tendency to realize their potential". Colloquially speaking, the self-actualization need is "what a person can become; they must become what they can become, and they must be loyal to their own nature". The key to personality development lies in forming and developing the correct self-concept. Normal self-development must have two basic conditions: unconditional respect and self-esteem. Unconditional respect is the foundation of self-esteem because only when others have a favorable impression (respect) of you can you have a favorable impression (self-esteem) of yourself. If the conditions for normal self-development are satisfied, you can act based on the truth itself, truly realize your potential, and become a self-actualizer, a functional perfectionist, and a psychologically healthy person.

The self-actualization of human potential is not achieved solely through education. Regarding the role of environment and education, humanists believe that "culture, environment, and education are just sunshine, food, and water, but not seeds", and that self-potential is the seed of human nature. The role of education is only to provide a safe, free, and humane psychological atmosphere, enabling the automatic realization of human inherent excellent potential (refer to 5.5.2).

2. Internal learning theory

Maslow believed that external learning relies solely on reinforcement and conditioning. Its focus is on indoctrination rather than understanding, and it belongs to a passive, mechanical, and traditional educational model. Currently, some students are imbued with a hostile attitude toward external learning. The only reason to read a book may be the external rewards it may bring. Obtaining a diploma or earning a degree can be summarized as the drawbacks of this external education.

According to Maslow, ideal schools should oppose external learning and advocate for internal learning. Internal learning relies on students' internal drive, fully develops their potential, and achieves self-actualization. Internal learning is a conscious, proactive, and creative learning mode.

Maslow advocated that learning cannot be derived from outside but from within. Teachers cannot force students to learn; learning activities should be chosen and decided by the students themselves. The task of teachers is only guidance. Students naturally have the potential ability to learn, but teachers' guidance must be appropriate, and students will grow because of learning with proper guidance. Otherwise, the students will shrink due to improper guidance.

# I. Review and reflection

- learning
- signal learning
- stimulus-response learning
- chained learning
- associative learning of speech
- stimulus discrimination
- discrimination learning
- concept learning
- rule learning
- Ausubel's classification of learning style
- reception learning
- discovery learning
- rote learning
- meaningful learning
- discovery learning

reception learning
Pavlov's classical conditioning theory
unconditioned stimulus
neutral stimulus (NS)
unconditioned response
law of acquisition
law of extinction
law of recovery
spontaneous recovery
law of generalization
stimulus generalization
law of discrimination
higher-order conditioning
two signal systems
Thorndike's connection and trial-and-error learning
law of readiness
law of exercise
law of effect
Skinner's operant conditioning theory
reinforcement
positive reinforcement
negative reinforcement
schedule of reinforcement
positive reinforcer
negative reinforcer
primary reinforcers
secondary reinforcers
Premack Principle
practical reinforcer
escape conditioning
avoidance conditioning
punishment
positive punishment
negative punishment
extinction
programmed instruction
connotation and basic theory of programmed instruction
principles of programmed instruction
behavior modification
behavioral shaping
Bandura's social learning theory
external reinforcement
vicarious reinforcement
self-reinforcement
gestalt-insight learning theory of gestalt school
gestalt
place learning
cognitive map
latent learning
cognitive learning view
cognitive structure
structural teaching view
discovery learning
reception learning
meaningful learning
mental set of meaningful learning
learning models
principle of gradual differentiation
advanced organizer
information processing model of learning
learning process and teaching events
views of knowledge
views of learning
situationality of learning
views of teaching
views of students
views of teachers

scaffolding instruction
anchored instruction
random entry instruction
cognitive apprenticeship
top-down instruction
detailed exploration
meaningful learning
student-centered teaching view
view of teaching
non-directive instruction
implementation stage of non-directive instruction
self-actualization personality view
external learning theory
internal learning

## II. Material analysis

Please analyze in English the differences of learning the poem of "悯农" between kindergarteners and middle school students using Ausubel' learning theory. (Refer to Appendix Ⅰ)

悯农

［唐］李绅

锄禾日当午，汗滴禾下土。

谁知盘中餐，粒粒皆辛苦。

# Chapter 5  Learning Motivation and Cultivation

*As a child, Li Bai was known for his playful spirit, often more interested in games than in his studies. His carefree nature led him to neglect his learning. One day, while wandering along a river, he encountered an elderly woman diligently grinding an iron pestle against a stone. Intrigued, he paused to observe her relentless effort. When he inquired about her work, she explained that she was determined to transform the iron pestle into a needle through sheer perseverance. Her unwavering dedication and the simplicity of her message — "With enough effort, even an iron pestle can be ground down to a needle" — struck a deep chord within Li Bai. This encounter ignited a spark of motivation for learning in him. Inspired by the old woman's determination, he realized that true mastery requires persistence and hard work. From that moment on, he committed himself to his studies, embracing the belief that dedication could lead to greatness. This pivotal experience not only transformed Li Bai's approach to learning but also laid the foundation for his future as a poet.*

Li Bai's story serves as a timeless reminder of how a single moment can inspire a lifelong pursuit of knowledge and self-improvement, highlighting the importance of motivation and cultivation in shaping one's destiny. Learning motivation is one of the most critical components of learning and also one of the most difficult to measure. What makes a student want to learn? The willingness to put effort into learning is a product of many factors, ranging from the students' personality and abilities to understand the characteristics of particular learning tasks, to incentives for learning, settings, and teachers' behaviors.

## 5.1  Overview of learning motivation

Motivation is the engine of behavior and plays an important role in the generation and maintenance of human behavior. Motivation is the factor that directs and energizes the behavior of humans and other organisms.

### 5.1.1  Learning motivation

Motivation refers to the internal psychological process or internal power that arouses and maintains individual activities and directs them towards a certain goal. In plain language, motivation is what gets you going, keeps you going, and determines where you are trying to go (Albert E. Slavin, 2017). Motivation is an internal process of motivating, guiding, and maintaining behavior, which includes three functions: activating function, directing function, and strengthening function.

Learning motivation is one of many human motivations, aiming to explore the motivation behind human learning behavior. **Learning motivation** refers to an internal process or psychological state that stimulates individuals to engage in learning activities, maintain the learning activities that have already been triggered, and orient behavior towards a certain learning goal. Motivation and learning promote each other. On the one hand, motivation promotes learning by enhancing behavior. On the other hand, what you learn can, in turn, enhance learning motivation.

### 5.1.2 Components of learning motivation

The two basic components of learning motivation are the need for learning and the expectancy of learning. They interact to form a learning motivation system.

#### 1. Need for learning and learning drive

Human beings act to satisfy their needs, which usually refers to the state caused by the imbalance between the present state and the ideal state of things. The need for learning refers to the psychological state in which an individual feels a certain lack in learning activities and strives to obtain satisfaction. The subjective experience of the need for learning is the learner's learning desire or learning intention. This desire or intention is the fundamental drive that motivates individuals to learn, which includes learning interests, hobbies, and beliefs. Learning interest is the most active component of learning motivation. From the function of need, the need for learning serves as the learning drive.

#### 2. Expectancy of learning and incentives

The expectancy of learning is an individual's subjective estimation of the goal to be achieved through learning activities. The expectancy of learning is closely related to learning objectives, but the two cannot be equated. A learning goal is the expected result that individuals want to achieve through learning activities, and before individuals complete these activities, this expected result exists in their minds in the form of ideas. Therefore, the expectancy of learning reflects the learning goal in an individual's mind.

Incentives refer to the external conditions or stimuli that can stimulate the orienting behavior of organisms and meet certain needs. Incentives can be simple objects or complex things. For example, the color and aroma of food are incentives for a hungry dog that is foraging. The expectancy of learning serves as an incentive for learning and is another basic element that constitutes the structure of learning motivation.

 3. Relationship between the need for learning and incentives

The need for learning and the expectancy of learning (incentive) are two basic components of learning motivation, and they are closely related. The need for learning is the drive for individuals to engage in learning activities and is one of the prerequisites for the expectancy of learning. The expectancy of learning points to the satisfaction of the need for learning and urges the learner to achieve the learning goal.

## 5.2 Classification of learning motivation

Learning motivation is a complex phenomenon that has been studied by many scholars. Different people have different ideas about learning motivation. Due to varying criteria for classifying learning motivation, the types of learning motivation also differ.

### 5.2.1 Intrinsic learning motivation and extrinsic learning motivation

According to the sources of the incentives, Edward L. Deci and Richard M. Ryan (1985) divided learning motivation into intrinsic learning motivation and extrinsic learning motivation. Both types of motivation can influence learning behavior and outcomes, but intrinsic learning is fueled by a genuine interest in learning and is often associated with deeper engagement, persistence, and enjoyment in the learning process, while extrinsic learning motivation stems from external factors and is driven by the pursuit of rewards or the avoidance of aversive consequences.

Intrinsic learning motivation refers to the internal desire or drive for learners to engage in learning activities for the inherent satisfaction, enjoyment, or interest provided by those activities, which comes from the learners themselves and their interest in the activity itself. Intrinsic motivation is driven by the intrinsic needs of individuals. The satisfaction of motivation lies in the activity rather than outside of it. Intrinsic motivation does not require external incentives or punishments to direct action toward a goal because learning itself is a form of motivation. Students' curiosity, thirst for knowledge, desire to improve their abilities, and other intrinsic motivational factors will promote active learning. Students with intrinsic learning motivation are naturally curious and find pleasure in exploring new ideas, solving problems, or mastering skills without the need for external rewards. For instance, some students enjoy English, so they listen attentively in class and study hard afterward.

Extrinsic learning motivation refers to external factors that motivate learners to engage in learning activities primarily to obtain external rewards or avoid punishment. Extrinsic motivation is driven by incentives outside of the learning task itself, such as grades, praise, or tangible rewards. Extrinsic motivation means that the satisfaction of people's learning motivation does not lie in the learning activity itself, but outside of it. At this time, people are not interested in learning itself, but in the results of learning. For example, some students learn to receive rewards, avoid punishment, or please their teachers.

Intrinsic motivation and extrinsic motivation determine whether students will continue to master what they have learned. Students with intrinsic motivation can find satisfaction in learning and actively participate in the learning process; they are curious, enjoy challenges, and are independent in solving problems. Once students with extrinsic motivation achieve their learning objectives, their motivation may decline. On the other hand, to achieve their goals, they often take measures to avoid failure or choose tasks without challenges. If they fail, they may struggle to recover.

In the process of education, more attention should be paid to the function of intrinsic learning motivation. Some students do not need any external incentives or rewards; teachers should properly guide students' interests and combine those interests with classroom content. However, the role of extrinsic learning motivation should not be ignored, as much of the learning content may not be inherently enjoyable or useful for most students. It can be challenging for students to maintain high enthusiasm for learning in day-to-day situations. Therefore, using some external stimuli in the teaching process, such as praise, scores, and rewards, can be beneficial for students' learning. However, the use of external rewards should be approached with caution, as excessive reliance on them may undermine students' intrinsic motivation.

### 5.2.2 Indirect learning motivation for long-term goals and direct learning motivation for short-term goals

According to the relationship between motivation, behavior, and goals, the American psychologist William James (1890) divided learning motivation into indirect learning motivation for long-term goals and direct learning motivation for short-term goals.

**Indirect learning motivation for long-term goals** refers to the drive for learners to learn or take action based on long-term goals or aspirations. This type of motivation is characterized by a focus on future outcomes and is often associated with personal values, ambitions, and vision. Individuals with indirect learning motivation for long-term goals are driven by the desire to achieve overarching objectives such as career success, personal growth, or societal contributions.

On the other hand, **direct learning motivation for short-term goals** involves the drive for the learner to learn or take action for immediate, tangible rewards or satisfaction. This type of motivation is centered around immediate needs, pleasures, or gratification. Individuals with direct learning motivation for short-term goals are motivated by the pursuit of instant benefits or solutions to current problems.

These two types of motivation influence individuals' behaviors and decisions differently. Indirect learning motivation for long-term goals emphasizes long-term objectives and personal growth, while direct learning motivation for short-term goals focuses on immediate rewards and satisfaction.

### 5.2.3 Cognitive drive, ego-enhancement drive and affiliated drive

Cognitive drive, ego-enhancement drive, and affiliated drive, proposed in School Learning by Ausubel & Robinson (1969), represent different motivational forces that influence human behavior. Cognitive drive propels learners toward intellectual pursuits. Ego-enhancement drive focuses on self-esteem and status enhancement. Affiliated drive revolves around the need for social connections and belonging.

**Cognitive drive** refers to the motivation for learners to seek out and engage with intellectually stimulating activities or challenges. It is driven by a desire for cognitive growth, learning, and understanding. Cognitive drive is also an intrinsic learning motivation and is considered the most important and stable learning motivation. Cognitive drive originates from students' innate curiosity and their psychological tendency to explore, manipulate, understand, and cope with the environment. The higher the students' cognitive drive, the better their persistence in learning, the more effective their learning, and the more eager they are for solutions in the problem-solving process. In the educational process, the best way to improve a student's cognitive drive is to make the learning situation attractive. The teacher's responsibility is to make the students interested in cognition itself, to create a connection between the new learning content and the students' cognitive structure, as well as an appropriate distance, which is the most effective way to enhance cognitive drive.

**Ego-enhancement drive** involves the motivation for the learner to enhance his self-esteem, self-image, or social status. Students with a strong ego-enhancement drive not only pursue knowledge itself but seek out opportunities to prove their competence, gain recognition, or achieve success in order to bolster their sense of self-worth, so it is an extrinsic learning motivation. The cognitive drive is directed toward the content of knowledge itself, and it is satisfied with acquiring knowledge and understanding things. The ego-enhancement drive points to a certain social status, which is satisfied with winning that status. As students grow older and become more self-conscious, they want to be respected in their families and school communities. This desire pushes students to work hard and strive for good grades in order to earn status commensurate with their achievements.

**Affiliated drive** refers to the need for learners to perform well in their work and studies in order to gain the praise or recognition of their elders (such as parents or teachers). The goal of affiliated drive is determined by others, and the school child gains derived status from the recognition and approval of others. School children with a strong affiliated drive are motivated by the desire for social belonging, acceptance, and intimacy. They may seek out social interactions, engage in group activities, or form bonds with others to fulfill their need for interpersonal connection. School children's affiliated drive is more manifested in studying hard to gain respect and recognition in peer groups. The motivation is not the pursuit of knowledge itself but the self-esteem satisfaction outside knowledge, so it is also an extrinsic learning motivation.

### 5.2.4 Interpersonal motivation and prestige motivation

American psychologist Sven Sorlie (1926) believed that in human social motivation, there are interpersonal motivation and prestige motivation, and learning motivation is derived from these two motivations, which have great significance for students' learning.

**Interpersonal motivation** refers to the drive for the learner to engage in activities or behaviors in order to gain acceptance, approval, affection, or favor from teachers, parents, and friends, and to avoid being cold and lonely. It involves seeking social connection and validation through interactions with others.

**Prestige motivation**, a higher level of social motivation than interpersonal motivation, is the motivation for learners to learn in order to receive recognition, admiration, praise, and respect from others. It is the manifestation of people's desire to achieve a certain status in society. Such motivation is the psychological basis for self-awareness and initiative in learning. Individuals with prestige motivation are driven by the pursuit of status, reputation, or social standing in their community or society.

Both interpersonal motivation and prestige motivation are fundamental aspects of human social motivation, influencing behavior and decision-making in various social contexts.

## 5.3 Functions of learning motivation

It is clear that students with higher-level learning motivation for achievement are more likely to succeed in school. Motivation and achievement affect each other. The function of learning motivation exists throughout the whole process of learning activities and has an obvious impact on the learning effect, while the learning effect has a feedback effect on the learning motivation. The relationship between learning motivation and learning is dialectical. Learning can generate motivation, and motivation can promote learning.

1. The function of arousing learning behavior

Learning motivation can stimulate individual learning activities. Students with high learning motivation will focus their attention on student-related activities, demonstrating high learning enthusiasm and great initiative. In learning situations, they will take the initiative to adopt a series of learning behaviors to accept and process relevant information, actively construct knowledge, and try to find ways to solve problems. However, students who lack learning motivation tend to focus their attention on stimuli other than learning and lack enthusiasm and initiative for learning. In learning situations, they seldom take the initiative to process information, construct knowledge, or solve problems. Learning motivation is the drive that triggers students' learning behavior, and it can stimulate students' learning actions.

2. The function of causing learners' learning behavior to point to a specific goal

Learning motivation can not only stimulate individual learning activities but also direct learning toward a certain goal. The difference between learning motivation and learning need lies in the fact that the learning need is not directed at a specific goal, while learning motivation is aimed at a certain goal (or incentive) and is guided by that goal. This relationship is like that between an engine and a steering wheel. Faced with abundant teaching information and educational resources, students tend to feel confused. Like a steering wheel, learning motivation can guide students' learning behavior toward a specific learning goal, enabling them to choose meaningful information from numerous and complicated resources, discard irrelevant information, engage in meaningful learning behaviors, and avoid adverse behaviors that hinder the realization of their goals until they achieve their learning objectives.

3. The function of maintaining the learning process

According to daily observation, students with strong learning motivation usually have a serious learning attitude and strong perseverance, which are important factors in maintaining learning behavior and directly affect the learning effect. After the emergence of individual learning activities, learning motivation can monitor the progress of learning and adjust the intensity and duration of learning activities. If they have strong learning motivation, students will consciously set learning objectives, formulate learning plans, and actively adjust their learning strategies according to the difficulty of the tasks. Students with strong learning motivation are often able to exercise strict self-discipline and consciously regulate their learning behaviors. When encountering difficulties and setbacks, they can actively mobilize their own resources, maintain and strengthen their learning activities, and ultimately complete learning tasks and achieve their learning objectives. If the intensity of students' learning motivation is low and their initiative and perseverance are poor during the learning process, they tend to follow others' arrangements for learning activities, rarely take the initiative to make a learning plan, seldom reflect on their learning strategies and effects, and are easily discouraged and fall by the wayside in the face of difficulties and setbacks.

4. The function of reinforcement

High-level learning motivation can lead to high-level academic achievements. In turn, high academic achievements can also improve motivation levels. In 1979, psychologist Walberg and his team studied the relationship between motivation levels and learning achievement. The results showed that subjects with stronger learning motivation have better learning achievements within a certain intensity range, and this positive correlation reaches a significant level of 98%. However, we should avoid excessively strong learning motivation and maintain the optimal level of motivation intensity. Only in this way can we play a positive role in reinforcing learning behavior.

## 5.4 Relationship between learning motivation and learning effect

Learning motivation can promote learning, and it is usually consistent with learning effect. However, learning motivation is not always consistent with learning effect. The relationship is not so simple in learning activities. The influence of learning motivation on learning effect can be divided into two aspects.

### 5.4.1 The relationship between learning motivation and learning effect is consistent

Learning motivation is usually consistent with learning effect. The stronger an individual's learning motivation, the higher his enthusiasm for participation in learning, the greater the persistence, the higher the learning quality, and the better the academic achievement. This correlation suggests that students with higher levels of motivation also have higher academic performance.

However, the relationship between learning motivation and learning effect is not always consistent. Some students have high levels of learning motivation, but their academic performance is not ideal because learning effects are not only influenced by learning motivation but also restricted by subjective and objective factors such as knowledge, intelligence, learning skills, and methods, which can affect the learning effect. Learning motivation is just one of the influencing factors.

Therefore, the relationship between learning motivation and learning effect is not completely proportional. Learning motivation is an important factor that affects learning behavior and improves learning effect, but it is not the only condition that determines learning activities. It is important to stimulate learning motivation, but we should also focus on improving various subjective and objective conditions to elevate the level of learning behavior.

### 5.4.2 The relationship between learning motivation and learning effect is not so simple in a specific learning activity

Only when the intensity of learning motivation is at the optimal level can the best learning effect be produced. The Yerkes-Dodson law shows that insufficient or excessive motivation will affect the learning effect (Figure 5-1).

1) The optimal level of motivation varies with the nature of the task. For easier tasks, the behavioral effect (work efficiency) increases with the improvement of motivation; however, as the difficulty of the task increases, the optimal level of

motivation tends to decline gradually.

2) Generally speaking, medium intensity of motivation is the optimal level, which is the most conducive to the completion of tasks.

3) The relationship between motivation level and behavioral effect shows an inverted U-shaped curve.

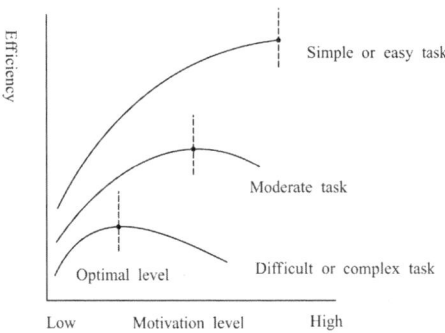

Figure 5-1  Yerkes-Dodson Law

Source: Kantowitz B. H. & Sorkin R. D., *Human Factors: Understanding People-system Relationships*, John Wiley & Sons, 1983, p. 606.

According to the Yerkes-Dodson Law, insufficient motivation or excessive motivation will lead to a decrease in work efficiency. That is to say, when the motivation intensity is at a medium level, work efficiency is the highest. Once the motivation intensity exceeds this level, it can hinder behavior. *For example, if your learning motivation is too strong and you are too eager for success, anxiety and tension may arise, interfering with the smooth progress of memory and thinking activities, which will reduce your learning efficiency. "Stage fright" in exams is mainly caused by excessive motivation.*

At the same time, the optimal level of motivation varies with the nature of the task. The optimal level of motivation is higher for easier tasks; it tends to decline gradually with the increase in task difficulty. That is, higher-level motivation in less difficult tasks is conducive to completing the task, while lower-level motivation in more difficult tasks is conducive to completing the task, and too high motivation will hinder task completion.

The Yerkes-Dodson Law has important implications for educators. In the learning process, if the learning tasks are difficult for students, such as algebra, geometry, and physics, a relatively low level of learning motivation will be conducive to their learning. If the difficulty of the learning task is moderate for students, a medium level of learning motivation is conducive to their learning. If the learning task is relatively easy for students, high learning motivation is more conducive to their learning. In school education, an important issue that should be considered is to ensure that the level of students' learning motivation is appropriate. Care must be taken to avoid setting too high a goal for students or putting too much pressure on them. Too high goals and too much pressure will not promote students' learning but may lead to psychological problems, psychological disorders, and even psychological illness.

## 5.5 Theories of learning motivation

The cognitive school, behavioral school, and humanistic school all agree that all behaviors are motivated, but different schools have different explanations for the reasons that cause motivation (Chen Qi & Liu Rude, 2007).

### 5.5.1 Reinforcement theory

The reinforcement theory of learning motivation was put forward by behaviorist psychologists. Behaviorism not only uses **reinforcement** to explain the occurrence of learning but also employs it to explain the generation of motivation. In their view, a person's tendency toward certain learning behaviors entirely depends on the previous solid connection between learning behaviors (R) and stimuli (S) (refer to 4.4.3). If an individual's learning behavior results in positive consequences, such as good grades, praise, affirmation, and reward, then the probability that the individual will exhibit the behavior again will increase. According to this view, the aim of any learning behavior is to gain some kind of reinforcement. That is, any learning behavior is aimed at obtaining some kind of reward. Therefore, in learning activities, utilizing various external means such as rewards, praise, scores, and competition can stimulate students' learning motivation and lead to corresponding learning behaviors. In this case, the reinforcer is the incentive.

1. External reinforcement and internal reinforcement

Reinforcement in school can be either external or internal. External reinforcement refers to the means of reinforcement, such as praise and rewards, given by teachers or others to students. Internal reinforcement, or self-reinforcement, means that students enhance their sense of success and self-confidence due to the satisfaction of success in learning, thereby improving their learning motivation. Both external and internal reinforcements can be divided into *positive reinforcement and negative reinforcement*. Generally speaking, both positive reinforcement and negative reinforcement play a role in enhancing learning motivation, such as appropriate praise and rewards, obtaining excellent results, or canceling annoying frequent exams, which are means of positive reinforcement or negative reinforcement. Regardless of whether they are positive or negative reinforcement, as long as they are appropriately applied in learning, they can help students improve their level of learning motivation, learning behavior, and academic performance (refer to Table 4-3).

The theory of reinforcement motivation has great limitations because it overemphasizes the external forces that cause learning behavior (external reinforcement) and ignores or even denies the self-consciousness and initiative of learning behavior (self-reinforcement). It should be noted that the motivational value of reinforcement and incentives is determined by many factors, which may vary from person to person. *For example, good grades, praise, and rewards are positive incentives for most school children, which can enhance their learning motivation, but they may not be important for others. Achieving good grades, praise, and rewards may not be their goals and may not stimulate their learning motivation.*

### 2. Using praise effectively

Praise serves many purposes in classroom instruction but is primarily used to reinforce appropriate behaviors and to give feedback to students on what they are doing right. Overall, it is a good idea to use praise frequently, especially with young children and in classrooms with many low-achieving students (Brophy, 1998; Evans, 1996). However, what is more important than the amount of praise given is the way it is delivered. Praise is effective as a classroom motivator to the extent that it is contingent, specific, and credible (Sutherland, Wehby, & Copeland, 2000). Contingent praise depends on students' performance of well-defined behaviors. *For example, if you say, "I'd like you all to open your books to page 92 and work problems one to ten," then only give praise to the students who follow directions.* Praise should be given only for appropriate behaviors. If used properly, praise can be an effective motivator in classroom situations (Table 5-1).

Table 5-1  Guidelines for effective praise

1. It is delivered contingently.
2. It specifies the particulars of the accomplishment.
3. It shows spontaneity, variety, and other signs of credibility; suggests clear attention to the student's accomplishment.
4. It rewards attainment of specified performance criteria (which can include effort criteria, however).
5. It provides information to students about their competence or the value of their accomplishments.
6. It orients students toward better appreciation of their own task-related behavior and thinking about problem solving.
7. It uses students' own prior accomplishments as the context for describing present accomplishments.
8. It is given in recognition of noteworthy effort or success at difficult tasks (for this student).
9. It attributes success to effort and ability, implying that similar successes can be expected in the future.
10. It focuses students' attention on their own task-relevant behavior.
11. It fosters appreciation of, and desirable attributions about, task-relevant behavior after the process is completed.

Source: Jere Brophy, "Teacher Praise: A Functional Analysis", *Review of Educational Research*, 1981, 51(1):26.

### 3. Principles of praise and criticism

For most students, punishment may be a negative incentive that hinders their learning motivation. However, for a small number of school children (such as those who are usually paid little attention to or even ignored), punishment can serve as a positive incentive (punishment means attention). The more teachers and parents punish them, the more frequently their behavior occurs. Specific problems need specific analysis. Therefore, in actual teaching, teachers should follow the principles of praise and criticism (Table 5-2), analyze specific problems, and take corresponding measures according to each student's unique situation.

Table 5-2  Principles of praise and criticism

| Principle | Explanation |
| --- | --- |
| Principle of seeking truth from facts | Both praise and criticism should align with reality and convince students, which will stimulate their intention to enhance their strengths and overcome their weaknesses; otherwise, it will have the opposite effect. |
| Principle of timeliness | If praise or criticism is delayed too long, it will weaken the strength and role of reinforcement. |
| Principle of appropriateness | Neither praise nor criticism should be too frequent or excessive. Too much praise for a student can easily lead to complacency or an inability to listen to criticism, while too much criticism and reprimand can cause students to feel inferior, timid, or oppositional. |
| Principle of infantilization | Do not simply apply rewards and punishments for adults, such as fines and criticism, to schools, because this will often damage children's minds or lead to counterproductive effects. |

Source: Jere Brophy, "Teacher Praise: A Functional Analysis", *Review of Educational Research*, 1981, 51(1):26.

In short, no matter which method of reinforcement is adopted, the educational consequences should be taken into account.

## 5.5.2 Theory of hierarchy of needs and its educational significance

### 1. Maslow's hierarchy of needs

The theory of the hierarchy of needs, put forward by Maslow, a famous American humanistic psychologist, elaborates on human needs in detail. Maslow believed that attention must be paid to people's needs in order to reveal the essence of motivation because all human behavior is driven by needs, and needs are hierarchical.

**Abraham Maslow**
**(1908-1970)**

The theory of the hierarchy of needs (Maslow, 1954) divides human needs into seven kinds: physiological needs, safety needs, belongingness and love needs, esteem needs, needs to know and understand, aesthetic needs, and self-actualization needs. The seven kinds of needs are not at the same level, and they are arranged in a certain order from low to high, forming a pyramid structure (Figure 5-2). According to Maslow, these needs are not only divided into high and low levels but also in sequence. Only when the low-level needs are basically satisfied can the high-level needs emerge.

Maslow divided the seven needs into deficiency needs and growth needs. Among them, the first four kinds of needs are deficiency needs, which are necessary for human beings to maintain survival activities. After they are satisfied, their intensity will be reduced. In contrast, growth needs, such as the need to know and understand things, to appreciate beauty, or to grow and develop in appreciation of others, can never be completely satisfied.

1) **Physiological needs**, at the bottom of the pyramid, refer to the most basic human needs and the foundation of human survival, such as food, water, air, sleep, and sex. Physiological needs are the most basic, primitive, and powerful.

2) **Safety needs** mainly refer to the needs of individuals for personal safety, life stability, and freedom from pain, threat, or disease. The safety need means that individuals require a stable and safe living or learning environment, free from fear and anxiety. As far as school children are concerned, their safety needs are mainly manifested in psychological safety; that is, they hope to feel relaxed in the learning process, have no anxiety, do not worry about reprimands from others (especially teachers and parents), and do not have to be wary of others at any time. Today's students experience varying degrees of psychological insecurity, mainly manifested in fear of teachers and campus bullying, etc. Therefore, if teachers want to cultivate and stimulate students' learning motivation, it is most important to meet students' safety needs and make them feel secure.

3) **Belongingness and love needs** refer to individuals' need to be accepted, loved, cared for, encouraged, and supported by others or groups and to establish emotional ties. Human beings are social animals. Individuals have a sense of belonging to a group and hope to belong to one or more groups. In this way, they can receive warmth, help, and love, thereby eliminating or reducing feelings of solitude and loneliness. Therefore, students yearn for a democratic, equal, and harmonious class, in which students are united and friendly, and the relationship between teachers and students is harmonious. This results in high learning enthusiasm and improves learning efficiency.

4) **Esteem needs** are the need to pursue one's own social value after the needs for physiology, security, belongingness and love are met, which includes self-esteem and

respect from others. Self-esteem is an emotional experience of self-love and self-worth generated and formed by individuals based on self-evaluation, and it requires respect from others, the collective, and society. Respect from others means that individuals hope that others will recognize and appreciate their work, valuing and praising them highly. Students and teachers should respect each other. Respecting students is the minimum attitude of teachers towards students. Students hope to receive respect not only from their peers but also from teachers and parents.

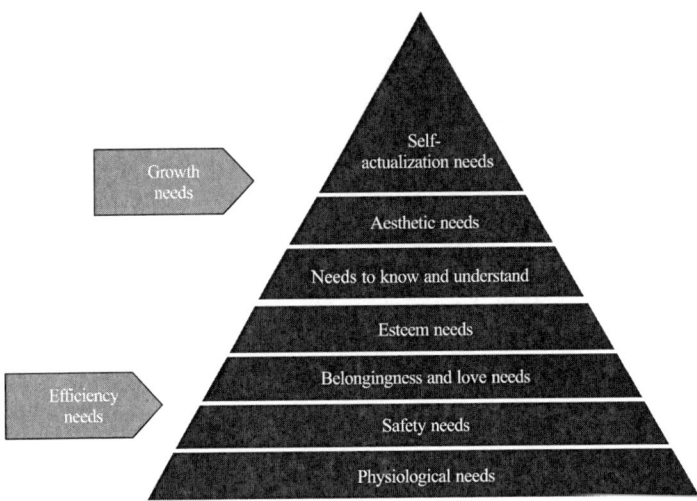

Figure 5-2　Maslow's hierarchy of needs

Source: Robert E. Slavin, *Educational Psychology Theory and Practice* (10th), Posts & Telecom Press, 2017, p. 289.

5) Need to know and understand, aesthetic needs, and self-actualization needs. Self-actualization, at the top of the pyramid, is the state of self-fulfillment in which people realize their highest potential in their own unique way. In fact, the need to know and understand and aesthetic needs must be satisfied first before self-actualization needs are met. Self-actualization includes cognitive needs, aesthetic needs, and creative needs; that is, the realization of a person's complete and full humanity and the full expression and manifestation of personal potential. According to the theory of the hierarchy of needs, people learn in order to pursue self-actualization. Through learning, they can fully realize their potential, express their personality, and achieve their value to the greatest extent. The self-actualization need belongs to growth needs, and it can never be fully satisfied. In other words, the need for self-actualization will not decrease with satisfaction but will be enhanced by it, so the pursuit of knowledge is endless. Therefore, the need for self-actualization is an important learning motivation (refer to 4.6.2).

## 2. Educational significance of the theory of hierarchy of needs

The theory of hierarchy of needs holds that the lack of students' learning motivation may be caused by the insufficient satisfaction of certain needs to a certain extent.

1) Understand whether students' low-level physiological needs are met. If students often have to worry about food and clothing, and if their families are poor and their needs for food and clothing cannot be met, the students' self-actualization needs will be hindered, and their learning motivation will be affected. For example, in some rural compulsory education stage schools in China, free breakfast has been implemented, which has solved the problem of students' meals and relieved their worries.

2) Create an orderly and standardized living environment and lifestyle for school children. If they are rejected and bullied, if they are often criticized and scolded, and if the pressure is too high, school children will feel that they are not accepted and respected, leading to negative emotional states such as fear and anxiety. The above situations are enough to make school children not only frustrated with their studies but also at risk of abnormal behavior.

3) Create a good and friendly learning environment for students. If they are afraid of being abandoned by their parents all day long, school children will have no intention to learn. Therefore, teachers and parents should love children as much as possible. Teachers should pay more attention to the interaction between themselves and school children, making them feel welcomed and accepted in the collective, and ensuring they are never rejected or excluded.

4) Make good use of school children's competitive consciousness, thirst for knowledge, self-esteem motivation, and desire to avoid failure, so that school children can have the opportunity to succeed, obtain praise, experience success, and cherish their progress and achievements.

5) Follow the educational objectives and cultivate school children towards self-actualization. Therefore, a teacher should not only care about school children's learning but also about their lives and emotions, trying to help them solve difficulties in life and stimulate their learning motivation.

### 5.5.3 Attribution theory of success or failure

Biden usually gets good grades, but he just received a low grade on his first examination in the new class, and the grade is inconsistent with his self-image and causes him to feel discouraged. He asked himself, "Why did I fail in the examination?" He might try to rationalize his low grade: "The questions were too tricky. I wasn't feeling well. The teacher didn't tell us the examination was coming. I wasn't really trying. It was too hot." Biden used these excuses to account for his low grade, which is called attribution.

1. Basic point of view

The attribution theory of success or failure was first put forward by American social psychologist Harold Kelley. Attribution is people's explanation and evaluation of their own or others' activities and their results. Weiner, B. (2000), an American psychologist, systematically discussed the attribution of behavior results and attributed the causes of the success or failure of people's activities to six factors: *ability*, *effort*, *difficulty of tasks*, *luck*, *physical condition*, and *external environment*. He also classified these six factors into three dimensions according to their respective properties: *internal attribution and external attribution*, *stable attribution and unstable attribution*, *controllable attribution and uncontrollable attribution* (Table 5-3).

Through the study of attribution theory, he drew some basic conclusions about attribution. When an individual attributes success to internal factors such as ability and effort, he will feel proud, satisfied, and confident, while when he attributes success to external factors such as an easy task and good luck, he will have less satisfaction. On the contrary, if a person attributes his failure to a lack of ability or effort, he will feel shame and guilt, while he won't feel ashamed when he attributes his failure to the difficulty of the task or bad luck.

Success or failure will produce strong emotional experiences. The success of hard work will produce a happy experience. Failure without effort will produce a shameful experience, and students with such experiences should also be encouraged.

Table 5-3　Six factors and three dimensions of Weiner's attribution of success or failure

| Dimension / Factors | Stability | | Source of factors (locus of control) | | Controllability | |
|---|---|---|---|---|---|---|
| | Stable | Unstable | Internal | External | Controllable | Uncontrollable |
| Ability | + | | + | | | + |
| Effort | | + | + | | + | |
| Difficulty | + | | | + | | + |
| Luck | | + | | + | | + |
| Physical condition | | + | + | | | + |
| Environment | | + | | + | | + |

Source: 莫雷,《教育心理学》,教育科学出版社,2007,第268页.

If a school child attributes the result of failure to stable factors such as poor ability or a too difficult task, his hope for future success will be relatively low. If he attributes the result of failure to unstable factors such as insufficient effort or bad luck, his expectation of future success is obviously higher. Similarly, if his success is attributed to stable factors such as strong ability or an easy task, the expectation of future success is relatively high. However, due to unstable factors such as great effort or good luck, the expectation of future success is obviously low. When making the same effort, those with lower ability should be rewarded more. School children with low ability who work hard receive the highest evaluation, while school children with high ability but who do not work hard should be regarded less favorably. A school child who always fails and attributes the failure to internal, stable, and uncontrollable factors (low ability) will form a sense of learned helplessness.

2. Learned helplessness

American psychologist Seligman put forward the theory of learned helplessness. **Learned helplessness** refers to the psychological state in which individuals feel powerless to control and do nothing about the behavioral results due to continuous failure experiences. According to his theory, the process of powerlessness can be divided into four stages(Table 5-4).

Table 5-4 The forming process of learned helplessness

| Stage | Specific event |
| --- | --- |
| Stage 1 | Get experience. |
| Stage 2 | Conduct cognition based on the experience. |
| Stage 3 | Form the expectation of "uncontrollable future results". |
| Stage 4 | Show the damage of motivation, cognition and emotion, affecting later learning. |

In school education, the following measures can be taken to prevent or eliminate students' learned helplessness (Table 5-5). The concept of learned helplessness derives from the theory that students might become academic failures through a conditioning process based on negative feedback from teachers, school experiences, peers, and themselves. Numerous studies show that when students consistently fail, they eventually give up. They become conditioned to helplessness. Teachers at both the elementary and secondary levels can help counter this syndrome in a variety of ways, including attribution training, goal restructuring, self-esteem programs, success-guaranteed approaches, and positive feedback systems. The following general principles are helpful for all students, especially those who have shown a tendency to accept failure.

Table 5-5  Helping students overcome learned helplessness

1. ***Accentuate the positive.*** Get to know the student's strengths and then use these as building blocks. Every student has something she or he does well. But be careful that the strength is authentic; don't make up a strength. For example, a student might like to talk a lot but write poorly. Have the student complete assignments by talking rather than writing. As confidence is restored, slowly introduce writing.

2. ***Eliminate the negative. Do not play down a student's weaknesses.*** Deal with them directly but tactfully. In the preceding example, talk to the student about problems with writing. Then have the student develop a plan to improve on the writing. Discuss the plan, and together make up a contract about how the plan will be completed.

3. ***Go from the familiar to the new, using advance organizers or guided discovery.*** Some students have difficulties with concepts, skills, or ideas with which they are not familiar. Also, students relate better to lessons that are linked to their own experiences. For example, a high school math teacher might begin a lesson with a math problem that students might face in the real world, such as calculating the sales tax when purchasing an iPod. Further, the teacher can ask students to bring to class math problems they have encountered outside of school. The whole class can become involved in solving a student's math problem.

4. ***Create challenges in which students actively create problems and solve them using their own knowledge and skills.***

Source: Robert E. Slavin, *Educational Psychology Theory and Practice* (10th), Posts & Telecom Press, 2017, p. 298.

## 5.5.4  Self-efficacy theory

Self-efficacy theory is a theoretical explanation of motivation proposed by American psychologist Bandura in 1982. **Self-efficacy theory** refers to people's subjective judgment on whether they can successfully engage in a certain achievement behavior. Bandura pointed out that human behavior is affected by the outcome factors and antecedent factors of behavior. The **outcome factor of behavior** is reinforcement. The **antecedent factor of behavior** is the expectation of the next reinforcement that individuals produce after recognizing the dependent relationship between behavior and reinforcement. Expectations include result expectations and efficiency expectations. **Result expectation** refers to people's speculation that their certain behavior will lead to a certain result. *For example, if children feel that paying attention to lectures in class will lead to the good grades they hope to achieve, they may listen attentively.* **Efficiency expectation** refers to people's speculation or judgment about their ability to implement a certain behavior, that is, their speculation about their own behavioral ability, which means whether people are sure that they can successfully carry out a certain behavior that will bring a certain result. When people are convinced that they have the ability to carry out a certain activity, they will have high **self-efficacy** and will engage in that activity. *For example, when students not only know that paying attention in class can lead to ideal grades, but also feel capable of understanding what the teacher is saying, they can listen attentively.*

Self-efficacy has many effects on school children's minds and behaviors:

1) it affects school children's choice of activities;

2) it affects the degree of effort and persistence, and determines their attitude in the face of difficulties;

3) it affects their mood during activities;

4) it affects whether they can complete the learning task.

The formation of self-efficacy is also restricted by many factors, such as direct experiences, vicarious experiences, verbal persuasion, and emotional arousal.

1) Direct experience of success or failure. School children's personal experiences have the greatest impact on self-efficacy. Success experiences will improve their self-efficacy, while repeated failure experiences will reduce their self-efficacy. However, the influence of success or failure experiences on self-efficacy also depends on their attribution of success or failure. If school children attribute success to external uncontrollable factors, they will not enhance their self-efficacy, and vice versa.

2) Vicarious experience. When a school child sees that a demonstrator at a level similar to his own has achieved success, he will enhance his sense of self-efficacy. Otherwise, he will reduce his sense of self-efficacy.

3) Verbal persuasion (verbal suggestion). Verbal persuasion is a way to enhance school children's sense of self-efficacy through persuasive suggestions, interpretations, and self-guidance. Research has shown that verbal persuasion without an experiential foundation has a fragile effect on forming a sense of self-efficacy. In other words, the self-efficacy formed by verbal persuasion is not durable. Whether people accept the persuader's opinion or not depends on the persuader's identity and credibility.

4) Emotional arousal. According to Bandura, emotional and psychological states will affect the formation of self-efficacy. In situations full of tension and danger or under heavy loads, emotions are easily aroused. High levels of emotional arousal and tense physiological states can hinder behavioral manipulation and reduce the level of expectation for success. When people are in a state of excessive anxiety and fear, a vicious cycle will occur. For example, if the mood is tense, the whole body will shake, fear will increase, and the sense of incompetence will grow.

### 5.5.5 Achievement motivation theory

The representatives of achievement motivation theory include Murray, McClelland, and Atkinson. Achievement motivation was first proposed by psychologist Murray. In the 1940s and 1950s, McClelland further developed the theory of achievement motivation based on Murray's foundation. Atkinson and Litwin conducted experimental proof of the theory of achievement motivation in the 1960s.

1. Basic viewpoints

According to Murray, achievement motivation refers to an individual's desire or tendency to strive to overcome obstacles, showcase their talents, and solve problems quickly and effectively. Achievement motivation, unique to humankind and acquired with social significance, can promote individuals to engage in achievement behavior and pursue social goals that people consider important under certain social conditions. Atkinson divided individual achievement motivation into two categories: the motivation to strive for success and the motivation to avoid failure.

The purpose of **people who strive for success** is to achieve success. Through various activities, they seek to improve their self-esteem and obtain psychological satisfaction. The task with a 50% probability of success is the one they are most likely to choose. **People who avoid failure** often seek to prevent their self-esteem from being hurt and to avoid psychological distress through various activities, and they tend to choose very easy or very difficult tasks. If the probability of success of a task is about 50%, they will avoid the task.

Atkinson believed that there are three variables that affect an individual's tendency to pursue success ($T_s$), namely, the motivation for success ($M_s$), the possibility or probability of success ($P_s$), and the incentive value of success ($I_s$). The formula is:

$$T_s = M_s \times P_s \times I_s$$

Generally speaking, those with a high level of achievement motivation have the following characteristics: they are challenging and creative; they have firm beliefs; and they have correct attributions.

2. Educational inspiration of achievement motivation theory

In educational practice, those who strive for success should be given novel and difficult tasks, arranged in competitive situations, and scored strictly to stimulate their learning motivation. People who avoid failure should be placed in no or less competitive situations. If they succeed, praise them promptly and reinforce their efforts. When grading, it is necessary to be more lenient and try to avoid blaming them for mistakes in public. Since the motivation to strive for success has greater initiative than the motivation to avoid failure, it is essential to increase the component of students striving for success, so that they are not merely satisfied with avoiding failure, but rather find joy in achieving success and truly mobilizing their enthusiasm.

## 5.5.6 Self-worth theory

Atkinson (1983) described achievement motivation from two independent dimensions: pursuing success and avoiding failure. Covington (1992) divided students into four categories according to their tendency to strive for success and avoid failure: high-strive and low-avoidance, low-strive and high-avoidance, high-strive and high-avoidance, and low-strive and low-avoidance (Figure 5-3). The term "strive" here means to strive for success; "avoidance" means to avoid failure.

### 1. High-strive and low-avoidance

People with high-strive and low-avoidance are also called success-orienteers. Schoolchildren with high-strive and low-avoidance are highly curious, highly engaged in learning, and less concerned with the impact of failure. They learn not only because learning is a means of their happiness but also because it is a way of life. They are learning tirelessly almost all the time. *For example, Wei Dongyi and Chen Jingrun are passionate about mathematics, and both are people with high-strive and low-avoidance.*

### 2. Low-strive and high-avoidance

People with low-strive and high-avoidance are also called failure-avoiders. Schoolchildren with low-strive and high-avoidance are afraid of challenges and the consequences of failure, so they adopt various self-defense strategies to blame their failures on objective factors beyond their control. They place greater emphasis on avoiding failure. They don't like learning, and although they don't necessarily have learning problems or difficulties, they simply don't show interest in the course. They fantasize about canceling the exam. They try to minimize the importance of the task, thinking that this course is not important at all and that it doesn't matter whether they study well or not. They make excuses for their failures, such as, "I was sleepless last night, so I failed the exam." They find fault with others to reduce their responsibility, saying, "If I had a good teacher, I would learn better." They doubt their abilities, fear being accused of incompetence, and feel a high degree of anxiety and tension.

### 3. High-strive and high-avoidance

People with high-strive and high-avoidance are also called over-strivers. Over-strivers are both tempted by success and afraid of failure. Schoolchildren with high-strive and high-avoidance love and hate tasks, pursuing and rejecting them, which often leaves them in a state of conflict. They have characteristics of both success-oriented individuals and failure-avoiders. They are smart and capable, and they study hard. When homework and curriculum are non-challenging, they set higher requirements and goals for themselves to win additional rewards from teachers. However, they are seriously troubled by mental issues such as tension and conflict. They try to appear carefree among their classmates and don't care about exams, but secretly they make an effort and study hard. In this way, once successful, their achievements are more valuable and demonstrate their exceptional abilities; even if they fail, they can still believe that they can find a good reason for their failure and not be considered incompetent.

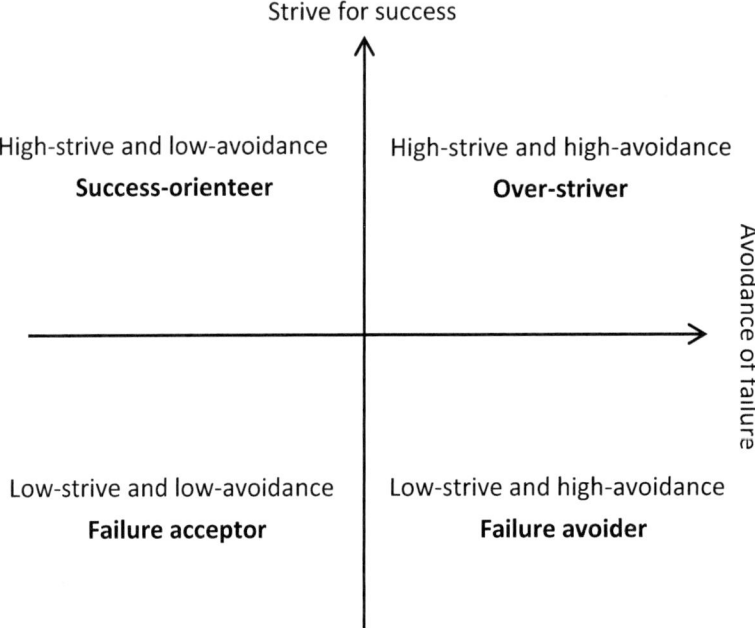

Figure 5-3 Classification of self-worth

4. Low-strive and low-avoidance

People with low-strive and low-avoidance are also called failure-acceptors. They show withdrawal and passive responses when facing academic challenges. They are neither proud of success nor ashamed of failure. They are indifferent to their achievements and do not accept any challenges related to their abilities, which prevents the evaluation of their incompetence.

They form the motivation to avoid failure mainly because individuals instinctively protect their sense of self-worth. Everyone has a need for self-acceptance. Only when we feel that we are valuable can we accept ourselves. The sense of self-worth usually comes from successful experiences. In other words, if individuals are competent, they can achieve success and thus gain a sense of self-worth. However, in the actual learning process, most school children have fewer successful experiences and more failure experiences in fierce competition. If school children fail to succeed in the long-term pursuit of success, they will develop self-protective behaviors, such as avoiding taking exams and trying to impress others that they have not worked hard. In this way, they avoid blaming their lack of ability for their learning failures, thus protecting their self-esteem. The motivation to avoid failure explains why some students refuse to work hard, while others hide or refuse to acknowledge their efforts. All of this essentially stems from a self-worth protective effect of attributing success to ability.

### 5.5.7 Relationship-behavior theory

Relationship-behavior theory, also known as the theory of relationship determining behavior, means that all behaviors are determined by relationships, which is discussed from four perspectives in this section.

**1. Any phenomenon in the universe is determined by relationships**

The universe is a vast and complex web of connections, where every phenomenon is intricately linked to others. Newton's law of universal gravitation states that every particle in the universe attracts every other particle with a force that is directly proportional to the product of their masses and inversely proportional to the square of the distance between them. This means that the more massive an object is, the greater its gravitational pull on other objects. The farther apart two objects are, the weaker the gravitational force between them. It explains why objects fall to the ground and why planets orbit the sun. It's a fundamental principle in physics that helps us understand the universe (Bergmann, 1958; Weinberg, 1972). Newton's law of universal gravitation, in fact, states the interconnection of everything in the world, that is, the relationship between everything in the universe. Connection mostly refers to the link between people or things, while relationship emphasizes the emotional bond and interaction between people. The former is broader, and the latter is deeper. Simply put, connection is the basis of relationship, and relationship is the deepening of connection.

The saying "All phenomena in the universe are determined by relationships" holds true and can be exemplified in various ways. Take the solar system, for instance. The planets, moons, and other celestial bodies are not isolated entities but are interconnected through gravitational forces. The distance between each planet and the sun, as well as their orbital paths, are all determined by these relationships, which Newton's law of universal gravitation can prove. Without these precise interactions, the solar system would cease to exist in its current form. Another example is the phenomenon of life on Earth. Every organism is dependent on other living beings and the environment around it. The food chain, symbiotic relationships, and ecosystem dynamics all showcase how various species are interrelated. For instance, plants rely on sunlight for photosynthesis, while animals consume plants or other animals for survival. These relationships shape the balance and diversity of life on our planet. Even on a subatomic level, particles interact with one another, forming atoms and molecules. The chemical bonds that hold matter together are based on specific relationships between elements. These interactions give rise to the diverse substances and compounds that make up our physical world.

In conclusion, the statement "All phenomena in the universe are determined by relationships" highlights the fundamental nature of the universe. From the largest celestial bodies to the smallest particles, and from nature to human society, relationships drive and shape the world around us. Understanding and appreciating these connections helps us better comprehend the complexity and beauty of the universe we inhabit.

### 2. Many behaviors in human society are determined by relationships

In human society, relationships also play a crucial role. Human beings are social creatures whose actions are deeply influenced by the various relationships they have. Interpersonal connections determine how we interact, communicate, and form communities. Families, friendships, and professional partnerships all influence our actions and decisions.

1) Urie Bronfenbrenner's bioecological theory

The American psychologist Urie Bronfenbrenner (1917-2005) identified five levels of environmental influence in his bioecological theory (Bronfenbrenner, 1979; 1986; 1994), ranging from very intimate to very broad: microsystem, mesosystem, exosystem, macrosystem, and chronosystem (Figure 5-4). A system is an integrated whole composed of a series of interrelated elements such as people and things. The people and things that make up the system will definitely have innumerable connections. Relationship refers to the connection and interaction between people or things. Simply put, a system is a combination of people or things, while a relationship is the bond between people or things.

The individual's development can be understood only in its social context. In this complex social context, the individual's development will be inextricably connected with others. The individual never develops as a separate entity interacting with the environment but as an inseparable part of it. The relationships in the social circle can greatly impact a person's upbringing, values, perspectives, and even all behavior.

We must see a person within the relationship context of these multiple environments to understand the complexity of influences on development.

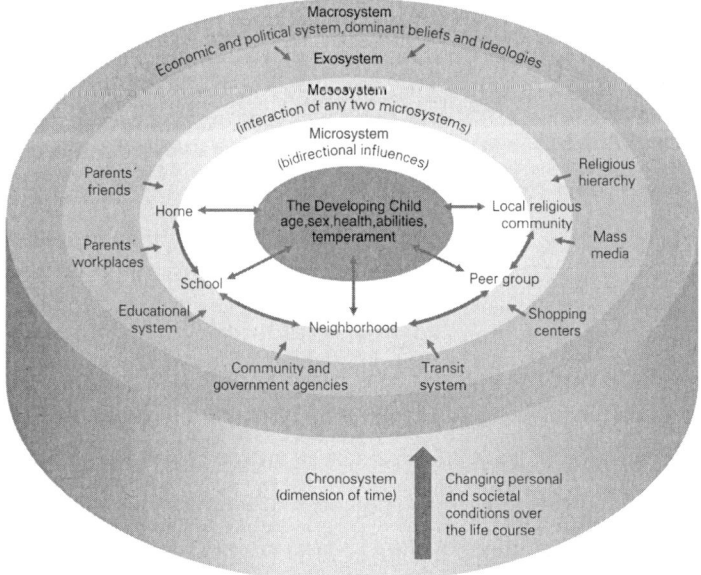

Figure 5-4　Bronfenbrenner's bioecological theory

Source: Diane E. Papalia & Ruth D. Feldman, *Experience Human Development* (12th), Posts & Telecom Press, 2014, pp. 35-36.

A **microsystem** is the everyday environment of home, school, work, or neighborhood, including face-to-face relationships with a spouse, children, parents, friends, classmates, teachers, employers, or colleagues. For example, parents affect their baby's growth, and the new baby, in turn, affects and even changes the parents' lives. Teachers' attitudes affect school children's performance in school, and school children, in turn, affect the teachers' teaching and lives.

The **mesosystem** is the interlocking of various microsystems. It may include linkages between home and school (such as parent-teacher conferences) or between the family and the peer group (such as relationships that develop among families of children in a neighborhood playgroup). For example, a parent's bad day at work might affect interactions with a child later that evening in a negative way. Despite never having actually gone to the workplace, the child is still affected by it.

The **exosystem** consists of linkages between a microsystem and outside systems or institutions that affect a person indirectly. Both the kicking cat effect and the butterfly effect show that relationships can influence or even determine the behavior of a person who seems to have nothing to do with it. For example, your community's transit system may affect job opportunities. The television programming that encourages prosocial behavior may make children more helpful.

The **macrosystem** consists of overarching cultural patterns, such as dominant beliefs, ideologies, and economic and political systems. For instance, a person is affected by living in a capitalist or socialist society.

Finally, the **chronosystem** adds the dimension of time: change or constancy in the person and the environment. This can include changes in family structure, place of residence, or employment, as well as larger cultural changes such as wars and economic cycles, such as periods of recession or relative prosperity. Vygotsky's sociocultural theory makes a specific, detailed, and thorough explanation of this problem.

No two leaves in the world are exactly the same. According to Bronfenbrenner, different people in different environments will produce different relationships with the environment and the people in it, and these relationships, in turn, shape a person's growth. By looking at systems that affect individuals in and beyond the family, this bioecological relationship of development helps us to see the variety of influences of relationships on mutual development.

2) Vygotsky's sociocultural theory

The Russian psychologist Lev Semenovich Vygotsky (1896-1934) focused on the social and cultural processes that guide children's cognitive development. Vygotsky's (1978) sociocultural theory stresses children's active engagement with their environment, and Vygotsky saw cognitive growth as a collaborative process. The collaborative process refers to the process of people collaborating to achieve common goals, while relationships are a key factor in the collaborative process. Good relationships can promote collaboration, improve efficiency, and the collaborative process can also deepen relationships. The collaborative process requires good relationships to support it, and relationships can also be strengthened through the collaborative process.

Social culture is the sum of values, beliefs, customs, behavioral norms, and ways of life commonly shared in a society or group. It forms and develops in a specific social environment and has a profound impact on people's behavior, thinking, and social relationships. Social culture includes but is not limited to language, art, religion, customs, moral standards, and social systems. Different social cultures may have differences, which reflect the history, traditions, geographical environment, and economic development of different social groups. Furthermore, the broader social and cultural context in which we live also dictates our behavior. Cultural norms, traditions, and societal expectations influence how we behave and what is deemed acceptable or unacceptable.

According to Vygotsky, people learn through social interaction. Social interactions in social activities are bound to produce complex social relationships. Good relationships are conducive for children to internalize their society's modes of thinking and behaving and make those folkways their own in shared social activities. According to Vygotsky, adults or more advanced peers must help direct and organize a child's learning before the child can master and internalize it. This guidance is most effective in helping children cross the zone of proximal development (ZPD), the gap between what they are already able to do by themselves and what they can accomplish with assistance. Responsibility for directing and monitoring learning gradually shifts to the child. For example, when an adult teaches a child to swim, the adult first helps the child in the water and then lets go gradually as the child can swim by himself. The metaphor of scaffolds—the temporary platforms on which construction workers stand—has been applied to this way of teaching. Scaffolding is the temporary support that parents, teachers, or others give a child in doing a task until the child can do it alone.

With a relationship, nothing matters; without a relationship, everything matters. Children's learning motivation and learning only happen in good relationships. In other words, good relationships determine children's learning motivation, learning, and learning effects.

3) Confucius' five cardinal relationships

Confucius' (551 BC-479 BC) five cardinal relationships theory refers to the five interpersonal relationships of monarch and subject, father and son, husband and wife, elder and younger brothers, and friends. He believed that these relationships are the foundation of social order, and everyone should fulfill their corresponding obligations and responsibilities according to their own identity and role (Confucius et al., 2012). In fact, the corresponding obligations and responsibilities that everyone should fulfill refer to behaviors that everyone should exhibit in the five cardinal relationships. In other words, the five cardinal relationships determine the behaviors everyone displays.

This ethical concept has an important position in traditional Chinese culture, has a profound impact on people's behavior and social harmony, and still holds significant importance in modern society. The family relationships include the relationships of father and son, husband and wife, elder and younger brothers, and so on. The relationships we have with our parents, siblings, and other family members shape our behaviors and values. For example, a loving and supportive family environment often leads to more positive and well-adjusted individuals. Conversely, dysfunctional family dynamics can negatively impact a person's behavior and mental well-being. Another significant example is that of friendships and social circles. The people we choose to associate with can greatly influence our behaviors and choices. Peer pressure, for instance, is a well-known phenomenon where we often conform to the behaviors and norms of our friends to fit in. In the workplace, relationships with colleagues and superiors also play a role in determining our behaviors. A positive work environment with good team dynamics encourages collaboration and productivity. On the other hand, a viciously competitive workplace can lead to stress and unproductive behavior. Relationships with significant others also have a profound impact. For instance, our romantic partners can influence our moods, decision-making, motivation, and even our long-term goals. A healthy and fulfilling romantic relationship can bring out the best in us, while a troubled one may have the opposite effect.

To sum up, it is evident that relationships play a crucial role in shaping our actions and determining the course of our lives. By understanding and consciously nurturing healthy relationships, we can strive to lead more fulfilling and meaningful lives.

### 3. Students' learning behavior, learning motivation and academic performance are determined by relationships

That school children's learning motivation is determined by relationships holds significant truth. Interpersonal connections and interactions have a profound impact on a student's desire and drive to learn. Relationships significantly shape a student's learning motivation. It is crucial for educators and parents to recognize the power of these relationships and strive to build good relationships effectively. By nurturing positive relationships with themselves, parents, teachers, peers, significant others, and their social and natural environments, we can create an optimal learning environment that encourages students to reach their full potential. Let's explore the relationships that affect students' learning motivation, learning, and academic performance with examples in the next section.

1) The relationship between the child and himself

The relationship between the child and himself is crucial. It involves self-awareness, self-acceptance, and personal growth. A child should learn to love and understand himself, develop his strengths, and build confidence. According to Freud, coordinating the relationship between the id, the ego, and the superego is also key to shaping good social behavior. Students should learn to reconcile with themselves. By nurturing this relationship, children can grow into individuals with a healthy sense of self and the ability to face life's challenges.

2) The relationship between the child and parents

The crucial relationship between the child and parents is based on love, trust, and mutual support. Parents are the guides who shape the child's life. Parents' support, expectations, and involvement in a student's education can greatly influence his motivation. When parents show interest in their child's studies, provide a conducive learning environment at home, and offer encouragement, it instills a sense of responsibility and motivation in the student. A healthy bond leads to the child's well-being and a strong foundation for a successful future. Nurturing this relationship is vital for a child's growth and development.

3) The relationship between the child and the teacher

A positive and supportive teacher-student relationship can stimulate students' learning motivation and inspire them to strive for better grades. A good teacher not only imparts knowledge but also guides and inspires students. When teachers show genuine care, provide constructive feedback, and encourage students, it boosts their confidence and motivation. Through interaction and communication, the teacher helps students grow, develops their potential, and builds a solid foundation for their future. Conversely, a strained or negative relationship may demotivate students and affect their academic performance.

4) The relationship between parents and teachers

The relationship between parents and teachers is crucial for a child's development. According to Bronfenbrenner, the mesosystem makes various microsystems interlocked, which includes linkages between home and school, so parent-teacher conferences are the bridge of the relationship between parents and teachers. Parents and teachers should communicate and work together to support the child's growth. Open communication, mutual respect, and a shared focus on the child's well-being can create a strong partnership that benefits the child's education and future.

5) The relationship between the child and the textbook

The textbook is a friend and guide for school children. It equips them with knowledge, opens up their minds, and helps them explore the world. They interact with the textbook, learn, grow, and build a foundation for their future. A good textbook can inspire a child's love for learning and set them on a path of discovery, so the good relationship between school children and textbooks is very crucial. Therefore, teachers and parents should try their utmost to make school children realize the importance of the textbooks and facilitate them to build good relationships with the textbooks.

6) The relationship between the child and classmates

A positive relationship with classmates helps a school child develop social skills and a sense of belonging. Classmates are an important part of a school child's social life. They build friendships, support each other, and grow together in the classroom. A good relationship with classmates can bring joy and support. School children learn to share, communicate, and cooperate through interactions. Peer relationships also play a vital role in school children's learning. Good relationships can give students a sense of belonging, which is conducive to the formation of a learning community. The learning community where school children work together in groups can enhance motivation. When school children feel a sense of camaraderie and shared purpose with their peers, they are more likely to be engaged and motivated in the learning process. *For instance, group projects or study sessions encourage active participation and foster a healthy competitive spirit.*

7) The relationship between the child and the school

The school is not only a place for learning but also a community for school children's growth. A positive and inclusive school community that values learning and celebrates achievements can create a motivating atmosphere. Children can make friends, develop their skills, and build their values in school. The school provides an environment for children to learn and grow, and the children also enrich the school with their unique presence. The social environment at school, including friendships and the overall school culture, can either motivate or demotivate a student. A good school should prevent bullying, offer school children a safe learning environment, give school children a sense of safety, and make them love their school. A good relationship with the school helps children have a fulfilling learning experience and is beneficial to foster their collective spirit.

8) The relationship between the child and society

The child and society are closely linked. Society provides children with various resources and opportunities for growth. Children also contribute to society through their learning and development. A healthy relationship helps children become responsible and contributing members of the community. Let's strive to create a nurturing environment for children to thrive in and make positive contributions to society.

9) The relationship between the child and the country

*"If the youth are wise, the country will be wise; if the youth are wealthy, the*

*country will be wealthy; if the youth are strong, the country will be strong; if the youth are independent, the country will be independent; if the youth are free, the country will be free; if the youth make progress, the country will make progress; if the youth excel in Europe, the country will excel in Europe; if the youth are the best in the world, the country will be the best in the world*" (Liang Qichao, 2001). The child is the future of the country. A strong country provides a stable and safe environment for children's growth. At the same time, we need to cultivate students' strong patriotism and enthusiasm. Children should be educated to love the country, contribute to its development, and work hard to make the country more prosperous. When the young Zhou Enlai issued the deafening cry of "reading for the rise of China", his patriotic enthusiasm sparked a strong learning motivation and desire to learn. The connection between the child and the country is interdependent and mutually reinforcing.

10) The relationship between the child and nature

The relationship between the child and nature is one of harmony and learning. They explore the world with curiosity and innocence. They learn to appreciate the beauty of nature and develop a sense of responsibility to protect it. By interacting with nature, children gain a deeper understanding of the environment and form a bond that lasts a lifetime. *For example, when heavy study tasks make a child overwhelmed, physically and mentally exhausted, or even cause mental problems, nature can heal the trauma and problems of this child.* Nature offers a space for children to relax, have fun, and gain a deeper appreciation of the world around them. It allows us to disconnect from the stress of daily life and reconnect with the simplicity and beauty of the world. Nature provides a calming and grounding experience that can help reduce anxiety, depression, and other mental health issues.

## 5.6 Stimulation and cultivation of learning motivation

The cultivation and stimulation of learning motivation are two different concepts: cultivating motivation is the process in which students are enabled to change the social and educational requirements into their own learning needs; stimulating motivation focuses on mobilizing the formed learning needs in order to improve the enthusiasm for learning. Cultivation is the premise of stimulation, and stimulation is bound to further strengthen the existing learning motivation. The cultivation of motivation focuses on developing interest and a thirst for knowledge.

### 5.6.1 Stimulation of learning motivation

The stimulation of learning motivation refers to the process of helping learners form learning motivation by using certain methods and means. According to different theories, there are several ways to stimulate learning motivation.

**1. Create problem situations, stimulate interest, and maintain curiosity**

Creating problem situations involves providing students with learning materials, conditions, and practices that encourage them to question, engage in activities, explore problems, and successfully solve challenges through effort. Effective instruction should constantly create problem situations to stimulate students' curiosity, thirst for knowledge, and internal learning motivation. Interest and curiosity are core components of intrinsic motivation, forming the foundation for cultivating and stimulating students' internal learning motivation.

To create problem situations, teachers must first familiarize themselves with the textbook, master its structure, and understand the internal connections between new and old knowledge. Additionally, teachers should fully understand the existing cognitive structures of students so that new learning content aligns appropriately with students' current levels, forming an appropriate zone of proximal development (ZPD) (Refer to 2.2).

The method of creating problem situations can manifest in various ways: it can be done through teacher questioning or by assigning homework; it can start from the connection between new and old knowledge, as well as from students' daily experiences. Furthermore, creating problem situations can occur at the beginning of teaching, during the teaching process, and at the end of teaching.

The principles for creating problem situations include: the problem should be small and refined; the problem should relate to students' actual life experiences; the problem should have appropriate difficulty and be enlightening.

**2. Set appropriate and specific goals and offer ways to achieve those goals**

When goals are set by students themselves, they usually put in more effort. Generally speaking, individuals are resistant to tasks imposed by others. They are more willing to accept and work hard for learning goals they participate in determining. Parents or teachers should guide students to set specific, short-term goals that can be achieved at a medium level of difficulty. Such goals enable students to see learning effects in the short term. Through their own efforts, students can complete these goals, promoting their confidence in learning and enhancing their interest in it. Teachers should help students identify achievable, challenging, realistic, specific, and short-term goals. When setting a goal, the teacher can discuss with the students how past goals have been achieved, what has worked, what has failed, and why, using this as a reference for setting new goals. Making students clearly aware of the learning goals is an effective way to cultivate their learning motivation, stimulating their learning needs and improving their learning efficiency. Conversely, blind learning leads to low efficiency. In the teaching process, teachers should ensure that students understand the significance of learning, know what they will learn, learn how to achieve these goals, receive specific suggestions for their goals, and be praised for setting and achieving them.

3. Control the difficulty of homework and the level of motivation appropriately

According to the Yerkes-Dodson Law, teachers should appropriately control the level of students' learning motivation based on the difficulty of learning tasks during teaching. When students study easier and simpler topics, they should try to focus their attention as much as possible and make themselves slightly nervous, allowing the level of motivation arousal to reach an optimal state from medium to high. When learning complex and difficult topics, it is necessary to create a relaxed and free classroom atmosphere, ensuring that the level of motivation arousal remains at a medium to optimal state. When students encounter difficulties or problems, teachers should guide them calmly and slowly to avoid excessive tension and anxiety. From this perspective, the common saying among students, "The bigger the exam is, the more you should play; the smaller the exam is, the less you should play; if there is no exam, you should never play", has positive significance to a certain extent.

4. Cultivate self-efficacy and enhance students' confidence in success

Self-efficacy refers to students' beliefs and judgments about their ability to complete certain tasks. Self-efficacy affects their choice of tasks, effort, persistence, and learning attitude. Students with high self-efficacy tend to choose challenging tasks, persist in difficult situations, and experience less fear and anxiety, while those with low self-efficacy are hesitant to choose challenging tasks and tend to give up when encountering difficulties or procrastinate and avoid difficult tasks. Students with poor academic performance usually have low self-efficacy and are prone to give up trying in their studies, making it difficult for them to improve their academic performance. Therefore, changing and improving self-efficacy is an effective way to stimulate students' learning motivation. Specifically, the following measures can be taken:

1) Select tasks of moderate difficulty so that students can continue to experience success.

2) Allow students to observe the successful learning behaviors of others with similar abilities. When they see the success of their classmates, their self-efficacy will be enhanced.

3) Help students learn from failures, improve learning skills, and gain confidence in their success.

### 5. Express positive expectations

Teachers' expectations of students greatly influence their motivation and results, as confirmed by the famous Pygmalion effect in psychology discovered by American psychologist Rosenthal. Rosenthal and his team visited a primary school, claimed to conduct a "future trend test," and provided a list of "most promising students" to the principal and teachers, stating that these students were all geniuses identified through the test, with limitless futures. Eight months later, when Rosenthal returned to the school, a miracle occurred: all the students on the list had made significant progress in their scores and excelled in various aspects. In reality, the list was chosen at random.

Clearly, the progress of these students was related to Rosenthal's "white lie," which led teachers to believe that these students possessed remarkable abilities. Teachers' psychological expectations were subtly transmitted to the students through emotions, language, and behavior, making them feel the love and expectations from their teachers, thus enhancing their self-esteem, self-confidence, and self-improvement, resulting in significant progress in all respects. In this process, teachers' expectations for these students were sincere, as they believed these students had the most potential for development.

Because of this, teachers' words and actions revealed their trust and expectations for these students, and such sincere expectations were something students could perceive. This phenomenon has significant implications for teachers. It reminds them to convey to students that they can learn well during the teaching process. Therefore, students need a clear understanding of what they should do, how they should be evaluated, and what they will gain after achieving success. It is crucial for teachers to clearly communicate their expectations to students.

### 6. Provide clear, timely, and frequent feedback

By providing feedback, students can promptly understand learning outcomes, including the effectiveness of using their knowledge to solve problems, the accuracy of homework, and the merits and demerits of exam results, which will have a significant motivating effect.

1) Feedback must be clear and specific, especially for young students, to help

them develop motivational attribution to their effort.

2) Feedback must be timely and closely follow individual learning outcomes to prevent students from making the same mistakes repeatedly.

3) Feedback must be frequent, encouraging students to put forth their best effort. Giving small rewards frequently promotes student learning more than offering large rewards occasionally.

### 7. Use rewards and punishments correctly

The correct use of rewards and punishments is one of the important means to stimulate students' learning motivation. When using rewards and punishments, teachers should pay attention to the following points:

1) It is necessary to help students establish correct concepts of rewards and punishments. Teachers should educate students to have a proper attitude towards rewards and punishments, viewing them as means rather than ends to enhance learning enthusiasm. Otherwise, the phenomenon of learning for rewards and avoiding punishments may arise, reducing intrinsic motivation.

2) Rewards and punishments must be fair and appropriate. If teachers' rewards and punishments are influenced by subjective impressions and lack fairness and reasonableness, they often lead to negative results.

3) Attention should be paid to students' age characteristics, personality traits, and gender differences. When implementing rewards and punishments, teachers must fully consider the individual differences of students to "have a definite object in view" and "treat the disease with the right medicine".

### 8. Use praise and criticism appropriately and effectively

Generally speaking, praise and rewards are more effective in motivating students to study than criticism and reprimand. Psychologist Hurlock (1925) conducted an experiment with 106 students in fourth and fifth grades, divided into four groups, each with similar abilities, who practiced addition exercises of equal difficulty in four different situations for 15 minutes per day over 5 days. The four groups were evaluated differently. The researchers gave the control group no ratings, isolating them from the other three groups and allowing them to practice alone. The praised group received constant praise and encouragement; the reprimanded group was criticized; and the listening group received neither praise nor criticism but listened to the other two groups being praised or criticized. The findings showed a significant difference in practice performance between these groups (Figure 5-5). On average, the three experimental groups performed better than the control group because it received no information.

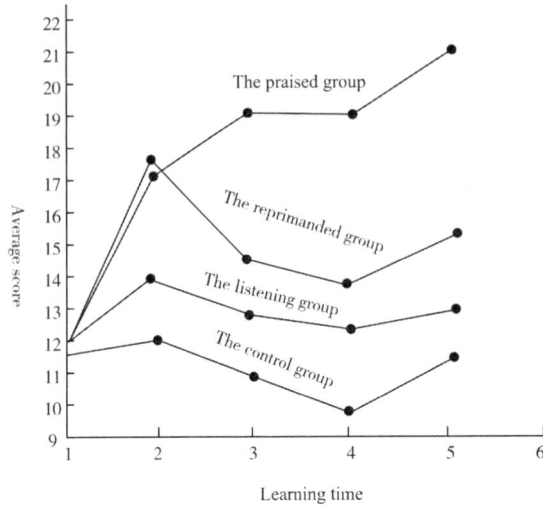

Figure 5-5  Impact of different evaluations on learning outcomes

Source：冯忠良等,《教育心理学》,人民教育出版社,2000,第 150 页.

The results of the praised group were better than those of the other groups and continued to rise in a straight line. The results of the reprimanded group went up at the beginning but then went down. This shows that the evaluation of learning results can stimulate students' learning motivation and promote their learning. The effect of appropriate praise is better than that of criticism, so students should be praised rather than criticized in teaching.

The way of praise is more important than the frequency of praise. Psychologists have put forward suggestions to make praise the most effective. 1) Praise should be directed at school children's good behaviors that are superior to conventional levels. 2) Teachers should make clear what kind of school children's behaviors are worthy of praise rather than general praise of their "good performance". 3) The praise should be sincere, come from the heart, and reflect the teacher's appreciation of students' grades, but should not be hypocritical. 4) The praise should convey the message that if students put in a certain amount of effort, there is still the possibility of success in the future. 5) The praise should tell students that they work hard and are praised because they enjoy the tasks.

According to the findings of Hurlock's (1925) experiment, the appropriate use of reasonable punishment in teaching can also play a role in stimulating the self-improvement drive, but the use of these negative incentives must be appropriate. Too severe punishment will make students lose self-confidence, damage their self-esteem, reduce their ideals and aspirations, and lead to withdrawal and avoidance. Therefore, these negative incentive measures must be used appropriately and differ from person to person. Appropriate criticism can be given to school children with enough self-confidence, strong will, strong psychological endurance, and certain potential but extreme laziness to stimulate their desire to win. Praise and encouragement should be used for younger school children whose psychological endurance is weaker and ability is lower.

Praise can be used in many ways in the classroom to reinforce appropriate behaviors. Generally speaking, praise should be used frequently, especially for lower-grade students and classes with more struggling students. However, excessive or inappropriate rewards can also have a negative effect. So more attention should be paid to the guidelines and principles of effective praise and criticism (Refer to Table 5-1 and Table 5-2).

**9. Conduct competitive education and appropriately develop learning competition**

Competition is an important means of stimulating learning motivation. Competition can greatly stimulate students' competitiveness and needs for success, enhancing their interest in learning and perseverance to overcome difficulties. Most people will significantly improve their learning and work efficiency in competitive situations. Through competition, school children can also obtain a more practical estimate of their own abilities, better discover their shortcomings and untapped potential, which can also stimulate motivation and improve grades.

Poorly organized competitions can also have negative effects. ① Frequent use of competitions can increase students' psychological tension and learning burden. ② Competition can cause students who have no hope of success to lose confidence; it not only fails to stimulate learning motivation for students who can win without effort but may also make them proud instead. ③ Individual competitions may cause students to develop a selfish mentality, encourage non-cooperative behavior, and weaken collective values. ④ Competition may cause students' motivation levels to be too high, which can interfere with the learning of complex courses.

When using competition, teachers need to pay attention to the following points. ① Teachers should educate students about the advantages and disadvantages of competition and teach them the means of fair competition. ② The competition should be based on the students' ability levels. ③ Multi-indicator competition should be conducted so that everyone has a sense of achievement. ④ Team competitions should be promoted. ⑤ Personal self-competition should be encouraged.

### 5.6.2 Cultivation of learning motivation

**1. Understand and meet school children's needs and promote the generation of learning motivation.**

Students' learning motivation arises from needs, which are the source of their learning enthusiasm. Teachers should understand students' learning needs through various methods and internalize learning requirements into students' own learning needs by adopting reinforcing and training methods. Research in educational psychology shows that new learning needs can be formed through two pathways. First, the pathway of direct generation. The original learning needs are constantly met, resulting in new, more stable, and more differentiated learning needs. Second, the pathway of indirect transformation. The new learning needs are transformed from the means and tools that previously met a certain need.

**2. Attach importance to the education of ambition and provide students with achievement motivation training.**

Through ambition education, students can enhance their sense of responsibility and mission, and they can be enlightened to consciously and diligently study. Research has shown that achievement motivation training has a great promoting effect on students' learning motivation.

**3. Help students establish a correct self-concept and gain a sense of self-efficacy.**

Self-efficacy is a subjective judgment that is closely related to the individual's self-concept. Cultivating students' self-efficacy should start with cultivating a correct self-concept.

1) Create conditions for students to experience success by selecting appropriate tasks for them and allowing them to continuously experience success.

2) Set a successful example for students. Let school children watch and imagine the successful operations of students who are similar to themselves, improve their self-efficacy by obtaining vicarious experiences and vicarious reinforcement, and make them believe that they are also capable of completing the corresponding learning behavior, thus promoting the progress of learning.

3) Change students' wrong judgment of their learning ability through attribution training and form a correct judgment of self-efficacy.

**4. Cultivate the view of attribution that effort leads to success.**

Believing in the inevitable connection between success and effort makes it less likely for people to show negative behavior and develop a sense of powerlessness, which helps cultivate students' learning motivation. The specific steps to cultivate the attribution of the inevitable connection between success and effort are as follows.

1) Understand students' attribution tendencies.

2) Encourage students to engage in certain activities and achieve successful experiences.

3) Ask students to attribute their success or failure.

4) Guide students to actively attribute.

**5. Cultivate school children's interest in learning.**

The most lasting motivation in learning activities comes from students' thirst for knowledge. When the thirst for knowledge becomes school children's personality characteristic, they can learn spontaneously and consciously and get pleasure and satisfaction from learning, with little or no need for external rewards, and they can still persist in learning after leaving school. The interest in learning is one of the most important components of learning motivation, and it is an internal motivation that points to the learning activity itself. Therefore, attention should be paid to cultivating students' broad cognitive interests in learning activities. In the development of students' interest in learning, the following ways can be adopted:

1) Make students understand the significance of the knowledge of every subject in real life in a lively way to evoke their cognitive need for further exploration. For example, discussing the wonderful uses of computers in modern life makes students eager to master the relevant skills.

2) Guide students to experience the sense of achievement and satisfaction brought by the process of knowledge acquisition, and encourage students to engage in self-reinforcement and self-reward.

3) Organize various extracurricular activity groups and interest groups to cultivate learning interest and enhance learning motivation.

**6. Utilize the transfer of original motivation to create learning needs.**

Some school children are indifferent to the study of cultural courses and even weary of studying. However, many of them have high enthusiasm and strong interest in sports, extracurricular interest groups, artistic performances, and other activities. An effective means to cultivate learning motivation is to guide school children to connect these positive factors with learning and transform them into learning needs and learning interests.

**7. Train the correct ability of attribution.**

The underlying assumption of attribution training is that students will continue to work hard as long as they believe that effort will lead to success. Therefore, the key to attribution training is to make students repeatedly experience the success or failure of learning, while also guiding them to learn and develop the attributional tendency to attribute success or failure to effort. People often attribute success to one of four factors: ability, effort, task difficulty, and luck. Each school child has their own unique attributional style when facing success or failure in learning. If they tend to attribute their success to their own abilities and their failure to difficult tasks and bad luck, they will develop a sense of pride and value in their success, and they will not doubt their own abilities and value when they fail in exams. If they tend to attribute success to task difficulty and luck, and failure to ability, then they will think they lack the ability to avoid failure, and a sense of learned helplessness will gradually develop during the learning process.

When school children first encounter setbacks in primary school, they tend to attribute failures to bad luck or difficult tasks. However, if they fail repeatedly, they will attribute failures to their own incompetence, and they will develop a sense of learned helplessness, which makes them unwilling to learn. Since the attributional style can be acquired, it can also be changed through certain training. After school children complete a learning task, teachers should guide them to make attributions of success or failure. On the one hand, school children should be guided to find out the real reasons for success or failure. On the other hand, more importantly, teachers should also make positive attributions in favor of future learning, even if the attributions are not true. For example, for those school children with poor academic performance, teachers can guide them to attribute their failure to insufficient effort. As long as they believe that effort can be controlled and will bring success, they will make unremitting efforts in the learning process and achieve ultimate success.

Changing students' incorrect attribution and improving learning motivation can be achieved from the following three aspects:

1) Effort attribution. Effort attribution means that whether school children have achieved academic success or failure should be attributed to whether they made efforts. When students attribute their success or failure to effort, it will improve their learning enthusiasm. When they meet learning difficulties or achieve poor grades in the future, they generally do not lower their expectations of future success due to temporary failures.

2) Reality attribution. Reality attribution means that teachers guide school children to make reality attributions based on specific issues in order to help them analyze what other factors affect academic performance besides effort, such as intelligence, learning methods, family environment, teachers, and so on, and to what extent these factors affect their academic performance. Teachers should also try

to point out ways to solve these problems to enhance students' courage to overcome difficulties and boost their confidence. The advantage of effort attribution training and reality attribution is that school children will connect their success or failure with reality when making "effort attribution", and they will emphasize effort when making "reality attribution".

3) Ability attribution. Psychologists believe that the optimal form of attribution is to attribute success to ability and failure to effort. When we attribute our success to our ability, the internal and stable attribution makes us feel capable and valuable, and we expect that we will succeed in the future. When we attribute failure to insufficient effort (internal and unstable attributions), we feel that if we work harder, we will do better in the future.

In conclusion, fostering learning motivation is essential for academic success and personal development. By creating supportive environments and encouraging self-directed exploration, educators and parents can inspire a genuine love for learning. Emphasizing intrinsic motivation and a growth mindset helps learners embrace challenges and view setbacks as opportunities. Ultimately, cultivating motivation not only enhances performance but also instills a lifelong passion for knowledge, empowering individuals to thrive in their educational journeys and beyond.

# I. Review and reflection

learning motivation
need for learning
learning drive
expectancy of learning
incentives
intrinsic learning motivation
extrinsic learning motivation
long-range indirect learning motivation
close-range direct motivation
cognitive drive
ego-enhancement drive
affiliated drive
interpersonal motivation
prestige motivation

function of learning motivation
function of reinforcement
relationship between learning motivation and learning effect
Yerkes-Donson Law
reinforcement theory
external reinforcement
internal reinforcement
guidelines for effective praise
principles of praise and criticism
Maslow's need hierarchy theory
physiological need
safety need
belongingness and love need
esteem need

need to know and understand
aesthetic need
self-actualization need
attribution theory of success or failure
low-strive and low-avoidance failure-acceptors
relationship-behavior theory
mesosystem
exosystem
macrosystem
chronosystem
Vygotsky's sociocultural theory
attribution
six factors and three dimensions of Weiner's
attribution of success or failure
learned helplessness
helping students overcome learned helplessness
self-efficacy theory
achievement motivation theory
high-strive and low-avoidance success-orienteers
low-strive and high-avoidance failure-avoiders
high-strive and high-avoidance over-strivers
Urie Bronfenbrenner's bioecological theory
microsystem
Confucius' five cardinal relationships
stimulation of learning motivation
cultivation of learning motivation

## II. Material analysis

1. Please make a brief explanation of "Learning is endless" using Maslow's hierarchy of needs theory. (Refer to Appendix I)

2. Please briefly discuss "There are a thousand Hamlets in a thousand readers' eyes" according to knowledge view and student view of constructivism. (Refer to Appendix I)

# Chapter 6  Learning Transfer and Cultivation

*One day in 2500 BC, Confucius asked Zigong, "Who do you think is better, you or Yan Hui?" Zigong replied, "How dare I compare with Yan Hui? Yan Hui infers ten from one, while I only infer two from one."* (Confucius et al., 2014) Here, "Yan Hui infers ten from one, while I only infer two from one" is considered a transfer, which is only one of the complex and diverse transfer phenomena. From a psychological point of view, learning transfer is widespread and has many types.

## 6.1  Concept of learning transfer

**Learning transfer**, also known as training transfer, refers to the influence of one type of learning on another or the impact of acquired experience on performing other activities. The meaning of "transfer" here is not "migration" or "movement" but rather "influence". Transfer is a common phenomenon in learning, widely present in the learning of knowledge, skills, behavioral norms, and attitudes. "Drawing inferences from one instance" and "thinking by analogy" are typical forms of transfer. With transfer, various experiences can be communicated, and the structure of knowledge can be integrated. *For example, people who can ride a bicycle can learn to drive a motorcycle more easily than people who cannot. At the same time, we can also see the opposite phenomenon. Learning Chinese Pinyin can interfere with the learning of some English letter sounds, which is also a type of learning transfer.*

## 6.2  Classification of learning transfer

The phenomenon of learning transfer is diverse, and different researchers have classified transfer from different perspectives, emphasizing different aspects of transfer.

### 6.2.1  Positive transfer, negative transfer, and zero transfer

According to the nature and results of transfer, it can be divided into positive transfer, negative transfer, and zero transfer. **Positive transfer**, also called "facilitative transfer", refers to the promotion of one kind of learning to another. For *example, learning mathematics is good for learning physics; learning abacus is beneficial for learning mental arithmetic; people who know English can easily master French, and so on.* **Negative transfer,** also known as "inhibitory transfer", means that one type of learning impedes another. *For example, with the mastery of Chinese grammar, we often cannot help using Chinese grammar to analyze English grammar when we learn English grammar, which affects the learning of English grammar.* The two kinds of learning that may not have any influence on each other are called zero transfer, which is a special form of transfer. *For example, learning to play badminton and learning programming; learning carving art and learning to drive a car.*

### 6.2.2 Forward transfer and backward transfer

According to the direction of transfer, it can be divided into forward transfer and backward transfer.

**Forward transfer** refers to the influence of previous learning on subsequent learning. *Learning the concept of "balance" in physics will have an impact on learning chemical balance, ecological balance, and economic balance in the future. "Drawing inferences from one example" and "reviewing what has been learned enables one to gain new understanding" belong to forward transfer.*

**Backward transfer** means that the later learning affects the experience structure formed by the previous learning so that the original experience structure is changed, enriched, corrected, reorganized, or reconstructed. The continuous improvement of one's knowledge structure also benefits from various levels of transfer. *For example, learning about microorganisms can affect the understanding of previously learned concepts of animals and plants.*

### 6.2.3 Horizontal transfer and vertical transfer

According to the level of abstraction and generalization of the content of transfer, it can be divided into horizontal transfer and vertical transfer.

**Horizontal transfer,** also known as lateral transfer, refers to the mutual influence between antecedent learning contents and subsequent learning contents that are both at the same level of difficulty, complexity, and generalization. The logical relationship between the learning contents is parallel. *After a baby learns to call a male neighbor "uncle", he may call any unfamiliar male he encounters "uncle". While reading newspapers, you can understand the new vocabulary learned in class. After you have learned the commutative law of multiplication, namely $A \times B = B$*

$\times A$, you can apply it to $3\times 5=5\times 3$.

**Vertical transfer**, also known as longitudinal transfer, refers to the mutual influence of experiences at different levels of difficulty, complexity, and generalization. Vertical transfer includes bottom-up transfer and top-down transfer. Bottom-up transfer means that the lower level of experience affects the upper level of experience learning. *For example, once you have learned number arithmetic, it is easy to learn letter arithmetic.* Top-down transfer means that the higher level of experience affects the lower level of experience learning. *For example, after mastering theorems and formulas, it is helpful to learn various examples.*

### 6.2.4 General transfer and specific transfer

According to the different contents of transfer, it can be divided into general transfer and specific transfer.

**General transfer**, also known as nonspecific transfer and universal transfer, refers to the influence of general principles, rules, and attitudes learned in one kind of learning on another kind of specific content learning, that is, the specific application of principles, rules, and attitudes. *For example, basic arithmetic skills and reading skills are acquired and then applied to the study of various specific subjects.*

**Specific transfer**, also known as special transfer, means that when learning transfer occurs, the original elements of the learner's experience and their structure do not change, but the experience elements acquired in one kind of learning are recombined, transferred, and used in another kind of learning. *For example, the influence of the learning of "日" and "月" on the learning of "明"; the influence of mastering addition and subtraction on doing mixed operations of addition and subtraction. For another example, mastering "mouth" may facilitate the learning of the new word "golden-mouthed."*

### 6.2.5 Self transfer, near transfer and far transfer

According to the degree of transfer, it can be divided into self transfer, near transfer, and far transfer.

That an individual's learned experience affects the operation of a task in the same situation belongs to **self transfer**. *For example, after you have learned to drive, you drive home.*

**Near transfer** refers to the application of acquired knowledge or skills in a situation similar to the original learning situation. *For example, when students solve a question in the exam, because they have previously conducted training on relevant* *types of questions, even if the question has changed in number and structure, they can still solve it quite smoothly. If you have learned to write the composition "My Mother", you can then write another, "My Father".*

**Far transfer** refers to the application of acquired knowledge or skills in new situations dissimilar to the original learning situations. *For example, the rules of logical reasoning that students have learned in mathematics are applied in physics or chemistry to solve problems. For another example, school children combine theory with practice, transferring the knowledge learned in school to actual life and production labor.* Far transfer is much more complex than near transfer in terms of its formation process and psychological mechanism.

### 6.2.6 Assimilative transfer, accommodative transfer and reorganized transfer

According to the different internal psychological mechanisms required in the process of transfer, it can be divided into assimilative transfer, accommodative transfer, and reorganized transfer.

**Assimilative transfer** refers to the direct application of the original cognitive experience to a class of things with the same essential characteristics without changing the original cognitive structure. The original cognitive structure does not change substantively in the process of transfer, but only gets some kind of enrichment. *For example, the concept of "fish" in the original cognitive structure is composed of such concepts as hairtail, grass carp, yellow croaker, etc. Currently, we need to learn about eel and incorporate it into the original structure of "fish", which not only expands the concept of fish but also gains the meaning of the new concept of eel. For another example, if you learn the formula for the area of a triangle through an example problem, then use this formula to solve the areas of other triangles.*

**Accommodative transfer** means that when the original cognitive experience is applied to a new situation, but the original experience structure cannot incorporate new things into it, it is necessary to adjust the original experience or summarize the old and new experiences to form a higher-level cognitive structure that can accommodate both the new and old experiences to adapt to external changes. *For example, after learning addition, we use addition to solve the problem of serial addition. When we encounter a situation where ten thousand 2s are added, we cannot solve this problem using addition. Therefore, we develop the concept of learning multiplication, use multiplication to solve this problem, and change the cognitive* *structure in our minds.*

**Reorganized transfer** refers to the reorganization of some constituent elements or components of the original cognitive system, that is, the adjustment of the relationship between the components or the establishment of new connections so as to apply to new situations. In the process of reorganization, the basic empirical components remain unchanged, but the combination relationship between the components is altered, meaning that the original components are adjusted or reorganized. *For example, adjusting or recombining some original dance and gymnastics movements to arrange new dance or gymnastics movements. For another example, after learning "tea" and then learning "eat", the constituent elements remain unchanged, but the order changes.*

### 6.2.7 Low-road transfer and high-road transfer

According to the different situations in which transfer occurs, learning transfer can be divided into low-road transfer and high-road transfer.

**Low-road transfer** is the automatic transfer of repeatedly practiced skills from one situation to another. "Rote problem-solving" is a type of low-road transfer, which allows students to recall the problems that they have done before when solving new problems, find similar problem-solving approaches, and thus successfully answer the questions. Memorizing essay templates also belongs to low-road transfer. *For example, plagiarism belongs to low-road transfer. For another example, if a person learns to type blindly on a computer keyboard, when they use a keyboard with a similar layout, they can easily transfer their typing skills and quickly type without much thought.*

**High-road transfer** is the conscious application of abstract knowledge acquired in a certain situation to a new situation. The key to high-road transfer is the conscious abstraction of rules, core concepts, or programs from the learning situation and the application of these to the new situation. *When you engage in high-road transfer while preparing to write a paper, you will first read the same type of articles included in the platform where you are planning to publish, extract a framework model of the journal's willingness to publish articles, and then select a topic to compose according to the framework model.*

## 6.3 Theory of learning transfer

Since the emergence of learning activities, learning transfer and learning have been closely related, and research on learning transfer, along with the emergence of learning activities, has always attracted people's attention. It was only in the middle of the 18th century that learning transfer was systematically explained and studied in theory. Psychologists have developed various theories based on their own experiments and research. Transfer theories mainly include early transfer theories and modern transfer theories. The early transfer theories include formal discipline theory, theory of identical elements, generalization theory, relationship transformation theory, learning set theory, and so on. The modern theories include situational theory, cognitive structure transfer theory, symbolic schema theory, and so on.

## 6.3.1 Formal discipline theory

Formal discipline theory is the earliest theory of learning transfer, and its psychological foundation is faculty psychology proposed by German psychologist Wolff. Faculty psychology believes that the human mind is made up of many different faculties, including attention, will, memory, perception, imagination, reasoning, and judgment. The different faculties are all entities, and they cooperate with each other to form a variety of psychological activities. Formal discipline theory holds that psychological faculties can be developed only through training; transfer is the result of mental faculties being trained and developed, and transfer is unconditional and spontaneous. Formal discipline theory also holds that training and improving psychological faculties is an important teaching goal, and the task of education is to enhance students' various faculties. The improved faculties can be automatically transferred to other learning, and the improvement of one kind of faculty can also enhance other faculties. Formal discipline theory emphasizes the cultivation of ability and the transfer of learning, and stresses the special training of effective memory methods, work and learning habits, and general effective work techniques.

This theory suggests that mathematics is beneficial for training reasoning ability, geometry is good for training logical thinking, and Latin and Greek are greatly beneficial for training memory. Knowledge is too vast to be imparted to students entirely, so the teaching of knowledge in school education is far less important than the training of faculties. If a student's faculties are developed through training, they can absorb knowledge at any time. Therefore, the mastery of knowledge is secondary, and the development of faculties is the most important. The value of knowledge lies in the material for the training of faculties.

However, formal discipline theory lacks a scientific basis, so it has aroused skepticism and opposition from some researchers.

## 6.3.2 Theory of identical elements

The theory of identical elements was proposed by Thorndike in the early 20th century. He argued that transfer is very specific and conditional, and that transfer requires identical elements. Only when there are identical elements between the original learning context and the new learning context can the original learning be transferred to the new learning. The amount of transfer depends on the number of identical elements in these two situations. In both situations, the more identical elements there are, the greater the amount of transfer; the fewer identical elements, the smaller the amount of transfer. For example, if you have learned how to ride a bicycle, then when you learn to ride a motorcycle, you can relatively easily transfer the experience of riding a bicycle to riding a motorcycle because there are some identical elements between the two, such as balance, control of direction, and so on.

Thorndike (1901) trained college students in an experiment to judge the area of paper of different sizes and shapes. First, subjects were asked to estimate the areas of 127 rectangles, triangles, circles, and irregular shapes. Each subject was then trained to estimate the area of 90 parallelograms with areas ranging from 10 to 100 square centimeters. The subjects were then divided into two groups. Group 1 needed to judge the areas of 13 rectangles similar to the previously trained parallelograms. Group 2 needed to judge the areas of 27 triangles, circles, and irregular shapes. The results showed that the training in estimating the area of parallelograms helped students to judge the area of rectangles better, but did not help them judge the area of triangles, circles, and irregular shapes (Thorndike & Woodworth, 1901).

Thorndike concluded that if there is any positive transfer between two learning situations, then the two situations must be very similar. Woodworth later changed the term "identical elements theory" to "common elements theory". According to the identical elements theory, if two kinds of learning activities contain common elements, there will be a transfer phenomenon whether learners are aware of the commonality of such elements or not. These theories have a positive impact on the research and practical teaching of learning transfer. However, these theories only see the function of learning situations but completely ignore the influence of subject factors on learning transfer.

## 6.3.3 Generalization theory

Generalization theory, also known as the theory of experience generalization, was proposed by the American psychologist Judd. Its main idea is that a person can complete the transfer from one situation to another as long as they have summarized their own experience. He believed that the transfer of previous learning to subsequent learning occurs when the general principles acquired in previous learning can be partially or completely applied to subsequent learning. The better the understanding and generalization of the principle, the better the transfer effect. Generally speaking, we can generalize specific methods and skills into more general principles and thinking modes, and then use these principles and modes to solve other similar problems.

Judd (1908) conducted a classic experiment called "underwater target shooting" with fifth- and sixth-graders as subjects. The students were divided into two groups to practice shooting targets that were in water. Group A was first taught the principle of light refraction in water and then practiced shooting. Group B only tried and practiced but was not taught the principle of light refraction. When they reached the same training results, the depth of the targets in water was changed, and they continued shooting. The practice performance of the group that had learned the principle was significantly better than that of the group that had not learned the principle. Judd believed that this was because the group who had studied the principle of light refraction generalized the principle, quickly adjusted, and adapted to targets at different depths in water, applying the generalized principle to special situations at varying depths. Generalization theory emphasizes the generalization of principles and experience. The generalization theory advocates that teaching should not just lie in explaining general and theoretical knowledge, but also in explaining principles in combination with practice. If attention is paid to how to generalize and how to think in teaching methods, the possibility of positive transfer will be increased.

### 6.3.4 Theory of relationship transformation

Gestalt psychologist Köhler (1938) put forward the theory of relationship transformation. He emphasized that insight—a sudden realization or understanding of something often after a period of confusion or struggle—is a decisive factor in learning transfer. He believed that transfer is the result of learners' sudden discovery of the relationship between two kinds of learning experiences, and it is the understanding and insight of various relationships in the situation, rather than the automatic generation due to common components or principles. The key point of learning transfer is not to master principles, but to be aware of the relationship between means and aims. He believed that students' insight into the relationship between principles and rules, especially the relationship between means and aims, is the fundamental condition for implementing transfer. Köhler's "chicken foraging" experiment is a classic experiment that supports the relationship transformation theory(Figure 6-1).

Köhler let chicks search for food under light gray paper and dark gray paper. Through conditioned reflex learning, the chicks learned that the food rewards could only be obtained under the dark gray paper. Then, the experimental situation was changed, keeping the original dark gray paper and replacing the light gray paper with black paper.

If the chicks still look for food under the dark gray paper, it proves that the transfer is due to the same elements; if the chicks look for food under the darker of the two sheets of paper (the black paper), it suggests that the transfer is a response to relationships.

The experiment showed that the chicks' response to the new stimulus (black paper) reached 70%, while the response to the original stimulus (dark gray paper) was 30%. In the same experiment, the infants consistently responded to the stimulus of black paper.

The experimental results prove that the relationship in the situation plays a role in transfer rather than the same elements. The subjects do not choose the absolute nature of the stimulus but compare the relative relationship. The subjects transfer the relationship learned in the previous situation—food is always under darker color paper—to the following situation and make the correct response.

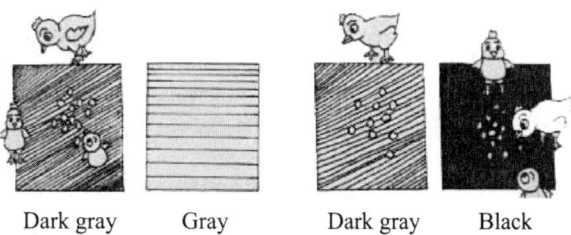

Dark gray    Gray    Dark gray    Black

**Figure 6-1　Experiment of chicken foraging**

## 6.3.5　Theory of learning set

The set is a state of mental readiness formed by an individual's previous activities. A student's learning transfer is often affected by their learning intention or learning set, which is the role of the learning set. Previous learning prepares the conditions for transfer in subsequent learning or puts subsequent learning in a state of readiness, which is conducive to transfer. The learning set theory is about the transfer of learning methods, and the formation or improvement of learning methods in antecedent learning, learning "how to learn", is conducive to learning transfer. *For example, if students are accustomed to a specific learning method, they may tend to use the same method when faced with new learning tasks and ignore other possibly more effective strategies.*

In 1949, American psychologist H. F. Harlow's famous "experiment of monkey discrimination learning" was a classic experiment of learning set theory. In this experiment, he presented the monkeys with two objects, such as a cube and a cone. The monkeys quickly "learned" that food was hidden under the cube, not under the cone. After they solved this problem, they were immediately presented with another similar problem, such as two different colored cubes: one was white, and the other was black. The monkeys had to undergo new learning to solve this new discrimination problem. After they had solved this problem, a new discrimination problem was presented for the third time. The monkeys continued the discrimination learning many times. After the monkeys solved many of these discrimination tasks, they solved new problems faster and faster, with fewer and fewer attempts. This phenomenon has been interpreted as the monkeys developing a "learning set" or learning how to learn. The monkeys learned the method of discrimination in the first several discrimination tasks or formed the discrimination learning set, and applied the acquired method or formed learning set to the subsequent learning, thereby improving the learning effect. Harlow also repeated the experiment on children and obtained the same results.

### 6.3.6 Theory of situational transfer

Greeno et al. put forward the theory of situational transfer. They argued that the transfer problem mainly illustrates how learning to engage in one activity in one situation will affect the ability to engage in another activity in a different situation. Learning is the interaction between the individual and the events in the environment, and it is an adaptation to the characteristics of a situation. What is formed through interaction is the motor schema, which is the organizational principle of the activity rather than a symbolic cognitive representation. Transfer lies in how to adapt the unchanged activity structure or motor schema to different situations (Greeno J. G., Collins A. M., & Resnick L. R., 1996). The establishment of these activity structures depends on both the initial learning situation and the subsequent transfer situation. *For instance, a child learns how to get along with family members at home. Then he transfers this way of getting along with family members learned in the family situation to getting along with classmates in the school situation. For another example, an employee has learned teamwork and communication skills in a specific project team of a company. When he is transferred to another project team and the working atmosphere, team member composition, and task nature of the new team are somewhat similar to those of the original team, he can transfer the teamwork and communication abilities he learned before and better adapt to the work of the new team. This is also an embodiment of the theory of situational transfer.*

### 6.3.7 Theory of cognitive structure transfer

On the basis of the theory of meaningful reception learning, Ausubel put forward the theory of cognitive structure transfer, which holds that all meaningful learning is produced on the basis of the original learning, and there is no meaningful learning without the influence of the original cognitive structure. In meaningful learning, the characteristics of students' original cognitive structure are always the key factors influencing new learning and retention. All meaningful learning necessarily includes transfer, and the transfer is mediated by cognitive structure. For instance, when we learn multiplication in mathematics, if we have already mastered the cognitive structure of addition, we can apply the operation method of addition to multiplication, thereby more easily understanding and mastering the operation method of multiplication.

Ausubel thought it is not only the similarity between the two kinds of new and old learning, but also the variables of cognitive structure stored in long-term memory that affect new learning. The cognitive structure is the learner's knowledge structure in the brain, that is, all the content and organization of the learner's thought. Each person's cognitive structure has its own characteristics. The characteristics of content and organization of an individual's cognitive structure are called cognitive structure variables. Ausubel believed that the main cognitive variables affecting individual transfer include availability, discriminability, and stability. Availability refers to whether there are concepts in an individual's cognitive structure that can be utilized as the fixed function. Discriminability refers to the degree of differentiation between the new learning content and the original knowledge that assimilates it. Stability refers to the degree of stability and clarity of the original thought with the fixed function.

The theory of cognitive structure transfer points out that a cognitive structure that possesses high availability, high discriminability, and strong stability can promote the transfer of new knowledge learning when students learn new knowledge. "Teaching for transfer" is actually about shaping students' good cognitive structure. In the teaching process, the goal of transfer can be achieved by reforming the content and presentation of textbooks and improving students' original cognitive structure variables.

### 6.3.8  Theory of symbolic schema

K. J. Holyoak, M. Bassok, and M. L. Gick put forward the theory of symbolic schema. The theory of symbolic schema believes that initial learning involves a process of forming abstract symbol schemas, namely abstract structural characteristics. The schema is a data structure that can be activated. When the new situational features match the symbols in the schema, the representation can be activated, extracted, and applied. In short, when the original representation (Representation 1) is the same as or similar to the new representation (Representation 2), transfer occurs, and schema matching or representational similarity is the determinant of transfer. In this view, learners need to acquire sufficient general symbolic schemas (abstract structural characteristics) in order to generate transfer and interpret schemas as the representation of the transfer situation. *For example, when students are learning mathematics, they form a symbolic schema about that type of problem by repeatedly practicing to solve the same type of problem. When they encounter a new problem, if the new problem is similar to their existing symbolic schema, they can use the previously learned methods to solve it. For another example, when learning to drive, one forms a symbolic schema about driving operations through learning and practicing. When driving on different roads and under various traffic conditions, one can make corresponding decisions and operations based on the existing symbolic schema.* The failure to transfer is due to a lack of enough experience in the learning activities and the failure to match the characteristics of different events to the symbolic schema. Symbolic schema theory has many applications in the field of artificial intelligence, such as machine translation, text generation, expert systems, intelligent robots, etc.

## 6.4  Factors (Conditions) affecting learning transfer

Transfer is not spontaneous and is subject to various conditions. Transfer is collectively affected by learners' personal characteristics, their initial learning level, the characteristics of learning materials, and the complex interactions among these factors.

1. Characteristics of learning materials

Learning materials, as the objects of students' learning and the main sources of knowledge, have a significant impact on learning transfer. According to Thorndike, identical elements are conducive to learning transfer. For example, English and French are the same or similar in font, pronunciation, and grammatical structure, and learning the two foreign languages has common requirements in terms of listening, speaking, reading, and writing, as well as mental processes such as thinking, so it is easy to produce positive transfer when learning. For another example, there are many common factors between plane geometry and solid geometry, so positive transfer will occur during learning. On the contrary, when learning objects that have no or lack common factors, negative transfer may occur. Although objects may have some common factors, if learners are required to make different responses, negative transfer may still occur. Common factors are objective and necessary conditions for the generation of learning transfer, but not the only condition.

### 2. Original cognitive structure

Ausubel's cognitive structure transfer theory suggests that the characteristics of the original cognitive structure directly determine the possibility and degree of transfer. The influence of the original cognitive structure on transfer is manifested in the following three aspects:

1) Whether the learner has the corresponding background knowledge is the basic prerequisite for the generation of transfer.

2) The level of generalization of the original cognitive structure plays a crucial role in transfer. Generally speaking, the higher the level of generalization of experience, the greater the possibility of transfer and the better the effect of transfer. The lower the level of generalization of experience, the smaller the scope of transfer and the worse the effect of transfer.

3) Whether learners have corresponding cognitive skills or strategies and meta-cognitive strategies that regulate and control cognitive activities has an important impact on transfer.

### 3. Understanding of the learning situation

Most psychological theories emphasize that the situation plays an important role in transfer. As for learning transfer, the central issue of the contextualized content of real learning activities in the school environment is to create a learner-centered practice field, in which the problems encountered by students and the practices carried out are consistent with the problems they will encounter outside the school. In addition, the situation of knowledge acquisition and experience is closely related to the situation of knowledge application in many aspects, such as the relationships between elements in the situation, the way problems are presented, and the spatial position, as well as the similarities between the two situations.

### 4. Mental readiness for learning (mental set)

Mental readiness formed in the course of past learning or activities will also impact the transfer of learning and activities. The impact can sometimes be positive and sometimes negative. A learning set is a kind of mental readiness state. The set refers to the often unconscious state of mental readiness formed by previous influences, which will govern school children to treat similar subsequent activities in the same way. The set occurs in successive activities, and the experience of previous activities forms a state of mental readiness for subsequent activities. The set predisposes school children to respond in a particular way in terms of cognition or explicit behavior. The set is actually a tendency to choose the direction of an activity. This tendency is itself a kind of experience of activities. It often provides ideas or clues for analyzing and solving problems, so the set will affect learning transfer. The role of set has two sides: the positive promoting effect and the negative hindering effect. The set can not only become a positive psychological background for positive transfer but also a negative psychological background for negative transfer, or a potential psychological background that hinders the generation of transfer.

### 5. Level of learning strategies

Learning strategies and methods have a wide range of influences on learning transfer, mainly including cognitive strategies and meta-cognitive strategies related to transfer. School children's learning strategies are mainly acquired spontaneously. The learning strategies of school children (preschool children, primary school children, and middle school children) are constantly developing, and the learning strategies of each period have different characteristics. Therefore, the level of learning strategy development in different periods will inevitably affect knowledge learning, problem-solving, and learning transfer. The influence of learning strategies on transfer is mainly reflected in the developmental level, the richness of learning strategies, and the flexible use of learning strategies according to changes in situations.

### 6. Intelligence and ability

The level of individual intelligence has a certain impact on the quality of learning transfer. School children with higher intelligence can easily find the same elements and correlations among learning situations, better summarize the general principles, and better apply the acquired learning strategies and methods to new learning situations.

### 7. Guidance from teachers

Teachers' conscious guidance can enable learners to make positive transfers. Teachers should inspire students to pay attention to the necessary summary of learning materials, directly teach students general principles, and effectively guide students' practice. Rather than giving someone a fish, it is better to teach them how to fish. Teachers should also pay attention to the teaching of learning methods and strategies so that students learn to learn.

## 6.5 Strategies of promoting school children's effective transfer

In daily teaching work, the educator applies effective transfer principles and laws for teaching so that the learner can learn faster and better in a limited time, actively and accurately apply original experience in appropriate situations, and prevent the inertia of original experience. The goal of teaching is to make students accept and master the experience, thereby forming and developing students' abilities and morals. Transfer is an effective way to achieve this goal and is also a reliable indicator to verify whether teaching has achieved the goal.

### 6.5.1 Reform the content of teaching materials and promote transfer

According to the theory of cognitive structure transfer, whether there are proper ideas that play a fixed role in cognitive structure that can be used is an important factor determining new learning and retention. In order to facilitate transfer, teaching materials must contain the basic concepts and principles that possess a higher level of generality and inclusiveness, as well as stronger explanatory effects.

1) Select high-quality teaching materials to improve the level of understanding of concepts and principles. According to the requirements of the law of learning transfer, the scientific achievements with extensive transfer value from various subjects should be taken as the main content of teaching materials. The materials with extensive transfer value include the basic concepts, basic principles, basic laws, basic methods, basic attitudes, and so on.

2) Arrange the teaching content reasonably and highlight the knowledge with organizational characteristics. The content of teaching materials also needs to be structured, integrated, and networked with unity in order to better promote the occurrence of transfer.

### 6.5.2 Arrange the teaching approach rationally to facilitate the transfer

Excellent teaching materials can give full play to their transfer efficiency only through reasonable teaching presentation and transmission; otherwise, the transfer effect is not significant and may even hinder the generation of transfer. When teachers organize teaching, on the one hand, they should grasp the core content of teaching materials, and on the other hand, it is necessary for teachers to arrange the teaching procedure reasonably so that students can thoroughly acquaint themselves with the learning content and improve the effect of transfer.

1) In the teaching process, gradual differentiation should be carried out from the general to the individual and from the whole to the details.

2) Attention should be paid to integrating various contents and promoting horizontal connections of knowledge.

3) According to the characteristics of students' learning, the teaching process should progress from shallow to deep, from easy to difficult, and from known to unknown.

4) In terms of specific operations, knowledge can be divided into several units, and each unit can be divided into several small steps, so that the learning of the latter step is built on the basis of the previous step, and the learning of the former step provides a fixed point for the latter step. When making a teaching plan, teachers must arrange the order of teaching content to optimize the connection of teaching content.

### 6.5.3 Teach learning strategies to improve students' transfer awareness

Learning not only requires students to master specific knowledge and skills in one or several subjects, but also to learn how to learn; that is, to master the knowledge and skills of learning methods. In fact, only when students master good learning methods can they successfully apply the knowledge and skills they have learned to promote wider and more general transfer. That is to say, learning how to learn can achieve the most common transfer.

Teachers should attach importance to guiding students to conduct in-depth analysis, synthesis, comparison, abstraction, and generalization of various problems in teaching, helping students to understand the relationship between problems, find the common characteristics of new and old knowledge or topics, and summarize the general methods of principles, laws, theorems, and knowledge and experience. To develop students' ability to analyze and generalize problems, emphasis must be placed on learning methods to facilitate more effective transfer.

### 6.5.4 Improve the evaluation of students

As a part of teaching activities, evaluation under teaching conditions is also educational. The effective use of evaluation means has a positive effect on the formation of students' positive learning attitudes and learning transfer.

In conclusion, learning transfer is the bridge between acquiring knowledge and applying it effectively in new contexts. By fostering a deep understanding of core concepts and promoting adaptable thinking, educators can enhance students' ability to transfer skills across diverse situations. Encouraging real-world application and reflective practice reinforces this process, ensuring learning remains relevant and impactful.

## Ⅰ. Review and reflection

| | |
|---|---|
| learning transfer | reorganized transfer |
| positive transfer | low-road transfer |
| negative transfer | high-road transfer |
| forward transfer | formal discipline theory |
| backward transfer | theory of identical elements |
| horizontal transfer | generalization theory |
| vertical transfer | theory of relationship transformation |
| general transfer | theory of learning set |
| specific transfer | theory of situational transfer |
| self transfer | theory of cognitive structure transfer |
| near transfer | theory of symbolic schema |
| far transfer | strategies of promoting school |
| assimilative transfer | children's effective transfer |
| accommodative transfer | |

## Ⅱ. Material analysis

*After Xiaoqiang learned Chinese Pinyin in grades one and two of primary school, when he learned the 26 English letters in grade three, he always got confused with Chinese Pinyin.*

According to the learning transfer theory, analyze why Xiaoqiang tends to confuse English alphabet letters with Chinese Pinyin.

(Refer to Appendix I)

# Chapter 7  Learning Strategies and Cultivation

In real life, many students have been unable to get good grades no matter how hard they study, so they think they are stupid and not good at learning. In fact, many students do poorly in school not because of intellectual problems, but because they do not master correct and effective learning strategies. Mastering and optimizing learning strategies is an important sign of "learning to learn" and an important task of school education. In the future, illiteracy will no longer refer to those who cannot read, but to those who have not learned to learn. Research in areas such as learning strategies and metacognition provides us with theoretical and practical guidance for learning to learn.

## 7.1  Concept of learning strategies

Different people have different understandings and definitions of learning strategies in the academic circle from various angles and emphases. To sum up, the definition of learning strategies can be broadly divided into three categories (Chen Qi & Liu Rude, 2007; Mo Lei, 2008; Peng Xiaohu, Wang Guofeng & Zhu Dan, 2013).

Mayer (1987) believed that a learning strategy is any activity used by people to improve learning efficiency in the learning process, including the use of memorization, marking, note-taking, retelling, and other methods. Nisbett and Shucksmith (1986) argued that a learning strategy is a series of processes or steps that can promote the acquisition and storage of knowledge and the utilization of information. According to their theories, a learning strategy is the process of conducting learning activities or steps, which is not merely an event, but an intelligent activity used to encode, analyze, and extract information to enhance learning efficiency, and is a set of operational processes for selecting and integrating the application of learning skills.

Weinstein (1985) believed that a learning strategy is helpful for learning and maintaining information effectively and is necessary for different abilities. According to Hu Binwu (1996), learning strategies refer to the sum of the methods that learners use to regulate the internal modes of the entire learning activity under the influence of metacognition, based on the characteristics of the learning situation, in order to achieve specific learning goals. In their view, learning strategies are the rules, abilities, and skills of learning.

According to Derry (1986), learning strategies are complex plans formulated by learners in order to achieve learning objectives. According to Sternberg (1983), the learning strategy in learning, also known as "intellectual skills", is formed by the integration of executive skills and non-executive skills. In short, learning strategies are learning plans.

Based on the opinions of domestic and foreign scholars, a learning strategy refers to the complex scheme of the learning process that learners purposefully and consciously formulate in order to improve the learning effect and efficiency (Chen Qi and Liu Rude, 2007), which is composed of rules and skills, and any learning has a corresponding plan. The definition clarifies the following four aspects of the characteristics of learning strategies.

## 7.2 Characteristics of learning strategies

### 1. Initiative

Generally, the use of learning strategies by learners is a conscious mental process. When learning, learners should first analyze learning tasks and their own characteristics, and then formulate an appropriate learning plan according to these conditions. For newer learning tasks, learners are always consciously and purposefully thinking about the planning of the learning process. Only when a strategy is used repeatedly can a level of automation be achieved.

### 2. Effectiveness

The so-called strategy is actually relative to effect and efficiency. When a person does something, even if he uses the most primitive method, he may eventually achieve the goal, but the effect will not be good, and the efficiency will not be high. *For example, if a student memorizes a set of words and reads them repeatedly, as long as there is sufficient time, he can eventually remember them, but the retention time is not too long, and the memory is not very firm. However, if he uses the method of spaced review or attempts to recite to memorize this group of words, the effect and efficiency of memorization will be greatly improved.*

### 3. Processuality

Learning strategy is related to the learning process. Processuality highlights that learning is an ongoing, adaptive process rather than a fixed outcome. It emphasizes the importance of flexibility and responsiveness to changing contexts and individual needs. A learning strategy stipulates what to do and what not to do, what to do first and what to do later, how to do it, to what extent, and various aspects of problems.

### 4. Procedurality

Learning strategies are plans developed by learners that consist of rules and skills. Every time a schoolchild learns, he will follow a different plan and use different learning strategies. However, when a schoolchild carries out the same type of learning, he will use basically the same plan, which is a common learning strategy. *For example, the PQ4R reading method* (refer to Table 7-8). Procedurality refers to the structured, systematic characteristic of approaches to acquiring knowledge and skills. It emphasizes the importance of following specific steps or procedures to achieve learning goals.

## 7.3 Classification of learning strategies

Because of the diversity of definitions of learning strategies, opinions on the structure of learning strategies are also different.

### 7.3.1 Dansereau's, Oxford's and Weinstein's classification

The structure of learning strategies has been discussed according to their practical *functions* by Dansereau (1985), Oxford (1990) and Weinstein (1985) (Table 7-1).

Table 7-1　Classification of learning strategies by Dansereau, Oxford and Weinstein

| Representative | Strategies | Concrete strategies and function |
|---|---|---|
| Dansereau (1985) | **Primary strategies** are specific operational information and learning methods. | strategies of understanding and storing information |
| | | strategies of extracting and utilizing information |
| | **Support strategies** are used to help the learner maintain a suitable internal mental orientation to ensure the effective functioning of the primary strategies. | planning and scheduling |
| | | concentration managing (mood setting and mood maintenance) |
| | | monitoring and diagnosing |
| Oxford (1990) | **Direct strategies** refer to the strategies that language learners can directly apply to the language learning. | memory strategy, cognitive strategy and compensation strategy |
| | **Indirect strategies** refer to the management and control of the learner's own learning process. | meta-cognitive strategies, affective strategies and social strategies |
| Weinstein (1985) | cognitive information processing strategies | elaboration strategies |
| | active learning strategies | examination strategies |
| | supportive strategies | strategies for dealing with anxiety |
| | meta-cognitive strategies | monitoring of the obtaining of new information |

## 7.3.2 Nisbett and Shucksmith's classification

Nisbett and Shucksmith (1986) discussed the structure of learning strategies according to the implementation process of learning strategies and believed that learning strategies were mainly composed of six steps (Figure 7-1).

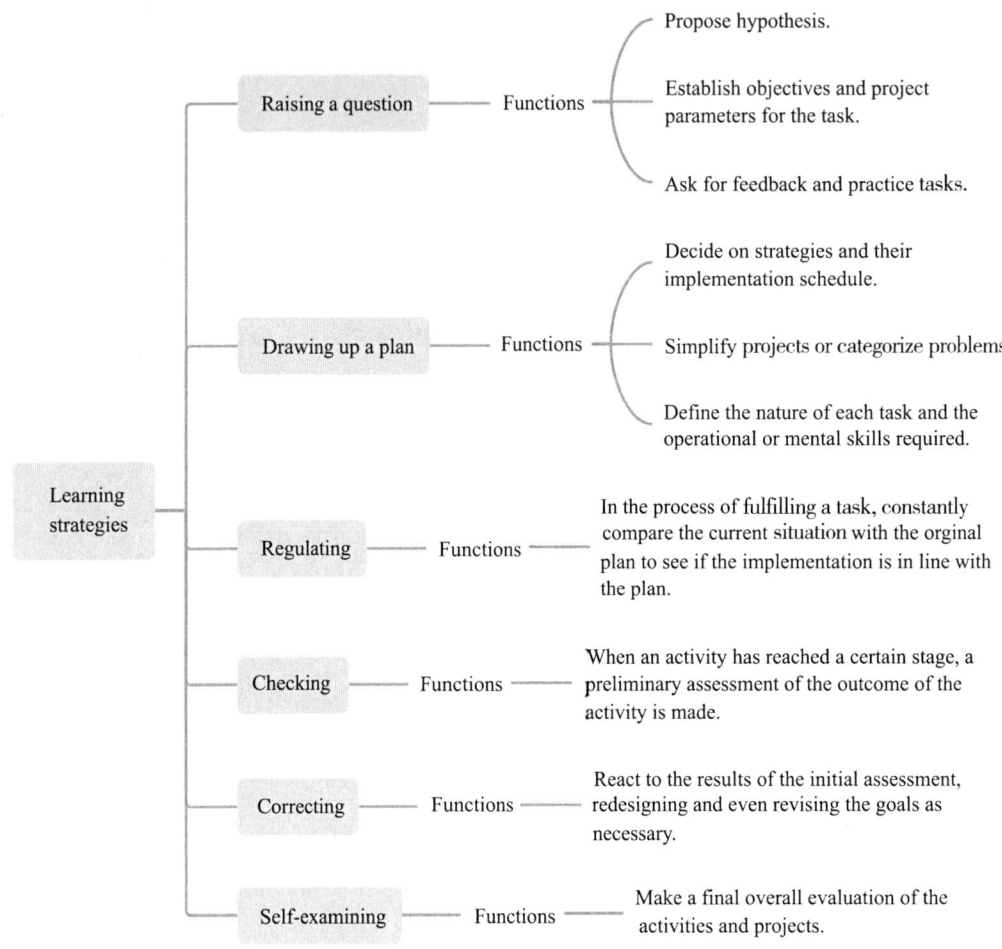

Figure 7-1　Classification of learning strategies by Nisbett and Shucksmith

## 7.3.3 McKeachie et al.'s classification

According to the components contained in learning strategies, McKeachie et al. (1990) divided learning strategies into cognitive strategies, meta-cognitive strategies, and resource management strategies (Figure 7-2). **Cognitive strategies** are the methods and techniques that learners use to process information in the learning process. Cognitive strategies have two basic functions: processing and organizing information effectively, and storing classified information systematically. Meta-

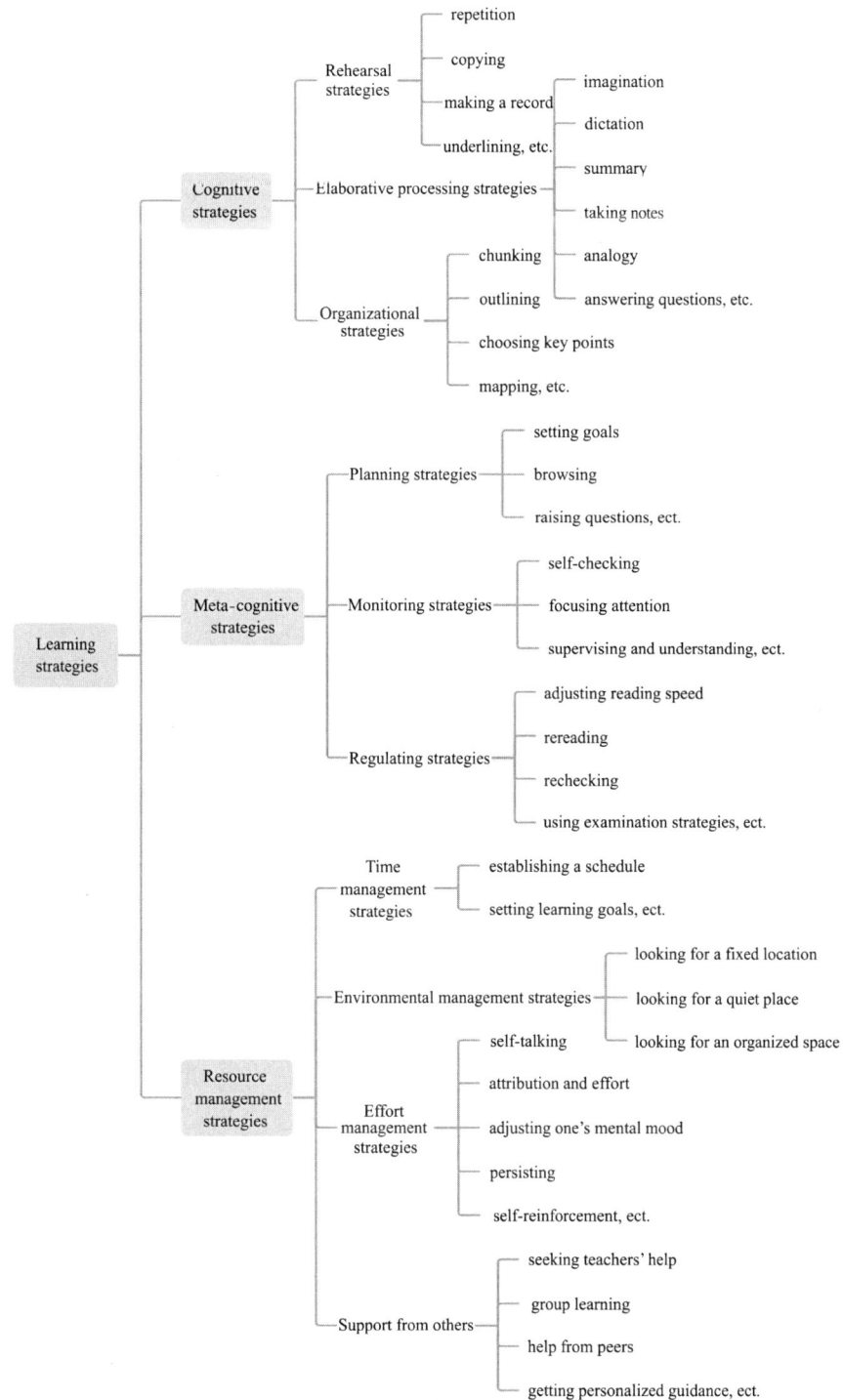

Figure 7-2  Classification of learning strategies by McKeachie et al. (1990)

Source: McKeachie W. H., et al, *Teaching and Learning in College Classroom: A Review of the Research Literature* (2nd ed.), the University of Michigan, 1990, p.160.

**cognitive strategies** refer to strategies that are mainly responsible for monitoring and guiding cognitive activities. **Resource management strategies** are strategies used to assist students in managing the available environment and resources, which play an important role in students' learning motivation. Successful students use these strategies to adapt themselves to the environment and adjust the environment to suit their needs.

## 7.4 Cognitive strategies

Cognitive strategies are of great significance to students' learning. Teachers should master the rules of their formation, develop students' cognitive strategies, and learn to improve the efficiency of students' learning and the quality of classroom teaching by cultivating and training students' cognitive strategies in teaching practice. Cognitive strategies include rehearsal strategies, elaborative processing strategies, and organizational strategies.

### 7.4.1 Rehearsal strategies

**Rehearsal strategies** refer to the methods of using internal language to reproduce learning materials or stimuli in the brain to retain information in working memory and maintain attention on the learning materials. They are key for information to transfer from short-term memory to long-term memory. Much new information, such as names of people, places, things, numbers, and words, can be stored in a short time only after repeated rehearsal. Here are some common rehearsal strategies.

1. Make a scientific review plan

Making a scientific review plan refers to arranging the time, amount, and method of review reasonably and regularly. The comprehensive review, which combines distributed practice with mass practice, is the most effective. The review interval should be dense at first and then sparse, and more at first and then less. The review content should be appropriate and should not be increased blindly. It is important for school children to review frequently and to avoid "one day of exposure brings ten days of cold" or "work in fits and starts". They should focus on distributed practice in daily life, accompanied by mid-term reviews and overall reviews in the later stage. What Confucius said—Is it not a joy to learn and practice what you have studied? —is the best interpretation of review.

2. Review scientifically in time

The Ebbinghaus forgetting curve shows that 66.3% of the content is forgotten after just one day (Figure 1-12), which means that almost two-thirds of the content has been forgotten. The forgetting curve, which follows a pattern of rapid initial forgetting (the quick loss of newly learned information shortly after it has been acquired) followed by a slower decline, necessitates learners to review promptly after learning. Therefore, learners must review newly learned content in a timely manner and make a review at least once a day to slow down the process of forgetting.

### 3. Utilize the cephalocercal echo review

Cephalocercal (from the beginning to the end) echo review refers to the method of placing the most important learning content at the beginning and end of the review period to promote memorization.

Due to the interference of *proactive inhibition* and *retroactive inhibition*, when reviewing and memorizing materials, the memory effect of the middle part is the poorest and the easiest to forget, because the middle part of the material is affected by both proactive and retroactive inhibition. When scheduling for the review, school children should try to prevent the influence of both types of inhibition and should try to stagger learning two kinds of easily confused materials. *For example, when school children learn English and Chinese Pinyin, it is necessary for them to avoid interference between them as much as possible.*

Due to the influence of the *primacy effect* and *recency effect*, when school children finish learning 20 words and take the test immediately, it is found that the words at the beginning and end are generally better remembered than the words in the middle. When arranging their review, it is better for school children to place important material at the beginning and end of the learning period. That is, they should start their review with important new concepts and summarize them at the end.

### 4. Adopt diversifying review forms

Review methods should be selected flexibly according to the nature and quantity of memory materials. Important poems and texts can be reviewed through "recitation". School children can regularly group and recurrently remember and review foreign words and chemical element symbols using the "cyclic memory method". When learning mathematics, physics, and chemistry, school children should adopt the "practice method", "experimental operation method", and "skill training method" to transform knowledge into operational skills to consolidate the learning content. Of course, applying knowledge in practice is the best review of knowledge.

### 5. Use unintentional memorization and intentional memorization

Unintentional memorization is the memory that has no predetermined purpose and requires no volitional effort. It is easier for school children to remember things or persons that are significant to them, closely related to their needs and interests, elicit a strong emotional response, or are vivid and distinct in image. In teaching, to strengthen unintentional memorization, teachers should try to cultivate students' interest in a subject, give great significance to a subject, and make a subject vivid, and so on. Thus, unintentional memorization gradually transforms into intentional memorization. Intentional memorization refers to purposeful and conscious memorization. Most learning content requires school children to remember consciously, mindfully, and repeatedly.

### 6. Mobilize multiple senses

A variety of senses such as eyes, ears, mouth, and hands should be mobilized for memorization simultaneously, which is conducive to enhancing memory. Trechler conducted research on the relationship between human perception and learning memory. The results indicate that our learning occurs 1% through taste, 1.5% through touch, 3.5% through smell, 11% through hearing, and 83% through vision. Moreover, people can generally remember 10% of what they read, 20% of what they hear, 30% of what they see, 50% of what they see and hear, and 70% of what they say during conversations (Chen Qi & Liu Rude, 2007; Personnel Department of the Ministry of Education of the People's Republic of China, et al., 2002). This result shows that the participation of multiple senses can effectively enhance memory.

### 7. Make chunk coding

A chunk is a grouping of information that can be stored in short-term memory (Robert S. Feldman, 2015). A grouping of information is a unit of information within the capacity of short-term memory. The short-term memory capacity is about $7\pm2$ chunks (Miller, 1956). A chunk can be a letter, a number, a word, a phrase, or even a sentence. When presented with unconnected letters, participants are usually able to remember about seven letters. If presented with a "three-letter word", participants can remember about seven words, equivalent to 21 letters (Lin Chongde et al., 2003; Robert S. Feldman, 2015). Thus, the way of chunking mainly depends on people's past knowledge and experience. An example of chunk coding memory is shown in Figure 7-3.

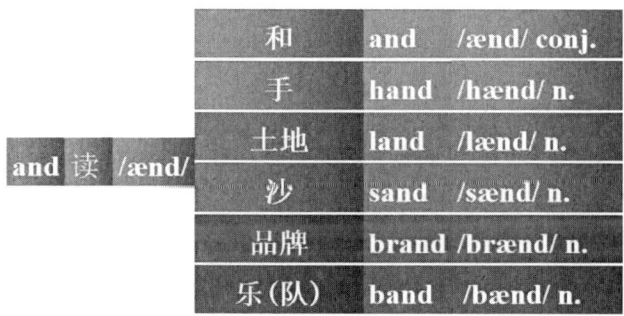

Figure 7-3　Chunk coding memory

Source：何心勇,《英语词经(中级版)》,中国科学文化音像出版社,2024,第3页.

*As for the names of Lu Xun's works, many students often cannot remember them correctly. If they are compiled into easy-to-read and easy-to-remember chunks like the following*:"热风华盖坟而已；三闲二心南北集；花边风月伪自由；两编且介集外集；集外拾遗又补编；译文古籍序跋集", *the names of sixteen essays are processed into six related chunks, and students can easily remember the names of these essays. If chunking the following six words* "and /ænd/ 和, land /lænd/ 土地, sand /sænd/ 沙子, hand /hænd/ 手, brand /brænd/ 品牌, band /bænd/ 乐队" *into seven chunks (Figure 7-4), school children can remember their spelling, pronunciation, and Chinese meanings easily and quickly* (He Xinyong, 2024).

### 8. Combine reading and reciting

The combination of reading and reciting means that the review of the material can be carried out by combining the attempt to recall with the reading process. For meaningless syllables and biographical articles, the optimal ratio between reading time and recall time is 20% for reading and 80% for attempt recall (Gates, quoted from Yi Keli, 2014). For meaningful material, the optimal proportion of time is 20% to 40% for reading and 60% to 80% for attempt recall, and thus the memory effect is the best (Ye Yiqian et al., 1988). *For example, in English teaching, teachers should guide students to attempt to recite in the process of reading and alternate between reading and reciting.*

### 9. Moderate over-learning

Over-learning refers to continuing to learn after learning just enough to recite. The effect of learning is the best when the over-learning reaches 50%, that is, the proficiency of learning reaches 150%. When the proficiency of learning exceeds 150%, the effect does not increase, which is likely to cause boredom and fatigue, becoming ineffective labor. *For example, the writing of Chinese characters and the spelling of English words both require over-learning.*

### 7.4.2 Elaboration strategies

**Elaboration strategies**, a type of deep processing strategy, refer to cognitive strategies that make new information more meaningful and promote the understanding and memory of the new information by forming additional connections between old and new information or establishing artificial connections between information that originally has no internal connection. Elaboration strategies can be divided into two categories: artificial association strategies and generative strategies (Lu Haidong, 2002).

1. **Artificial association strategies**

Artificial association strategies refer to the strategies of using association to give some artificial meaning to meaningless materials in order to promote the maintenance of knowledge. Artificial association strategies mainly include the following strategies:

1) Prosodic syllable method

**Prosodic syllable method** refers to the method of compiling difficult materials into ballads or doggerels that are rhythmic, cadenced, and catchy like poems or songs so as to facilitate memorization (Figure 7-4).

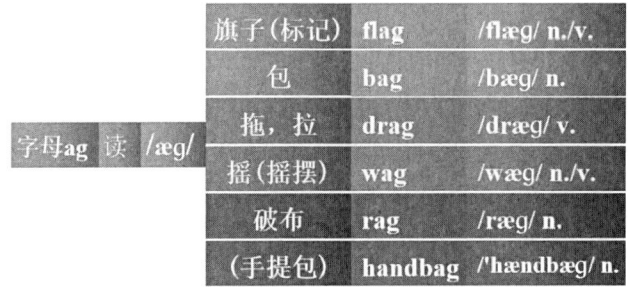

Figure 7-4　Rhythmic chant memory

Source：何心勇,《英语词经(中级版)》,中国科学文化音像出版社,2024,第 2 页.

2) Method of loci

**The method of loci** refers to a technique in which the learner first determines a familiar route in their mind and then identifies specific points along that route. The information to be remembered is connected to these specific points, and when recalling, each piece of information is retrieved from each point along the route. The method of loci also involves fixing the information to be remembered in "the fixed positions of the body". It is particularly useful for memorizing sequential series of items. *For example, you can use the "body fixation method" to remember the following words: tree, baseball, doctor, duck, balloon, witch, water gun, crayon, superman, tricycle. You can connect these ten words to each of the ten parts* *of the body and convert them into images for memory. You can imagine that your hair is a big tree on the top of your head; your eyebrows are shaped like a baseball; something is wrong with your eyes, and you go to see the doctor; you have a duck on your nose; your mouth is blowing a balloon; then your ears grow long, making you look like a witch; you have a water gun around your neck; on your shoulder lie two boxes of crayons; your arms become very sturdy like Superman; and you push the tricycle forward.*

3) Analogy method

**Analogy method** is a method that promotes memory retention by comparing familiar information to new material. In other words, analogy refers to a deduction that is made based on similarity or identity in some properties between two objects. By analogy, school children can create similarities between things that have no obvious connections to enhance understanding and memory. *For example, when teaching the circulatory system in a physiology class, a teacher might use an analogy: "Our circulatory system pumps blood around the body like a pumping system. The blood vessels are like water pipes, and the heart is like a pump."* In this example, the new information about the blood circulatory system is compared to the familiar pumping system, which makes it easier for school children to remember the components and functions of the blood circulatory system.

4) Reduction method

**Reduction method** is a memory method of simplifying each piece of memorizing material into a keyword, and then combining keywords into things that you are familiar with and can remember easily so as to connect the new material and previous experience. The combination of reduction method and prosodic syllable method is often used to achieve better memory results. *For example, first, we can induce Jin Yong's fourteen martial arts novels into fourteen Chinese characters using reduction method*: 飞:《飞狐外传》; 雪:《雪山飞狐》; 连:《连城诀》; 天:《天龙八部》; 射:《射雕英雄传》; 白:《白马啸西风》; 鹿:《鹿鼎记》; 笑:《笑傲江湖》; 书:《书剑恩仇录》; 神:《神雕侠侣》; 侠:《侠客行》; 倚:《倚天屠龙记》; 碧:《碧血剑》; 鸳:《鸳鸯刀》. *Second, we chunk them into the following two rhymed chunks using prosodic syllable method*: "飞雪连天射白鹿,笑书神侠倚碧鸳", *and it's easy to remember the complete works of Jin Yong's martial arts novels. For another example*, "两湖两广两河山, 四江云贵福吉安, 川藏二宁青甘陕, 海疆内蒙北上天, 重庆港澳和台湾", *thus it's easy for school children to remember all the provinces, municipalities and autonomous regions of China.*

5) Homophonic association method

**Homophonic association method** is a memory technique that uses the same or similar pronunciations to transform meaningless material into meaningful material to aid memory. *For example, pregnant* （怀孕的）—扑来个男的；*ambulance*（救护车）—俺不能死；*pest*（害虫）—拍死它；*family*（家庭）—伐木累；*knowledge*（知识）—脑累积. *It's easy for school children to remember* π = 3.14159265358979323846264338327 *like this*：山顶一寺一壶酒（3.14159），尔乐苦煞吾（26535），把酒吃（897），酒杀尔（932），杀不死（384），遛尔遛死（6264），扇扇刮（338），扇尔吃酒（3279）.

6) Semantic association method

**Semantic association method** is a memory technique that associates new materials with existing knowledge in the mind through connections and endows them with more meanings. *For example, the teacher asks students to remember the following words in order: paper basket, mountain, telephone, desk, fire, pigeon, envelope, police, car, an old lady, ditch, hospital, doctor, pen, bubble gum, picture books, newspaper, symbol, peace. A student used semantic association method to remember the words quickly in order like this: A <u>paper basket</u> fell from the <u>mountain</u> and hit the <u>telephone</u> on the <u>desk</u>. The telephone burst into <u>fire</u>. The <u>pigeon</u> took the <u>envelope</u> to the <u>police</u>. The police rushed in a car and crashed <u>an old lady</u> into a <u>ditch</u>. The old lady was soon taken to the <u>hospital</u>. A <u>doctor</u> examined the old lady with an instrument like a <u>pen</u> and then said that the old lady would be well if she went back to eat <u>bubble gum</u> and read <u>picture books</u>. The next day, the news appeared in the <u>newspaper</u>, and the pigeon became a <u>symbol</u> of <u>peace</u>.*

7) Initial acronym method

**Initial acronym method** is a memory technique in which an abbreviation is formed by using the first letter of each English word. *For example, CEO is the acronym for "Chief Executive Officer"; WTO is the acronym for "World Trade Organization"; NBA is the acronym for "National Basketball Association".*

In Chinese, the initial acronym method is a memory technique in which an abbreviation is formed by using the first Chinese character of each word, phrase or sentence. *For example,* "春夏秋冬" *is the acronym for* "春雨惊春清谷天,夏满芒夏暑相连。秋处露秋寒霜降,冬雪雪冬小大寒".

**2. Generative strategies**

Generative strategies are active learning approaches that encourage individuals to create, construct, or generate new knowledge, ideas, or solutions. These strategies facilitate deeper understanding and retention by involving learners in the process of knowledge creation. Some commonly used generative strategies include:

1) Self-questioning method

**Self-questioning method** means that learners ask themselves thought-provoking questions to promote the connection between new and existing knowledge, thereby deepening their understanding of new knowledge. Teachers should train students to talk to themselves, ask themselves questions, or ask each other questions during learning activities. For example, in a literature class, "What could have happened if the main character made a different choice?" This prompts students to imagine alternative scenarios and generate deeper insights into the story. Trained students can successfully use self-questioning in math problem-solving, spelling, composing, and many other subjects.

2) Underlining method

**Underlining method** means that learners can quickly find important information in the learning material by underlining, which is a cognitive strategy often used in reading.

3) Abstracting strategy

**Abstracting strategy** refers to a method or approach used to extract and summarize the main points and essential information from a larger body of data or text. In literature analysis, students can abstract main themes from a novel. In science, they can abstract key concepts from a research paper. In history, they can abstract significant events from a time period.

4) Annotation strategy

**Annotation strategy** is the act of adding notes or comments to a text to enhance understanding. For example, highlighting important points and writing explanations in the margins of a book. An annotation strategy might involve:

Highlighting key terms: Marking important terms or concepts with a specific color or underline to draw attention to them.

Adding definitions: Providing brief definitions or explanations for complex terms or ideas.

Commenting on methodology: Offering insights or critiques on the research methods used in the paper.

Summarizing sections: Writing concise summaries of each section to help readers understand the main points quickly.

5) Drafting a summary

**Drafting a summary** involves condensing learned information into concise statements or paragraphs. For example, after reading an article, summarizing its main points in one's own words helps to solidify understanding and retention.

Mind mapping, writing a title, analogizing, self-testing, taking notes, brainstorming, role-playing, and card method all belong to generative strategies. By employing these generative strategies, learners can actively engage with the material, construct their own understanding, and enhance their learning outcomes.

## 7.4.3 Organizational strategy

**Organizational strategy** is a cognitive strategy in which the learner sorts and categorizes memory materials to form a new knowledge structure based on the characteristics and categories of the memory materials during the process of encoding and storage. The most important characteristic of organizational strategies is integrating the intrinsic connection between new knowledge and existing knowledge to form a new knowledge structure. There are many types of organizational strategies, mainly including concept maps, comparison charts, diagrams, hierarchy charts, and outline methods.

### 1. Outlining

**Outlining** refers to an organizational strategy in which the learner organizes and expresses the key points of the learning material in a certain way and outlines them to promote material learning based on summarizing and extracting the main knowledge points of the learning materials. An outline commonly includes numerical outlines and diagrammatic outlines.

1) Numerical outline

**A numerical outline** is an organizational strategy that uses numbers to represent the hierarchy of the materials and reflects their logical relationship. *About "A Blessing in Disguise", the following four-tier numerical outline can be listed:* ① *the horse was lost;* ② *it came back with more;* ③ *his son was disabled by riding a horse;* ④ *he saved his life because of disability.*

2) Diagrammatic outline

**A diagrammatic outline** is a method that uses diagrams, lines, arrows, or other means to show the inner relationship of knowledge. Its characteristics are imagery, intuitiveness, and strong generalization, which are conducive to grasping the complex relationships and internal connections of knowledge at a glance. *For example, we can use a diagrammatic outline to explain "Surrounding Wei to Rescue Zhao"* (Figure 7-5).

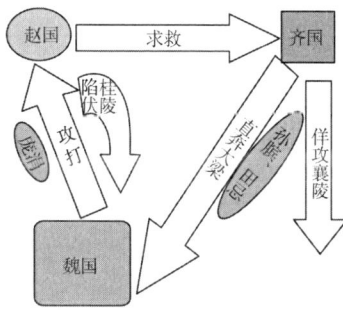

Figure 7-5 Diagrammatic outline of Surrounding Wei to Rescue Zhao

## 2. Drawing graphics

**Drawing graphics** refers to the use of visual representations, such as diagrams, flow charts, illustrations, and mind maps, to organize and structure information in a way that is easy to understand and remember. This strategy helps to visually depict relationships, hierarchies, and connections between different pieces of information, making it easier to grasp complex concepts and ideas. By drawing graphics, individuals can better visualize and internalize the material, enhancing their understanding and retention of the information. There are many types of these organizational strategies, such as concept maps, comparison charts, schematic diagrams, hierarchy diagrams, outline methods, mind maps, etc.

1) System structure diagram

After the learner has learned the content of a unit or a subject and classified and arranged the learning materials, the system structure diagram is formed by classifying the main information into different parts with different levels. Once complex information is organized into a pyramid-like hierarchy, it is easy to understand and remember. In a pyramid structure, more specific concepts are placed under more abstract concepts (refer to Figure 5-2).

2) Flow chart

A flow chart is a sequence diagram that can be used to represent steps, events, and phases. The flow chart is generally expanded from left to right, with arrows linking the steps. For example, the complex audit work can be explained by the flow chart of audit work (Figure 7-6).

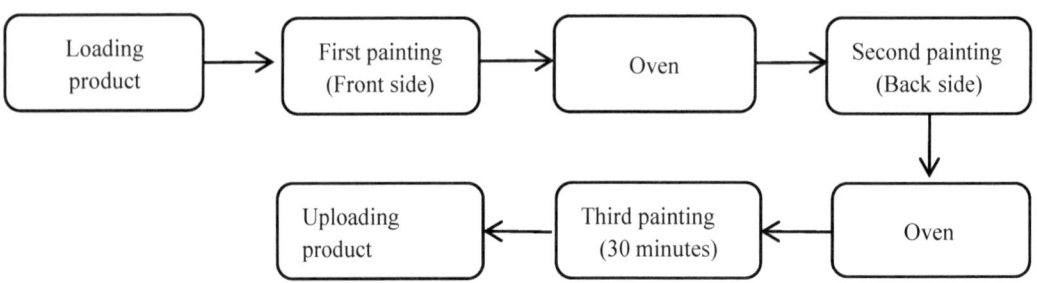

Figure 7-6　Process flow chart

3) V-model diagram

A v-model diagram (pattern diagram) refers to the diagrams used to illustrate how elements are related to each other in a process(Figure 7-7). A model diagram does not necessarily take time as a reference but focuses on illustrating the relationship between various elements or links in a process.

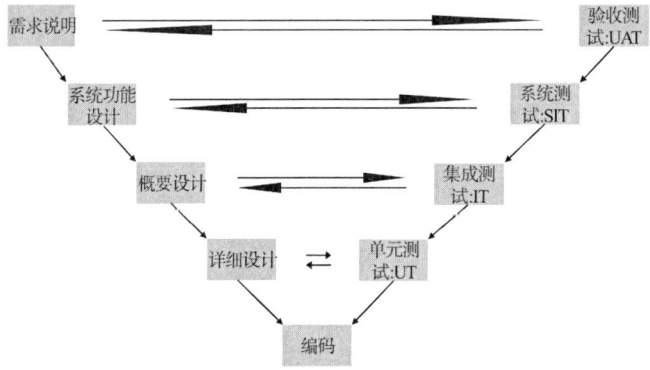

Figure 7-7　V-model diagram (software development model)

4) Network diagram

A network diagram, that is, a network relationship diagram or concept diagram, is a tool for visualizing the relationships between different entities(Figure 7-8). In a network relationship diagram, each node represents a different entity, such as an individual, an organization, an item, etc. The connecting lines between nodes represent specific relationships between entities. These relationships can be diverse, such as cooperative relationships, superior-subordinate relationships, social relationships, business transaction relationships, and so on.

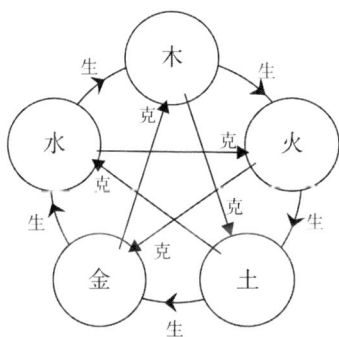

Figure 7-8　Network relation diagram of five elements

5) Mind map

Mind map is a visual tool that helps organize and structure ideas. It allows you to see connections and relationships between different concepts, making it easier to understand and remember information. A mind map can also enhance creativity, as it encourages you to think outside the box and explore new ideas. Additionally, it is a useful method for planning and prioritizing tasks, as well as for note-taking and brainstorming (refer to Figure 7-2; Figure 7-4).

### 3. Creating tables

Tables are often used to organize learning content. A table is a useful tool for presenting and organizing information. It allows for easy comparison and analysis of data. Tables are visually appealing and can make complex information easier to understand. They provide a clear and organized way to present data, making it easier for readers to find and use the information they need. Tables include schedules (Table 5-5) and two-way tables (see Table 5-3). A schedule is a simple list that shows related information in one row or column, while a two-way table is more complex with multiple rows and columns, used to compare and analyze data between two or more factors.

### 4. Classifying

Classifying refers to a strategy of organizing and categorizing materials according to their characteristics or categories to make them easy to remember. *For example, it's easy to remember the following words by classifying:* "TV, rice, suit, cotton-padded jacket, bread, lion, policeman, banana, mouse, actor, egg, soybean, schoolbag, shoes, stereo, flour, weasel, potato, teacher, cake, manager, writing brush, hat, air-conditioner, eraser, fan, refrigerator, spinach". The classification of these things is shown in Table 7-3.

Table 7-3  Classification of things

| Appliances | Animal | Clothing | Stationery | Food | Characters |
|---|---|---|---|---|---|
| TV, stereo, fan, air-conditioner, refrigerator | mouse, lion, weasel | suit, hat, cotton-padded jacket, shoes, | schoolbag, eraser writing brush | rice, bread, egg, banana, soybean, flour, potato, cake, spinach | policeman, actor, teacher, manager |

## 7.5  Meta-cognitive strategies

In the information processing system of learning, there is also a process of monitoring and regulating information processing, which is mainly responsible for monitoring and guiding cognitive activities. The basis of this executive control function is meta-cognition.

### 7.5.1  Overview of meta-cognition

Meta-cognition is gradually developed in long-term learning activities. Meta-cognition generally increases with age. Meta-cognitive abilities begin to develop at the age of 5 to 7 years and continue to rise throughout primary and secondary school. It gradually shifts from external control to internal control. Meta-cognition develops from unconsciousness to consciousness, and then to automaticity. Meta-cognition expands from local monitoring to overall monitoring.

1. Meta-cognitive concept

The American psychologist J. H. Flavell first proposed the concept of meta-cognition. He pointed out that meta-cognition is the cognition about cognition, as well as the self-awareness and self-regulation of cognitive activities (Mo Lei, 2002). In essence, it is a process of an individual's awareness and understanding of their own cognitive processes, including their thoughts, learning strategies, memory, and problem-solving abilities, by selecting appropriate strategies, monitoring the process of cognitive activities, continuously giving feedback, and analyzing information according to the requirements of cognitive activities. It involves the ability to reflect on and regulate one's own thinking and learning, enabling individuals to monitor their comprehension, identify areas of confusion, and adjust their strategies accordingly. Meta-cognition encompasses both the knowledge of one's own cognitive abilities and strategies, as well as the monitoring and control of these cognitive processes during various cognitive activities.

2. Meta-cognitive structure

According to Flavell, meta-cognition is composed of three elements: meta-cognitive knowledge, meta-cognitive experience, and meta-cognitive monitoring, which are interrelated and inseparable.

1) Meta-cognitive knowledge

**Meta-cognitive knowledge** is learners' general knowledge about the processes, results, and influencing factors of their own and others' cognitive activities, that is, knowing what to do (stored in long-term memory). Meta-cognitive knowledge mainly includes: ① knowledge of cognitive subjects, namely cognition of the internal cognitive level, personality characteristics of individuals, individual differences, and the influence of various subjective factors on cognitive activities; ② knowledge about cognitive tasks, that is, learners' understanding of the purpose, materials, and processes involved in executing cognitive tasks; ③ knowledge of learning strategies and their applications, that is, learners' understanding of the categories, attributes, advantages, and disadvantages of learning strategies, as well as the conditions and scope for using these learning strategies.

2) Meta-cognitive experience

**Meta-cognitive experience** refers to the cognitive or emotional experiences that arise during the learner's cognitive activities. The type of experience produced is directly related to learners' position in cognitive activities, the progress that has been made, and the potential for further progress. The experience can be simple or complex; it can also be the experience of "knowing" or "not knowing"; and it can be an experience that the learner is aware of or unaware of.

3) Meta-cognitive monitoring

**Meta-cognitive monitoring** means that learners actively and consciously manage and control cognitive behavior to achieve predetermined goals, that is, to know when and how to do it (stored in working memory). Meta-cognitive monitoring is the core component of meta-cognition. Meta-cognition operates in working memory and mainly involves three links: making plans, implementing monitoring, and effective regulation.

## 7.5.2 Meta-cognitive strategies

Meta-cognitive strategies of learning refer to the classic strategies that learners use to effectively monitor and control their cognitive activities in order to achieve the best cognitive outcomes. Meta-cognitive strategies mainly involve planning strategies, monitoring strategies, and regulating strategies.

1. Planning strategies

Planning strategies refer to the meta-cognitive strategies that an individual, before the start of cognitive activities, plans to complete various activities involved in the task according to the specific objectives of cognitive activities. This includes predicting the results, selecting strategies, considering problem-solving methods, and predicting their effectiveness. Planning strategies include setting learning goals, arranging time, browsing reading materials, predicting key and difficult points, generating questions to be answered, and analyzing how to complete learning tasks. *For example, if you would like to learn the passage "Puma" in New Concept English Ⅲ, firstly you will set the learning aims — learning the new words and expressions, getting the main idea, reciting the passage, and so on; secondly, you should arrange learning time; thirdly, you browse the passage quickly and predict the key and difficult points; fourthly, you will encounter some questions and difficulties that need to be solved; finally, you should analyze the questions and find methods to solve the problems.*

2. Monitoring strategies

Monitoring strategies refer to the strategies that the learner uses to detect the cognitive process in a timely manner according to the cognitive goal, identify the difference between the cognitive process and the cognitive goal, and adjust the learning process as needed to successfully achieve effective learning. Monitoring strategies include comprehension monitoring, strategy monitoring, and attention monitoring.

1) Comprehension monitoring

Comprehension monitoring is a specific monitoring strategy that is commonly used in reading. A skilled reader has a comprehension goal in mind, such as discovering a particular detail or finding out the main point, so they browse the text with that comprehension goal. If comprehension monitoring ultimately shows that the goal has not been achieved, the reader will take remedial action, such as rereading or reading more carefully. Many school children who lack the comprehension monitoring strategy just mechanically resort to rereading or endlessly taking notes, but they don't know how to take better measures. Devine (1987) suggests that learners use four strategies to monitor and improve comprehension (Table 7-4).

Table 7-4　Devine's methods to improve comprehension monitoring strategy

| Strategies | Explanation |
| --- | --- |
| Change reading speed | Vary the reading speed to accommodate the differences in comprehension abilities for different texts. For easier chapters, read quickly and grasp the author's overall point of view; for more difficult chapters, slow down. |

**Continued table**

| Strategies | Explanation |
|---|---|
| Tolerate ambiguity | If you don't understand something, just keep reading. The author may fill in the gap later, add more information, or clarify in subsequent passages. |
| Guess | When you don't understand something you read, get into the habit of guessing. Guess what the paragraph means and read on to see if your guessing is correct. |
| Reread more difficult paragraphs | Reread difficult paragraphs, especially when the information seems contradictory or ambiguous. The simplest strategy is often the most effective. |

Source: 陈琦、刘儒德,《当代教育心理学(第 2 版)》,北京师范大学出版社,2007,第 386 页.

2) Strategy monitoring

After students learn to use learning strategies, the most common problem is that they set aside the strategies they have learned and revert to using the less efficient and less thought-provoking strategies they previously relied on, which are, of course, less troublesome. To ensure that the learned strategies become truly effective tools that can be easily used at any time, monitoring training for the use of learning strategies must follow the teaching of these strategies. There are many training methods, but the most commonly used method is the self-questioning method.

When using the self-questioning method to train school children to monitor their use of learned strategies, teachers should first create a "Question List" that reflects the procedure for the effective use of efficient learning strategies. For example, to help school children become accustomed to using the learned "problem-solving strategies", the following self-questioning list can be made (Table 7-5).

Table 7-5  Self-questioning list

1. How can I characterize this problem?
2. Which method is the most suitable to solve the problem?
3. Did I make two-way reasoning when solving the problem?
4. Did I pay attention to divergent thinking and convergent thinking?
5. (for difficult problems) Have I summarized my ideas?

3) Attention monitoring

The attention monitoring of metacognition means that learners ensure they always pay attention to the content related to the current learning activity and prevent themselves from being disturbed by irrelevant content during the learning process. Attention is the beginning of mental activities, and an important prerequisite for successful learning is that school children are good at focusing on learning activities. School children who excel at concentrating will not only consciously remind themselves to focus on the learning activities and take the initiative to avoid distractions during the learning process, but they will also actively create an environment conducive to concentration for themselves. However, school children with attention disorders are unable to concentrate on what they are learning and cannot actively regulate their behavior, resulting in generally poor academic performance. The following methods can be used to help maintain students' attention (Table 7-6).

### 3. Regulating strategies

**Regulating strategies** mean that school children, based on the monitoring results of cognitive activities, discover cognitive deviations and timely adjust strategies or modify the goals during the learning process. At the end of learning activities, school children evaluate cognitive results, take corresponding remedial measures to correct mistakes, and summarize experiences and lessons. Regulating strategies can help students correct their own learning behaviors and remedy deficiencies in understanding.

Table 7-6　Ways to improve attention

| Ways | Explanation |
| --- | --- |
| Pay attention to learning objectives in advance | Teachers tell the students the goals they should pay attention to before class, and the students will learn better. |
| Mark the key points | In teaching, teachers raise or lower their voices or use gestures to express key information. Textbooks often use different colors or typography to highlight the main points. |
| Increase the emotionality of the material | Choose emotionally charged words to grab attention. That's why newspaper headlines say "Senator XX shot down an education bill" instead of "Senator XX vetoed an education bill". |
| Use unique stimuli | For example, science teachers can often make demonstrations in class to arouse students' curiosity and thus attract their attention. |
| Inform the importance | Many students anticipate questions on subsequent tests to identify important information in the lesson. This skill can enhance students' attention to relevant materials. To prevent students from reviewing only the key points presented by the teacher, they can be informed about the type and scope of the test questions. It is also necessary to tell students which materials are not important so that they can improve their learning efficiency. |

Source:陈琦、刘儒德,《当代教育心理学(第 2 版)》,北京师范大学出版社,2007,第 387 页.

Meta-cognitive strategies always work together with cognitive strategies. To be a successful learner, learners must not only know how to use many different cognitive strategies but also understand how to use meta-cognitive strategies to help them decide which strategy to use in a given situation.

## 7.6　Resource management strategies

Resource management strategies refer to the learning strategies that assist school children in managing available environments and resources, which include time management strategies, learning environment management strategies, effort management strategies, and academic help-seeking strategies.

### 1. Time management strategies

Time management strategies mean that school children arrange time reasonably and make effective use of learning resources through certain methods. Time is a very important learning resource. Effective time management promotes learning efficiency and enhances self-efficacy, while ineffective use of time weakens confidence and reduces learning efficiency.

1) Making an overall arrangement of learning time

Time is limited, but using the limited time to learn as much as possible does not mean that the more you learn, the better the learning effect. According to Macan et al. (1990), school children should prioritize tasks according to their importance and allocate time and resources accordingly. Teachers should guide each schoolchild to make an overall arrangement of time according to their overall goals and implement it through a phased timetable. They should also create a priority list of activities for each day. When making the learning plan, they should pay attention to the learning outcomes. When implementing the learning plan, they should effectively prevent procrastination.

2) Using the best time efficiently

Because people's mental state and attention change with the progress of learning, each person should arrange the learning content according to their own patterns to ensure that they learn the most important content when they are in the best condition. When learning, you should arrange learning activities ① according to your biological clock; ② according to the changes in learning efficiency during the week; ③ according to the changes in learning efficiency during the day; ④ according to your own work curve.

3) Utilizing spare time flexibly

Firstly, you can use your spare time to deal with learning chores. Secondly, short stories or newspapers and magazines can be read to broaden your knowledge, and poems and foreign words can be recited. There are many skills in using spare time. *Ouyang Xiu, one of the Eight Great Litterateurs of the Tang and Song dynasties, said, "Most of my articles in my life have been written on the horse, on the pillow, and on the toilet seat." This shows that Ouyang Xiu was an expert in time management.*

## 2. Learning environment management strategies

The learning environment can affect students' mood during learning and thus impact learning efficiency. Firstly, to better ensure the effectiveness of learning, it is usually necessary to ensure that the learning environment is a fixed, special, quiet place. Secondly, school children should take the initiative to avoid contact with TV, radio, mobile phones, and other entertainment devices. Thirdly, they should try to choose a quiet and simple place, such as a classroom or library, and should not learn in bed, dormitories, or other places closely related to daily life. Fourthly, they can also learn with students who have good grades, high learning efficiency, and strong self-control to supervise and promote each other and form a learning community.

## 3. Effort management strategies

To help school children maintain their will to study hard, it is necessary to encourage them to engage in self-motivation. ① Stimulating intrinsic learning motivation; ② establishing the correct learning beliefs; ③ choosing challenging tasks; ④ regulating the criteria for success or failure; ⑤ attributing success or failure correctly; ⑥ self-reward.

## 4. Academic help-seeking strategies

Academic help-seeking strategies refer to the behaviors of asking others for help when school children encounter difficulties in learning. Academic help-seeking, an important learning strategy, is not a sign of a lack of ability but a way to obtain the ability for knowledge growth (Pang Guowei, 2003). Academic help-seeking includes two aspects: ① the use of learning tools, such as effectively using reference materials, instrumental books, libraries, computers, and mobile phones; ② the use of social human resources, such as making good use of help from teachers and cooperating and discussing with students to deepen the understanding of learning content.

Nelson-Le Gall S. (1985) divided help-seeking strategies into two kinds according to the purpose of help-seeking (Table 7-7).

Table 7-7  Academic help-seeking strategies

| Help-seeking forms | Characteristics | Purpose |
| --- | --- | --- |
| Executive help-seeking | Others solve difficulties *instead of* the help-seeker himself or herself. | The help-seeker just wants the answer or hopes to complete the task as soon as possible. Without making any attempt, he gives up his ability to achieve success and chooses dependence instead of independent mastery. |
| Instrumental help-seeking (adaptive help-seeking) | Others provide ideas and instruments. | In order to learn independently, he uses the power of others to solve problems or achieve his goals. |

Source: Nelson-Le Gall S., Help-seeking Behavior in Learning, in Gordon, W. (Eds.), *Review of Research in Education* (Vol. 12), American Education Research Association, 1985, pp. 55-90.

## 7.7 Training and teaching of learning strategies

One of the goals of education is to help students learn to use effective learning strategies. Many struggling school children have never been taught how to learn. A foreign study found that primary school teachers only spend about 3% of their time recommending some memory and learning strategies to students (Chen Qi & Liu Rude, 2007). The principles, methods, and patterns for teaching learning strategies should necessarily be discussed.

### 7.7.1 Teaching principles of learning strategies

Learning strategy is a kind of procedural knowledge that teaches students how to learn, which cannot be taught by "teaching" in the general sense. Therefore, in order to make students really learn how to learn and enable them to flexibly and appropriately use various methods and strategies in different learning situations and tasks, a set of effective learning principles suitable for specific learning methods will be introduced, combining Thomas and Rohwer's opinions (1986).

1. **Principle of subjectivity**

The principle of subjectivity means that the subjective role of school children should be given full play in the teaching of learning strategies. Any use of learning strategies depends on the full engagement of students' initiative. The training of learning strategies still requires students to exert their own subjectivity, which is not only the purpose of learning strategy training but also a necessary method.

2. **Principle of internalization**

The principle of internalization means that school children constantly practice various learning strategies, gradually internalizing them into their own learning ability, and can use them flexibly in new situations during the learning process.

3. **Principle of concretization**

The principle of concretization means that learning strategies must be suitable for learning objectives and school children's types. The same strategy can be used differently by different school children. Therefore, in the teaching process, teachers should explain a variety of learning strategies suitable for different students according to various teaching objectives.

4. **Principle of generativity**

The principle of generativity means that school children use learning strategies to reprocess the learning materials to generate something new in the learning process.

Two signs of knowledge understanding are that school children can express the knowledge in their own words and that they can apply it. Therefore, school children are also required to establish the awareness of processing the learning materials to better understand and absorb them.

### 5. Principle of effective monitoring

Effective monitoring means that school children should know when and how to apply their learning strategies and be able to reflect on and describe their own use of these strategies. They can recognize their own learning strategies in the process of applying them, which is the so-called metacognition, allowing them to monitor the results caused by the strategies they use to determine whether the strategies are effective.

### 6. Principle of personal efficacy

The principle of personal efficacy means that learners should be given the opportunity to feel the effectiveness of learning strategies and their ability to use them in the teaching of these strategies. Because of the close relationship between learning attitude and performance, if learners are psychologically unwilling to use these strategies, their learning ability will not improve. Those who use strategies effectively, however, tend to believe that the use of learning strategies will enhance their academic performance. Therefore, teachers must help school children realize that their academic performance will improve as long as they grasp and use the learning strategies. In the teaching process, teachers can constantly ask school children questions and check their understanding, then evaluate their achievements in using strategies, so that they can feel the benefits of using learning strategies and enhance self-efficacy to promote the active use of these strategies.

## 7.7.2 Teaching models of the training of learning strategies

Learning strategies can be taught and transferred. Many teaching models of learning strategies have been proposed both at home and abroad. Several representative teaching models are introduced.

### 1. Direct instructional mode

The direct instructional mode consists of stimulation, explanation, practice, feedback, and transfer. The basic idea of this mode is that school children learn relevant learning strategies under the guidance of teachers, which is similar to the traditional teaching method. Teachers first explain the specific steps and conditions of the selected learning strategy to school children during the teaching process. Then, in the specific application process, teachers continuously prompt the school children, asking them to report aloud and clearly explain each step they have performed as well as their own thinking process. Their perception, understanding, and retention of learning strategies are strengthened through the repetition of internally oriented thinking. At the same time, teachers select many appropriate examples according to each strategy in teaching to illustrate the various possibilities of its application, helping students form a figurative and profound understanding of the strategy. This allows for the development from the application of a single strategy to the comprehensive application of a variety of strategies, thereby cultivating the ability to apply learning strategies comprehensively.

## 2. Programmed training mode

According to Gagne's learning hierarchy theory, the programmed training mode involves decomposing the basic skills of activities into several organized small steps, which are used as a fixed procedure within its appropriate scope. Schoolchildren should carry out activities according to the program and practice repeatedly until the use of the basic activity skills reaches the level of automation. The basic steps of the programmed training mode are: ① Decompose an activity skill into small steps that are executable and easy to operate according to relevant principles, and use concise wording to indicate the meaning of each step; ② Demonstrate each step through activity examples and require students to carry out activities step by step; ③ Ask students to memorize the steps and keep practicing until they are automated. For example, the teaching of the PQ4R (Thomes and Robinson, 1972) reading strategy belongs to a typical programmed teaching mode (Table 7-8).

Table 7-8  PQ4R Reading Method

| Steps | Explanation |
| --- | --- |
| Preview | Quickly browse the materials and gain an understanding of the basic organization, theme, and sub-theme of the materials. Pay attention to the headlines and subheadings, and identify the information you want to read and learn. |
| Question | Ask yourself some questions as you read. Formulate questions based on the title using interrogative words such as "who," "what," "why," "where," "how," etc. |
| Read | Read the materials, don't take notes in general, and try to answer your questions. |
| Reflect | Try to understand the information and make sense of it through the following ways: ① connect the information with what you know; ② connect the subtitles in the textbook with the main concepts and principles; ③ try to eliminate distractions from the presented information; ④ use these materials to solve similar problems associated with them. |
| Recite | Practice remembering this information over and over again by stating it aloud and asking and answering questions. You can ask questions using headings, underlined words, and notes on key points. |
| Review | Actively review the materials mainly by asking yourself questions. Only when you are sure you can't answer them should you reread the materials. |

Source: Robert E. Slavin, *Educational Psychology Theory and Practice* (10th), Posts & Telecom Press, 2017, p. 171.

### 3. Gestalt teaching mode

The basic content of the gestalt teaching mode is that teachers provide students with complete materials of different degrees after the direct explanation of a learning strategy and urge them to practice a certain component or step of the learning strategy. They then gradually reduce the degree of completeness of the materials until the students can entirely complete all components or steps by themselves. The basic steps of the gestalt training mode are: ① to provide an almost complete outline and require students to fill in some supporting details while listening to the lecture or reading; ② to provide a theme-only outline and require students to fill in all supporting details; ③ to provide only supporting details and ask students to fill in the full point of view. The gestalt teaching mode can make students pay attention to every detail or step in the learning strategy, and the psychological effort required for each step of training is manageable for students. More importantly, each step of training gives students an overall impression of strategy application.

### 4. Reciprocal teaching mode

The reciprocal teaching mode is conducted by teachers and a group of students together, which mainly aims to externalize the mental model of students who are good at reading into a program that students who are not good at reading can operate through strategies, thus helping students with poor grades to understand reading. The reciprocal teaching mode teaches students four strategies (Table 7-9), and the specific teaching procedure includes five steps (Table 7-10).

Table 7-9  Four strategies of reciprocal teaching mode

| Reading strategies | Explanation |
| --- | --- |
| Summarize | Summarize the content of the paragraph. |
| Ask questions | Ask questions about key points. |
| Clarify | Clarify the difficulties in materials. |
| Predict | Predict what will happen next. |

The teacher first sets up some sample behaviors that he wants the students to do on their own, then changes his role to that of an organizer and facilitator, providing support and assistance to students by offering clues, guidance, encouragement, etc., when the students encounter problems. Ultimately, he enables the students to use these strategies independently in reading.

Table 7-10  Specific teaching procedure of reciprocal teaching mode

| Serial number | Teaching procedure |
|---|---|
| Step 1 | The teacher introduces a variety of these strategies at the same time or one at a time. |
| Step 2 | The teacher demonstrates the strategies. *For example, the teacher reads a paragraph of a text, asks questions about the core content of the paragraph, and finally summarizes the main idea of the paragraph.* |
| Step 3 | The teacher encourages students to practice themselves. *For example, the teacher assigns a student to act as a "teacher" and imitate the steps as the teacher has done, and leads the students to analyze the next paragraph.* |
| Step 4 | The teacher provides demonstrations again by summarizing, questioning, elaborating, or anticipating based on reading. |
| Step 5 | The students take turns to act as the "teacher", and the teacher becomes a member of the learning group and achieves the role transition. |

### 5. Reciprocal cooperation teaching mode

According to Dansereau (1985), the reciprocal cooperative learning mode means that two students form a group and take turns summarizing the material section by section. In the reciprocal cooperative learning activity, when one student gives the lecture, the other student listens and corrects mistakes and omissions. The two students then change roles with each other until they finish learning the material. Both participants in the reciprocal cooperative learning activity benefit from this learning experience, and the presenter benefits more than the listener.

In conclusion, learning strategies serve as the cornerstone for efficient and effective learning. By adopting and refining these strategies, learners can enhance their comprehension, retention, and application of new knowledge. Whether through active engagement, reflective practice, or collaborative efforts, the utilization of learning strategies is essential for achieving academic success and fostering a lifelong passion for learning.

In conclusion, effective learning strategies are essential for students to enhance their academic performance and develop lifelong skills. By utilizing techniques such as active learning, time management, and self-assessment, students can tailor their approaches to meet individual needs. Emphasizing collaboration and open communication further enriches the learning experience. Ultimately, mastering these strategies not only boosts confidence and motivation but also prepares students to navigate future challenges with resilience and adaptability, fostering a passion for continuous learning.

# I. Review and reflection

learning strategy
characteristics of learning strategy
initiative
cognitive strategies
rehearsal strategies
elaboration strategies
organizational strategies
make a scientific review plan
review scientifically in time
the cephalocercal echo review
adopt diversified review forms
unintentional memory
intentional memory
mobilize multiple senses
make chunk coding
combine reading and reciting
moderate over-learning
elaborative processing strategies
artificial connection strategy
rhythmic chant method
loci method
analogy method
reduction method
homophonic association method
semantic association method
initial acronym method
generative strategies
self-questioning method
underlining method
card method
organizational strategies
outlining
numerical outline
diagrammatic outline
drawing a graph
system structure diagram
flow chart
model diagram
network diagram
mind map
using tables
classifying
meta-cognitive strategies
meta-cognitive concept
meta-cognitive structure
planning strategies
monitoring strategies
comprehension monitoring
strategy monitoring
attention monitoring
regulating strategies
resource management strategies
time management strategies
learning environment management strategies
effort management strategies
academic help-seeking strategies
training and teaching of learning strategies
teaching principles of learning strategies
principle of subjectivity
principle of internalization
principle of concretization
principle of generativity
principle of effective monitoring

principle of personal efficacy  
direct instructional mode  
programmed training mode  
gestalt teaching mode  
reciprocal teaching mode  
reciprocal cooperation teaching mode  

## II. Material analysis

*Middle school students use two methods to remember the following five English words: introduce, produce, reduce, induce, deduce. One way is to remember them in a traditional method like this: i-n-t-r-o-d-u-c-e, p-r-o-d-u-c-e, r-e-d-u-c-e, i-n-d-u-c-e, d-e-d-u-c-e. Another way is to remember them in the "Prosodic syllable method" like Figure 2. Figure 1 shows Memory Retention Percentage.* Please analyze which method is more effective according to memory retention percentage and elaboration strategies. (Refer to Appendix I)

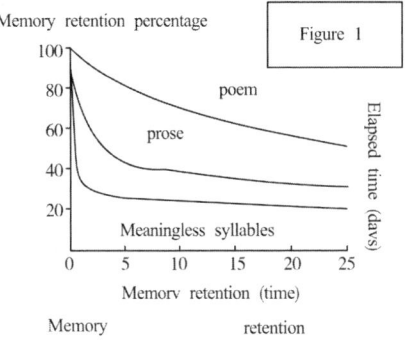

Figure 1

Memory retention

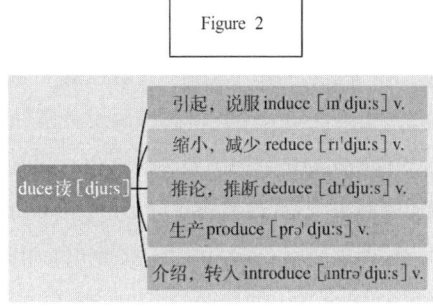

Figure 2

# Chapter 8　Learning Styles and Cultivation

*In a vibrant classroom, two students, Mia and Alex, approached their lessons in distinctly different ways. Mia, a visual learner, thrived on diagrams and colorful notes, often creating mind maps to grasp complex concepts. Alex, an auditory learner, preferred listening to lectures and discussing ideas with peers, finding that he retained information better through conversation. As the semester progressed, both students faced a challenging science project. Mia's visual aids helped her articulate her ideas clearly, while Alex's discussions enriched his understanding of the subject matter.*

Their contrasting approaches not only reflected their unique learning styles but also revealed the importance of recognizing individual preferences in education. Some students excel in visual learning, while others excel in auditory learning, which reflects the comprehensive performance of individual differences in learning and has a direct regulatory impact on the learning process, efficiency, and outcomes. This chapter will delve into various learning styles, illustrating how understanding one's preferred methods can enhance learning efficiency. By tailoring strategies to fit these styles, students can optimize their study habits and unlock their full potential.

## 8.1　Concept and characteristics of learning styles

Since Herbert Thelen (1954) first put forward the concept of learning style, the study of learning styles has garnered significant attention. Learning styles refer to the ways in which a learner prefers or often uses to learn, along with the corresponding characteristics they display in the learning process. These learning styles, tendencies, and characteristics are stable over a long period of time (persistence) and consistently show stability (consistency) when performing similar tasks. It is these stable, lasting, consistent, and unique learning manners and tendencies that constitute learners' learning styles.

According to the concept, the characteristics of learning styles include uniqueness and stability, which can help teachers predict what mental activities a learner will engage in under certain circumstances.

1. Uniqueness

Due to different physiological and psychological conditions, as well as the influence of family life, school education, social culture, and so on, each school child will gradually form his own unique learning style in learning activities. This is a comprehensive basic orientation and overall characteristic manifested in thoughts and behaviors, forms, and methods when completing learning tasks.

2. Stability

Learning style is a learning approach with individual characteristics that school children gradually develop in the long-term learning process. In a sense, it can also be described as the comprehensive response of learners' personality traits in learning activities. Therefore, once a learning style is formed, it will frequently and stably manifest in learning activities and rarely change due to alterations in learning tasks and environments. Of course, the stability of learning style does not mean that the learning style is unchangeable.

## 8.2 Theories of learning styles

According to their personal understanding of learning styles, the researchers spare no effort in putting forward various theories about learning styles.

### 8.2.1 The Dunns' model and theory

In the view of Mr. and Mrs. Dunn (1986), American psychologists, school children in the same class, grade, age, and cultural background show different learning preferences, which is the embodiment of learning styles. The learning style model proposed by the Dunns is an important analytical framework for exploring the types of school children's learning styles, which has strong universality. The Dunns put forward a learning style model from five aspects: environment, physiology, psychology, emotion, and society, which consists of 21 independent elements (Table 8-1). Although a schoolchild is not influenced by all the factors, generally speaking, 6-14 factors influence their learning.

Table 8-1  Elements of the Dunns' learning style and learners' performance

| Dimensions | Specific elements | Learner's performance |
|---|---|---|
| Environmental elements | Sound | The learner's preference for background music: Does he prefer silence or background sound? |
| | Light | The learner's preference for light: Does he prefer gentle, dim, or bright light? |
| | Temperature | The learner's requirements for the temperature during learning or activities. |
| | Sitting posture | The learner's sitting posture, which is related to the learners' environment and furnishings: Does he prefer formal tables and chairs or informal ones? |
| Emotional elements | Motivation | Is the learner's learning motivation driven by internal factors; does he learn because he is interested in peer interaction or influenced by adults' feedback? |
| | Persistence | The learner's attention persistence on a task: Does he prefer to complete tasks one by one, or start multiple tasks simultaneously? |
| | Responsibility | Does he need a small amount of adults' supervision, guidance, and feedback when he carries out tasks; doesn't he need any supervision, guidance, or feedback from adults when he completes tasks independently or does he require timely feedback and guidance from adults? |
| | Organizational degree of learning content | Does the learner prefer well-organized learning activities (specifically instructing on how to proceed), or prefer goal-only activities (leaving it up to themselves to decide the steps to achieve the objectives)? |
| Social elements | Self | The learner likes to work alone. |
| | Companionship | The learner enjoys having companions. |
| | Peer, team | The learner enjoys participating in activities as part of a team and being with the group. |
| | Adult | The learner enjoys working with adults such as parents or teachers to carry out tasks. |
| | Diversity or standardization | Does the learner prefer standardized tasks or tasks with uncertain processes? |
| Physiological elements | Sensory perception | The learner learns by sight, hearing and kinesthesia, and has different preferences for the presented materials. |
| | Ingestion | The learner enjoys eating snacks, drinking beverages, and chewing gum while learning. |
| | Time | The learner prefers different times of a day. |
| | Activities | Does the learner prefer to sit still or need to stand up and move constantly when carrying out a task. |

| Dimensions | Specific elements | Learner's performance |
|---|---|---|
| Psychological elements | Analysis and synthesis | Does the learner focus on the overall meaning, outcome and big picture of the task, or focus on the details and integrate the details to understand the big picture. |
| | Left and right hemisphere of the brain | Those who tend to use the left brain are analytical learners, who prefer successive tasks. Those who tend to use the right brain are holistic learners, who prefer multitasking simultaneously. |
| | Meditation and impulse | The learner's preference for thinking speed: Does he prefer to make decisions quickly or to deliberate carefully before making decisions? |

Source: Carbo M., Dunn R. & Dunn K, *Teaching Students to Read Through Their Individual Learning Styles*, Prentice Hall, 1986, pp. 2-20.

## 8.2.2 Keefe's model and theory

Keefe's (1989) model of learning style involves three levels of indicators: cognitive style, emotional style, and physiological style (Table 8-2).

Table 8-2 Keefe's model of learning style

| First level indicators | Second level indicators | Third-level indicators |
|---|---|---|
| Cognitive style | Accept conceptualization of style and maintain style | Preference for sensory channels (sight, hearing, and kinesthesia)<br>Field dependence and field independence; scanning and focusing<br>Functional fixation and flexibility; tolerance for non-present experiences<br>Degree of automation; sensory and rational activity<br>Conceptualization speed; conceptualization style; width of classification<br>Cognitive complexity and simplicity; divergence and convergence |
| Emotional style | Focus on style expectations and motivational styles | Rationality level; curiosity; persistence; anxiety; frustration tolerance<br>Locus of control; achievement motivation; self-actualization; imitation; adventure and caution<br>Competition and cooperation; aspiration level; response to reinforcement; social motivation; personal interests |
| Physiological style | | Male-female behavior<br>Health-related behavior<br>Time rhythm<br>Environmental factors |

Source: Keefe J. W., *Learning Styles Profile Handbook: Accommodating Conceptual Study and Instructional Preferences*, NASSP, 1989, p. 6.

## 8.2.3 Curry's onion model and theory

Curry's (1987) onion model of learning styles is composed of four layers (Figure 8-1). The first layer is the outermost layer, known as the "teaching preference layer." This layer is the most visible, the most unstable, and the most easily influenced by the learning environment, students' aspirations, teachers' expectations, and other external characteristics. The second layer is called the "social interaction layer". In this layer, it is believed that learning is accomplished through avoidance and participation, competition and cooperation, dependence and independence between students and teachers, students and peers, students and the learning environment, as well as between students and their learning. Learning is a response to classroom activities and not an evaluation of learners' personalities, so it's extremely unstable. The third layer, known as the "information processing layer", is more stable than the first and second layers but can still be modified by learning strategies. This layer is at the intersection of individual differences at basic personality levels and the social environment, and it is the way learners process information. This layer emphasizes the importance of information acquisition, organization, storage, and use. It is combined with Howard Gardner's theory of multiple intelligences and is the mental activity mode for learners to absorb information. The fourth layer, the innermost and core layer, is the "personality style of cognition", which is the tendency of the learner to modify and assimilate information and does not directly interact with the environment.

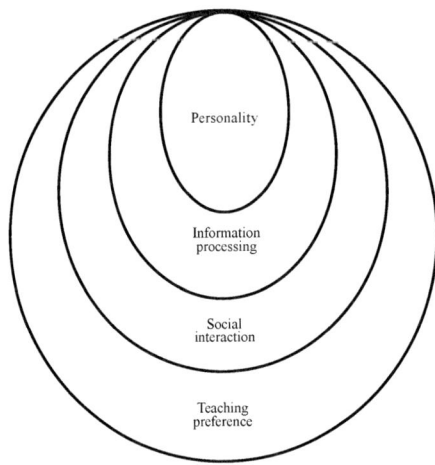

**Figure 8-1 Curry's onion model of learning style**

Source: Curry L. , "An Organization of Learning Style Theory and Constructs", in J. L. Curry (Ed.), *Learning Style in Continuing Education for the Health Professions*, Canadian Medical Association, 1983, pp. 115-131.

### 8.2.4 Sternberg's theory of mental self-government

Sternberg (1997) studied learning styles from an integrated perspective based on previous style theories and proposed the concept of thinking style and the theory of mental self-government. This theory draws an analogy between human cognition and national governance: it posits that just as different countries have different government styles, individuals also have their own unique "thinking styles" for self-organization and management, which manifest in various aspects of a person's learning, life, and work. The theory of mental self-government includes five aspects: function, form, level, scope, and tendency. A person's self-government style is a combination of multidimensional thinking styles, and each aspect reflects different styles (Table 8-3).

Table 8-3 Sternberg's model of learning style

| Dimensions of mental self-government | Learning styles | Specific description |
| --- | --- | --- |
| Function of mental self-government | Legislative style | Learners with legislative style like to create and propose plans and to do things in their own way according to their own thoughts and concepts, and like to make decisions by themselves, but do not like structured work or problems and do not like to execute tasks constructed by others. |
| | Executive style | Learners with executive style like to follow the routine and to do things according to the given procedures and rules, but don't like to create while they are willing to do what others ask them to do. |
| | Judicial style | Learners with judicial style like to analyze and judge existing things and methods, and like to evaluate rules and procedures. |
| Form of mental self-government | Oligarchic style | Learners with oligarchic style can only have a single goal or deal with one thing at a time for a period, complete one thing before doing another, and they are not easily disturbed by the outside world when doing things. |
| | Hierarchical style | Learners with hierarchical style can simultaneously have multiple goals or deal with multiple tasks, prioritize tasks according to their importance, and have a good sense of order to organize their affairs methodically. |
| | Monarchic style | Learners with monarchic style often have multiple goals simultaneously but struggle to prioritize them by importance, and they often feel stressed or indecisive because they cannot allocate time, resources, and other elements effectively. |
| | Anarchic style | Learners with anarchic style often oppose authority and prefer to work extremely actively, flexibly and freely, doing as they please. They perform best in unstructured situations without clear procedures to follow and enjoy tasks that lack rules and constraints. |
| Level of mental self-government | Global style | Learners with global style prefer dealing with large, overall and abstract concepts to ignoring details, and they often "see the forest but not the trees". |
| | Local style | Learners with local style prefer dealing with concrete and detailed things, and they are more practical but often "see the trees but not the forest". |

**Continued table**

| Dimensions of mental self-government | Learning styles | Specific description |
|---|---|---|
| Scope of mental self-government | Internal style | Learners with internal style are task—oriented and they prefer to work independently and are not sensitive to interpersonal issues. |
| | External style | Learners with external style are interpersonal—oriented, they enjoy working with others or completing tasks in groups, and they are sensitive to interpersonal issues. |
| Tendency of mental self-government | Conventional style | Learners with conventional style prefer to follow existing rules and procedures, enjoy doing familiar work and avoid ambiguous and changing situations. |
| | Radical style | Learners with radical style enjoy facing unfamiliar and uncertain situations, surpassing existing rules and procedures, and having a high tolerance for change. |

Sternberg R. J., *Thinking Styles*, Cambridge University Press, 2001, pp. 15-78.

In summary, Sternberg's theory of psychological self-management identifies 13 types of thinking styles. Sternberg believes that these 13 styles manifest to varying degrees in everyone, with differing intensities among individuals. Furthermore, the intensity of a particular thinking style can change depending on the task and situation.

## 8.2.5 Riding et al's theory of two-dimensional structure

Riding et al.'s (1997, 2000) theory of two-dimensional structure proposes that individual differences in cognitive styles can be understood through two primary dimensions: holistic-analytic and verbal-imagery (Table 8-4).

Table 8-4 Dimensions of representative studies on learning/cognitive styles

| Dimension One Holistic-analytic | | |
|---|---|---|
| Field dependence-field independence | The individual's dependence on the whole field when analyzing the structure or form of a part of the perceptual field. | Witkin & Asch (1948) Witkin (1964) |
| Flattening-sharpening | Quickly assimilate and ignore detailed differences, or emphasize details and changes in new information. | Klein (1954) Gardner et al. (1959) |
| Impulsivity-reflectivity | Tend to react quickly or react after contemplation. | Kagan et al. (1964) Kagan (1966) |
| Convergence-divergence | The tendency toward meticulous, focused, logical, and inductive thinking, or the tendency toward broad, open-minded, and associative thinking in the problem-solving processes. | Guilford (1967) Hudson (1966, 1968) |
| Holistic-serial | The global and holistic approach, or a serial and detailed approach, in learning and problem-solving. | Pask & Scott (1972) Pask (1976) |

Continued table

| Dimension One Holistic-analytic | | |
|---|---|---|
| Concrete and orderly/ concrete and random/ abstract and orderly/ abstract and random | Learners learn with a random or sequential approach through concrete or abstract experience. | Gregorc(1982) |
| Assimilator-explorer | Individuals prefer to seek familiarity or novelty in the processes of problem-solving or creation. | Kaufmann c1989) |
| Adaptive-innovative | Solve problems according to traditional, existing procedures or solve problems according to reconstructive procedures and in new ways. | Kirton (1976, 1987) |
| Reasoning-intuitive active-contemplative | The preference for understanding through reasoning or intuition and active participation or passive response in learning activities. | Allinson & Hayes (1996) |
| Dimension Two Verbal-imagery | | |
| Abstraction-concretization Verbalization-visualization | The preference level and ability of abstraction according to the degree of using verbal or imaginal strategies in representing knowledge and thinking processes. | Harveyet al. (1961), Paivio (1971), Riding & Taylor (1976), Richardson (1977) |

Source: 杨治良、郭力平,《认知风格的研究进展》,《心理科学》,2001(3):326—329.

The holistic-analytic dimension reflects how individuals process information. Holistic individuals tend to perceive and process information holistically, focusing on the big picture and relationships between elements. Analytic individuals, on the other hand, tend to break down information into smaller components, focusing on details and analyzing each part separately.

The verbal-imagery dimension pertains to the representation of information. Individuals who tend to think in the form of visual images are called imagery thinkers. Individuals who tend to think in the form of words are called verbal thinkers. Verbal thinkers prefer processing information in linguistic or verbal forms, such as words or symbols. In contrast, imagery thinkers prefer processing information in non-verbal or visual forms, relying on mental imagery and spatial representations.

By considering these two dimensions, Riding et al.'s theory provides a nuanced understanding of cognitive styles, highlighting how individuals vary in their approaches to processing and representing information.

## 8.3  Factors of learning styles

The factors of learning styles can be divided into three levels: social factors, physiological factors, and psychological factors.

### 8.3.1  Social factors

The social factors of learning style refer to the preferences of learners in the social interaction forms of learning activities, such as learning alone, learning in pairs or in groups, learning in competitive or cooperative environments, or learning with adult support. Learning always takes place in a certain social environment and inevitably involves interactions with teachers, peers, and others. However, due to the different growth experiences and personality traits of learners, their ways of interacting with others and situations in learning activities are inevitably different. For example, some learners are very sensitive to external interference, so they prefer to study alone rather than with others; on the contrary, some learners feel cold and lonely when studying alone, so they prefer to study with classmates and friends. Similarly, some learners are in a higher state of arousal in terms of emotion, intelligence, and physical strength in an appropriate competitive environment, so they tend to promote learning through competition, while some learners feel that mutual promotion and common improvement with peers can better stimulate their learning motivation, thus they prefer collaborative learning.

Due to differences in physiological structure and function, learners also have different requirements for their surrounding learning environment, such as sound, light, and temperature. Learners have varying preferences or tolerance for background sound (or noise) during learning. Some learners require absolute silence when studying, while others need background sound (such as music or radio) to concentrate. The difference in these tendencies is manifested in reading: the former prefers silent reading, while the latter prefers reading aloud. Individual sensitivity to light varies, leading to different requirements for brightness. Some require bright light, while others prefer soft light. Strong light can make individuals who prefer dim light feel tense, while dim light can dampen the spirits of those who prefer bright light. Different students have different requirements for temperature, which also affects their learning. Both too hot and too cold can affect students' attention.

## 8.3.2 Physiological factors

The physiological factors of learning styles refer to learners' preferences for various factors in the learning environment, such as learning conditions and learning places. External stimuli can evoke individuals' different perceptual responses, so learners will adopt different perceptual modes when receiving information, which results in preferences for different senses, such as visual preferences, auditory preferences, or kinesthetic preferences. Similarly, individuals' different responses to environmental factors can also lead to different biological rhythms, which manifest in rhythmic learning times and varied requirements for external learning environments. For example, some people are mentally alert and efficient in learning in the early morning, while others prefer studying late at night. Some enjoy studying in quiet, well-ventilated, well-lit environments, while others prefer learning in "noisy" environments through "debate" and "hands-on" approaches to acquire information and knowledge.

## 8.3.3 Psychological factors

The psychological factors of learning styles refer to learners' preferences in cognition, emotion, and volition. The cognitive factors of learning styles reflect an individual's cognitive style in learning. Cognitive style, also known as cognitive mode, refers to the preferred way an individual processes information, which is manifested in perception, attention, thinking, memory, and problem-solving. In terms of cognitive factors, the most studies focus on field-independent and field-dependent cognitive styles, impulsive and reflective cognitive styles, and so on. The emotional and volitional factors of learning styles mainly manifest in individuals' learning interests, achievement motivation, anxiety levels, learning willpower, and hands-on operations. In terms of emotional and volitional factors, the most studies are on internal and external motivation related to learning, normal anxiety and hypersensitive anxiety, as well as persistence in learning.

Obviously, understanding the constituent factors of learning styles is beneficial for us to understand the individual differences of students in learning methods, so as to consciously adjust the teaching styles and strategies to adapt to the learning preferences of different learning groups, and then better give full play to the learning advantages and subjective initiative of students.

## 8.4 Learning styles and their learning characteristics

Learning styles are the preferred information processing modes in cognitive activities and relatively stable psychological features with great differences. There are no good or bad learning styles. Learning styles are simply students' preferences for information processing, which mainly affect their learning methods.

### 8.4.1 Field independence and field dependence

During World War II, pilots often lost their sense of orientation due to the fuselage tumbling in the clouds, resulting in plane crashes. In order to reduce the occurrence of such accidents, it was necessary to test the candidates' ability to perceive and judge spatial orientation when selecting and training pilots. In the 1940s, American psychologist Herman Witkin became interested in how Air Force pilots determined their own orientation. He designed a room that could tilt and asked participants to sit in a chair with a rotating handle, which could tilt in the same or opposite direction as the room (Figure 8-2). When the room tilted, participants were asked to rotate the handle to position the chair in a vertical position. The results showed that some participants, even at a 35-degree deviation from vertical, still insisted they were completely vertical, while others were able to position the chair very close to vertical despite the apparent tilt of the room. Witkin concluded that some individuals perceive more from environmental cues, while others rely more on internal bodily cues. He termed those highly influenced by environmental factors as "field dependent", who tend to rely on external references (external objects), and those less influenced or unaffected as "field independent", who tend to rely on internal references (subjective sensations). Field-dependent individuals may struggle to decompose a pattern into many parts or may focus only on a specific aspect of a situation. Field-independent individuals excel in analysis and organization (Witkin et al., 1977).

According to Herman Witkin et al., learning styles can be divided into field dependence and field independence. According to psychologists, "field" here refers to the external environment.

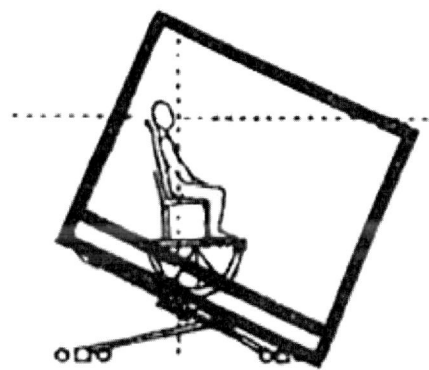

Figure 8-2 Witkin's "Tilted room experiment"

Source: Witkin H. A., et al, *Personality Through Perception: An Experimental and Clinical Study*, Harper & Brothers, 1954, p. 73.

**Field independence** refers to the learning style of individuals who rely more on their own internal references, are less susceptible to the influence and interference of external factors, and independently make judgments about things. According to perceptual selectivity, when facing many stimuli, learners automatically divide the stimuli into objects and backgrounds and distinguish the perceptual objects from the perceptual background preferentially. Field independence also refers to the perceptual characteristics and cognitive styles that make it easy for learners to separate a perceptual target from its background. Field-independent students often judge objective things based on their own internal clues (experience, values), and they are not easily affected or disturbed by the surrounding environmental factors. They tend to judge things independently, and their behaviors often lack social orientation. They have lower social sensitivity, are not good at communicating, care about abstract concepts and theories, and prefer to be alone. They prefer to learn general principles rather than specific knowledge. They achieve a higher degree of generalization than field-dependent students, but there is no significant difference in the amount of knowledge they obtain. *For example, Li Lang is accustomed to studying alone and is less susceptible to the influence and interference of the surrounding environment when facing problems. He tends to make judgments based on his own internal clues and shows a tendency to learn casually, independently, and innovatively, with a greater interest in natural sciences. A conclusion can be drawn that Li Lang is a field-independent student.*

**Field dependence** refers to the learning style of learners who take their own environment as an external reference and obtain knowledge and information from the stimulation and communication within the environment. According to perceptual selectivity, field dependence also refers to the perceptual characteristics and cognitive styles that make it difficult for learners to separate a perceptual target from its background. Field-dependent students often make judgments about objective things based on external cues, and their attitudes and self-cognition are easily affected by the surrounding environment (especially by authoritative people) or background. It is often not easy for field-dependent students to make judgments about things independently, but they tend to follow others' opinions and obtain standards from others. Their behaviors are often socially oriented. They have high social sensitivity and are fond of social activities. *For example, Elizabeth is more interested in people than things, likes to learn in a collective environment, and is easily influenced by complex background factors when facing problems. She shows a learning tendency of following rules, seeking common ground, and being organized, and she prefers social sciences. That is to say, Elizabeth is a field-dependent student.*

Field-independent students and field-dependent students have different learning characteristics (Table 8-5).

Table 8-5  Learning characteristics of field-independent students and field-dependent students

| Learning characteristics | Field-dependent students | Field-independent students |
|---|---|---|
| Preference for learning interests | They like the humanities, social sciences, and specific knowledge; they rely on external feedback, and their academic performance is prone to decline when criticized. High school students with field independence are better off choosing the humanities. | They like mathematics, natural sciences, and abstract, theoretical, as well as unorganized materials; they have a keen interest in the learning materials themselves. High school students with field independence are better off choosing sciences. |
| Academic achievement tendency | Poor grades in natural sciences; good grades in the humanities and social sciences. | Good grades in natural sciences; poor grades in the humanities and social sciences. |
| Preference for learning strategies | They like to discuss things with peers or engage in collaborative learning, and they are easily dominated by extrinsic motivation. | They do not like external influences very much and are dominated by intrinsic motivation. |
| Preference for teaching styles | They like the teaching method that has a rigorous, systematic, and organized structure. They need to be provided with external structures and clear guidance and explanations from teachers. | They prefer teaching methods with a relatively free, less structured, and less rigorous format and enjoy learning unstructured materials. They will achieve better learning outcomes in the big-step teaching mode. Nonetheless, in the small-step teaching mode, there is no notable significant difference in learning outcomes between the two types of learners. |

**Continued table**

| Learning characteristics | Field-dependent students | Field-independent students |
|---|---|---|
| Preference for cognitive styles | They are good at grasping the whole and are fond of general and holistic perception. | They are good at analyzing various factors as a whole and prefer perception-based analysis. |

## 8.4.2 Reflective learning style and impulsive learning style

According to Jerome Kagan et al. (1964), reflective learning style refers to a cognitive style with which a learner tends to carefully consider the observed phenomena and problems when he is in an unfamiliar situation and is committed to contemplating problems clearly before taking action. Reflective students always approach cognitive tasks by carefully and thoroughly examining hypotheses and giving answers only when they are sure there are no doubts. When they encounter a problem, they tend to think deeply, spend enough time considering and examining the problem, weigh various solutions to the problem, and then choose the best solution that meets multiple conditions, so they make fewer mistakes.

Impulsive learning style refers to the cognitive style of individuals who tend to answer questions with the first answer that comes to mind when they are in an unfamiliar situation. Impulsive students are always eager to give answers to problems when solving cognitive tasks but do not usually consider all the possibilities of solving problems and sometimes begin to solve problems before they fully understand. They have an advantage in using low-level factual information to solve problems. However, although the speed of their problem-solving is very fast, the error rate is high, and they mostly use the holistic processing mode. When encountering a problem, they tend to test hypotheses quickly, make hasty decisions based on partial information or incomplete analysis of it, react quickly, but are likely to make mistakes.

Table 8-6  Learning characteristics of reflective students and impulsive students

| Learning characteristics | Reflective students | Impulsive students |
|---|---|---|
| Response and accuracy | Slow response; high accuracy | Fast response; poor accuracy |
| Information processing strategy characteristics | Detailed processing mode | Holistic processing mode |
| Academic achievement tendency | Better grades on learning tasks that require detailed analysis | Better grades on learning tasks that require holistic explanations |

|  |  | Continued table |
| --- | --- | --- |
| Learning characteristics | Reflective students | Impulsive students |
| Preference for problem-solving | Examine carefully and ensure that there is no problems before giving answers. | Be not used to thinking holistically the possibilities of solving problems before they are fully understood. |

The learning characteristics of reflective students and impulsive students are of great difference (Table 8-6). The difference between them is particularly significant for school education because students with different cognitive styles can improve their current situation to a certain extent through certain training. It is worth learning from the example of how Confucius educated students based on their cognitive styles 2,500 years ago.

*Zilu once asked his teacher Confucius: "Do I act immediately as soon as I hear anything?" Confucius said, "Because your father and brother are still alive, how can you proceed without first consulting them as soon as you hear it?" Ran You asked, "Do I act immediately as soon as I hear anything?" Confucius said, "Do act as soon as you hear it." Gongxi Hua said, "Zilu asked, 'Do I act as soon as I hear anything?' You said, 'As long as your father and brother are still alive, how can you not ask them to do something as soon as you hear it?' Ran You asked, 'Do I act as soon as I hear anything?' You said, 'Act as soon as you hear it.' I have been a little confused and I'd like to know why." Confucius said, "Ran You often hesitates to do things in everyday life, so I encourage him to proceed; Zilu is braver than others, so I want to remind him to be cautious." We can draw a conclusion from the story that Zilu was a student with an impulsive cognitive style while Ran You had a reflective cognitive style.*

### 8.4.3 Holistic type and serial type

The holistic learning style and serial learning style reflect differences in cognitive logical reasoning modes in learning. According to the English psychologist Pask et al. (1976; 1988), the **holistic type** refers to the cognitive way in which a learner achieves an overall grasp of the learning material by using illustrative examples and analogies when learning it. The serial type refers to the cognitive way in which a learner grasps each part of the learning material by focusing on a series of material details continuously or successively when learning it. Holistic students tend to adopt holistic strategies, and their cognitive characteristics are "hypothesis oriented". Serial learners tend to adopt sequential strategies, and their cognitive characteristics are "step-by-step". The specific learning characteristics of holistic students and serial students are illustrated in Table 8-7.

Table 8-7  Learning characteristics of holistic students and serial students

| Learning characteristics | Holistic-type students | Serial-type students |
|---|---|---|
| Preference for information processing | In a free learning context, they treat the task as a whole when remembering and generalizing information and strive to grasp the "high-level relationship". | They focus on the smaller details, break the problem down into smaller parts, and establish a lower sequential relationship. They are used to absorbing lengthy sequential data and cannot tolerate irrelevant information, so they connect information based on simple relationships when learning, memorizing, and summarizing. |
| Preference for cognitive style | They study the learning material as a whole, consider multiple hypotheses, and take into account all possibilities simultaneously in the problem-solving process. They believe that the whole is greater than the sum of its parts. | They tend to analyze problems step by step and only consider one hypothesis or attribute at each step. After the first hypothesis is established, the second is further considered, the results of the problem are deduced one by one, and each hypothesis has its own chronological order. |
| Preference for problem solving | They consider multiple assumptions and various possibilities from a broad perspective in the process of solving problems. They like to browse through a lot of information to find paradigms or relationships and test a large number of predicted or related hypotheses. They are used to taking big steps and independently searching for answers. They are often able to combine seemingly unrelated materials in novel ways to solve complex problems faster, but they cannot clearly explain their problem-solving steps. | They focus on exploring specific and clear materials without looking up information and use a step-by-step approach to confirm or deny their hypotheses. They are used to solving problems in linear steps and tend to search for answers step by step, with each step logically following the previous one; thus, they can clearly explain their problem-solving steps. |
| Preference for learning strategies. | They prefer the holistic strategy and the simultaneous processing strategy. They construct the overall meaning framework according to their own understanding, grasp the main idea, and then analyze the relationship between the specific meaning and the overall meaning based on the positions of the details. | They prefer the serial strategy and the successive processing strategy. They move from one topic to the next sequentially in a straight line when reading and understanding material. They often concentrate their attention on operational details and procedures and build knowledge bit by bit to learn the whole material. |
| making mistakes | They gain a superficial understanding through cursory observation; they are satisfied with a superficial knowledge of a subject; they easily draw hasty conclusions. | They lack foresight; they do not see the forest for the trees; they are afraid of using analogies, do not try to build a big picture, are poor at coming up with their own hypotheses, and are afraid to take cognitive risks. |

### 8.4.4 Deep processing and surface processing

According to Fergus I. M. Craik and Robert S. Lockhart (1972), school children process information in two ways: one is deep processing and the other is surface processing. Deep processing refers to a thorough understanding of the learned content and connecting it with a larger conceptual framework to obtain a deeper meaning. Surface processing refers to memorizing superficial information about the learned content without connecting it to a larger conceptual framework. Deep processing is conducive to focusing on understanding, while surface processing is conducive to focusing on factual learning and memory.

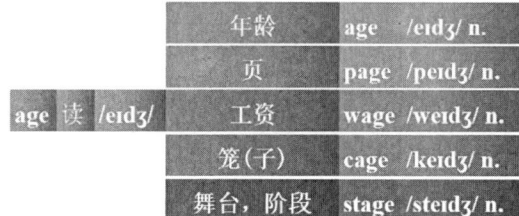

**Figure 8-3  Deep processing of English vocabulary memory**

Source：何心勇，《英语词经（初级版）》，中国科学文化音像出版社，2024，第 34 页．

*For example, when a school child learns the word "age /eɪdʒ/," does he notice that it has something to do with other words such as "page /peɪdʒ/", "wage /weɪdʒ/", "cage /keɪdʒ/", "stage /steɪdʒ/", and "cabbage /ˈkæbɪdʒ/"? Does he find the difference between the pronunciation of "cabbage" and those of the other words? If he only memorizes the spelling, pronunciation, and meaning of "age /eɪdʒ/" without exploring further, he is using surface processing. Instead, if he not only realizes the relationships and differences between "age /eɪdʒ/" and the others but also uses complex memory strategies such as the rhythmic chant method and chunking method as follows (Figure 8-3), he is using deep processing.*

### 8.4.5 Convergent cognitive style and divergent cognitive style

According to Ellis Paul Torrance (1974), convergent cognitive style refers to the cognitive style of learners who often show the characteristics of convergent thinking in the process of solving problems. This is manifested in collecting or synthesizing information and knowledge, using logical laws to narrow the scope of solutions until the most appropriate and only correct solution is found. Learners with a convergent cognitive style focus on finding a single answer and prefer a single solution to a problem.

In daily life, learners with a convergent cognitive style may also be more inclined to use logical thinking and solve problems in a targeted manner. *For example, when faced with a math problem, learners with a convergent cognitive style may carefully analyze the problem, gather necessary information, and use logical reasoning to reach a precise answer. They may look for specific rules, patterns, or methods to solve the problem, avoiding too much irrelevant information.* Therefore, individuals with this convergent cognitive style are more likely to take a direct and purposeful approach to problem-solving, aiming for clear and definitive results.

**Divergent cognitive style** refers to the cognitive style of learners who often show the characteristics of divergent thinking in the process of solving problems. Their thinking develops in many different directions, leading them to believe that a concept can develop into all relevant aspects, eventually producing a variety of possibilities rather than a single correct answer, thus easily generating creative and novel ideas. *For example, learners with a divergent cognitive style believe that there are many solutions to one problem and that all roads lead to Rome.*

In daily life, learners with a divergent cognitive style may be more inclined to think and deal with problems creatively, emphasizing the diversity and innovation of ideas. *For example, when facing a creative project, they may adopt different perspectives, explore various possibilities, and try to find novel solutions. They may involve many different concepts, ideas, and viewpoints, rather than being limited to specific rules or patterns. In team discussions, they may propose many different ideas and viewpoints, promoting diversity and creativity in team thinking.* Therefore, individuals with this divergent cognitive style tend to adopt open, innovative, and diverse approaches to problem-solving in order to stimulate new thinking and creativity.

## 8.4.6 Simultaneous cognitive style and successive cognitive style

According to Hermann Ebbinghaus (1885), the simultaneous cognitive style refers to the cognitive style of learners who adopt a wide-field approach when solving problems, consider multiple hypotheses at the same time, and take into account various possibilities for solving problems.

In daily life, individuals with the simultaneous cognitive style may tend to handle multiple tasks or sources of information and can effectively switch between these tasks. *For example, when doing household chores, individuals with the simultaneous cognitive style may simultaneously handle several tasks, such as cooking while tidying up the kitchen or listening to music while organizing files.*

These individuals may prefer working in an environment with a certain degree of chaos or diversity rather than a completely orderly one. They may be better at handling multiple tasks simultaneously and can flexibly shift attention between different tasks to accomplish them effectively.

**Successive cognitive style** refers to a cognitive style with which learners often analyze problems step by step when solving problems. They consider only one hypothesis or one attribute at each step, and the proposed hypothesis has a clear sequence in time. The second hypothesis is tested only after the first hypothesis is established until the answer to the problem is found. Both verbal manipulation and memory are successive processing, and some studies suggest women are better at this type of processing.

In daily life, individuals with the successive cognitive style may tend to use sequential thinking, gradually processing information and tasks. *For example, when individuals prepare a dish, they may follow the steps in a recipe, first preparing the ingredients, then cooking each dish step by step according to the instructions, and finally completing the entire dish.* Those who act in this way belong to the successive cognitive style. They may prefer to complete tasks according to a fixed plan and sequence, solving problems step by step until they achieve the desired outcome. Therefore, individuals with the successive cognitive style are more inclined to proceed with tasks methodically and achieve goals through gradual actions.

The differences between successive processing and simultaneous processing are not in the processing level but in the cognitive mode. Learning is more effective when the learning material matches students' cognitive styles better.

### 8.4.7 Extroversion and introversion, sensing and intuition, thinking and feeling, judging and perceiving

The theory of four pairs of dimensions, proposed by Carl Jung (1921) and further developed by Isabel Briggs Myers and Katharine Cook Briggs (1995) in the MBTI (Myers-Briggs Type Indicator), delineates fundamental aspects of personality that significantly influence learning styles and behaviors, and offers insights into how individuals perceive and process information differently. Based on Jung and Myers et al., Jin-Kei Kise (2009) believes that students' cognitive styles can be inferred by observing their behavioral clues. He categorizes students' behavior into four aspects: extroversion and introversion, sensing and intuition, thinking and feeling, judging and perceiving.

1. Extroversion style and introversion style

**Extroversion** refers to a personality trait characterized by an outgoing, sociable, and energetic nature, with a tendency to seek external stimulation and derive energy from interacting with others. Extroverts tend to seek social interactions, thrive in group settings, and enjoy external activities. They are often characterized by their assertiveness, talkativeness, and preference for external stimulation. In the learning context, extroverts may thrive in collaborative environments where they can engage in discussions, group projects, and interactive learning activities. *For example, in a classroom setting, an extroverted student may enjoy participating in group discussions, working on team projects, and actively engaging with peers during lectures.* Whether doing homework in the classroom or at home, extroverted students are often restless, tapping on the desk, sharpening pencils, drinking water, going to the toilet, or trying to leave their seats from time to time.

On the other hand, **introversion** is a personality trait characterized by a focus on inner thoughts and feelings rather than seeking stimulation from the external environment. Introverts typically require time alone to rejuvenate and often prefer deep, meaningful conversations to small talk. They tend to be reflective, observant, and concentrated on internal thoughts and feelings. In the learning environment, introverts may excel in quiet, solitary settings where they can concentrate deeply on their studies without being distracted by external stimuli. *For instance, an introverted learner may prefer studying alone in a quiet library or working on individual assignments where they can focus without interruptions.* Students with an introversion style don't necessarily sit still all the time; they may speak loudly and participate in group discussions, but they need more time for reflection and preparation.

In summary, the extroversion and introversion theory provides valuable insights into how individuals interact with their environment, approach social interactions, and engage in learning activities. By understanding these personality dimensions, educators can create inclusive learning environments that cater to the diverse needs and preferences of students, fostering optimal learning outcomes for all.

2. Sensory style and intuitive style

**Sensory style** is a cognitive preference characterized by a reliance on concrete and tangible information obtained through the five senses—sight, sound, touch, taste, and smell—and an emphasis on present and factual details. Individuals tend to focus on the here and now, relying on factual data and details. *For instance, in a classroom setting, a student with a sensory style might prefer hands-on activities, where they* *can directly interact with materials to understand concepts.* In daily life, they might excel in tasks that require precise instructions or involve practical skills, such as cooking, where following step-by-step directions leads to a successful outcome. Students with a sensory style always ask the teacher to give examples and provide clear guidance until a solid "bridge" is established between their existing knowledge and the new knowledge they want to learn.

On the other hand, intuitive style refers to a cognitive preference characterized by a focus on abstract thinking, patterns, and future possibilities rather than relying on concrete and factual information or immediate sensory experiences. They look beyond the immediate facts to envision possibilities and connections. In a learning environment, they might enjoy brainstorming sessions or creative projects where they can explore different ideas and perspectives. *For example, when faced with a problem, they might prefer to brainstorm various solutions rather than following a linear approach.* In real-life situations, they may excel in professions that require innovative thinking, such as entrepreneurship or design, where they can envision new concepts and solutions. Students with the intuitive style always ask questions that go beyond the scope of the guidance or beyond the topic that teachers are teaching. They either want to showcase their uniqueness or connect two unrelated things. They may also perform poorly on simple assignments such as math exercises or fill-in-the-blank tasks.

In essence, while individuals with the sensory style prefer concrete, factual information and focus on the here and now, individuals with the intuitive style thrive on abstract thinking and contemplate future possibilities. Understanding these cognitive preferences can be beneficial in various contexts, from educational settings to professional environments. By recognizing and accommodating the different learning styles, educators can create inclusive learning environments that cater specifically to diverse cognitive preferences, ultimately improving learning outcomes for all students.

### 3. Thinking style and feeling style

**Thinking style** refers to the cognitive approach individuals employ when engaging with information. Those who lean towards a thinking style tend to prioritize logic, analysis, and objective reasoning in their decision-making processes. They may rely on the systematic evaluation of facts and evidence to arrive at conclusions. *For example, in a learning context, a student with a thinking style might excel in subjects like mathematics or science, where logical reasoning and problem-solving skills are paramount. They may prefer structured learning environments that* *emphasize critical thinking and deductive reasoning.*

On the other hand, the **feeling style** pertains to the emotional and intuitive aspect of cognition. Individuals with a feeling style are more attuned to their emotions, values, and interpersonal relationships when making decisions. They may prioritize empathy, compassion, and subjective experiences over strict logic. *For instance, in a group discussion, a person with a feeling style might focus on fostering harmony and understanding among group members, valuing emotional connection and empathy rather than purely rational arguments.* In a learning context, students with a feeling style may excel in subjects like literature, social sciences, or the arts, where subjective interpretation and emotional engagement play significant roles. They may thrive in environments that encourage creativity, collaboration, and self-expression, valuing personal connections and emotional resonance within their learning experiences.

Overall, understanding the thinking style and feeling style provides insights into how individuals approach learning tasks, solve problems, and interact with others. By recognizing and appreciating these differences, educators can design more inclusive and effective learning environments that cater to diverse cognitive and affective needs.

### 4. Judging style and perceiving style

**Judging style** refers to a cognitive preference employed by individuals who prefer structure, organization, and decisiveness in their lives. They tend to have a systematic approach to learning and prefer clear goals and deadlines. These individuals are inclined towards planning, making schedules, and following them diligently. In a learning context, they are likely to excel in tasks where there are clear guidelines and a step-by-step process to follow. *For example, a student with a judging style might prefer to study for exams by creating detailed study schedules, setting specific goals for each study session, and adhering strictly to their plan.* However, students with the judging style are not necessarily better at drawing conclusions (judgments). They quickly search for answers to each specific question and complete assignments quickly.

On the other hand, perceiving style refers to a cognitive preference characterized by adaptability, spontaneity, and openness to new experiences and information. Individuals with the perceiving style prefer to keep their options open, enjoy exploring new ideas, and tend to be more comfortable with uncertainty. In learning, they may thrive in environments that allow for exploration and creativity, where there is room for improvisation and spontaneity. *For instance, a student with a perceiving style might prefer to approach studying by exploring various resources, adapting their study methods based on their interests and intuition, and being open to new information and perspectives.* Students with the perceiving style are not necessarily more perceptive than others but are open to new information (perception). They tend to scroll through the material slowly, and if they see pictures or content that interest them, they stop and read it carefully until they finish reading, and then jump to something else. Students with the judging style may have already finished the assignment, while students with the perceiving style may not have finished a single question.

In summary, individuals with a judging style prefer structure and organization, while those with a perceiving style lean towards flexibility and spontaneity. Understanding these cognitive styles can help educators tailor their teaching methods to accommodate different learning preferences. By providing structured learning environments for judging-style learners and more flexible and open-ended opportunities for perceiving-style learners, educators can create a more inclusive and effective learning experience for all students.

## 8.5 Identification on cognitive styles

Cognitive style identification refers to the process of identifying and understanding an individual's preferred ways of perceiving, processing, and organizing information. In teaching practice, an indispensable link from theoretical research to the application of cognitive styles is to identify school children's cognitive styles, of which the important prerequisites are a correct identification attitude and reliable identification tools.

The correct identification attitude refers to maintaining an objective and open-minded approach while assessing an individual's cognitive preferences. It involves avoiding bias and preconceptions to accurately identify the individual's unique way of perceiving and processing information. The correct identification attitude is not to label students, but to help teachers better understand students and assist students in understanding their own cognitive styles so that teachers' teaching and students' learning can be aligned.

Reliable identification tools are assessment instruments or methods that have been validated through research and demonstrated to consistently measure cognitive styles accurately. These tools provide consistent and dependable results, thereby enhancing the validity and reliability of the identification process.

## 8.5.1 Observational method

The observational method is a research technique whereby researchers observe subjects in their natural environment or in controlled settings to gather data. The observational method can be used to observe students' behaviors, reactions, and problem-solving approaches in learning activities. Researchers can record how students interact with learning materials, how they approach tasks, and how they respond to challenges. By analyzing these observations, researchers can identify patterns and tendencies in students' cognitive styles, such as whether they prefer holistic or serial processing, whether they rely more on external cues or internal cues, and whether they exhibit convergent or divergent thinking. These observations help categorize students into different cognitive style types, facilitating a deeper understanding of individual learning preferences and informing personalized teaching strategies.

Based on Jung (1921) and Myers et al. (1995), Jin-Kei Kise (2009) believes that students' cognitive styles can be inferred by observing their behavioral clues. He categorizes students' behavior into four aspects: extroversion and introversion, sensing and intuition, thinking and feeling, and judging and perceiving (refer to 8.4.7). By observing their behaviors (Table 8-8), students' cognitive styles can be identified.

Table 8-8  Behavioral clues and cognitive style tendencies

| Extraverted style and introverted style: How do students gain energy for learning? | |
|---|---|
| Learners with extraverted style: <br>➤ May speak louder and be more restless than introverted students. <br>➤ May forget the answer while raising their hand and being asked to speak-they need to think before speaking. <br>➤ May perform better when whispering with other students or in group cooperation if conditions permit. <br>➤ May prefer to readin their spare time. <br>➤ May say whatever comes to mind-answers, feelings, ideas, etc. <br>➤ May prefer to try first and then read. <br>➤ Will not be disturbed by interruptions. | Learners with introverted style: <br>➤ May respond relatively slowly in class discussions unless they are familiar with the topic of discussion in advance. <br>➤ May prefer reading and writing to discussing. <br>➤ May prefer to do homework alone or select partners independently. <br>➤ May need a slight pause to formulate a response even in one-on-one conversations. <br>➤ Tend to keep their answers, thoughts, and feelings to themselves unless asked. <br>➤ May prefer to read first and then try. <br>➤ Can be easily annoyed by interruptions. |
| Sensory style and intuitive style: What information do students notice first? | |
| Learners with sensing style <br>➤May interrupt during your guidance sessions, asking about things you plan to mention later. <br>➤ Find it difficult to come up with ideas for research projects. <br>➤ May request more examples from the teacher and dislike vague objectives. <br>➤ Seem to learn more from hands-on experience than from textbook learning. <br>➤ Might ask "Is it really like this?" | Learners with intuitive style <br>➤Might not read instructions, starting on tasks before you have finished verbal instructions. <br>➤ May suggest research ideas that are too complex or impractical for them to carry out. <br>➤ May be careless and make mistakes. <br>➤ Might ask if they can choose their own assignments. <br>➤ May enjoy "unrealistic" or fictional topics. |
| Thinking style and feeling style: How do students make decisions? | |
| Learners with thinking style <br>➤May enjoy criticizing and pointing out faults. <br>➤ Prefer to have control over things. <br>➤ Might not continue (they need to feel capable to take risks), if they feel they cannot succeed in doing something well. <br>➤ Seem to always argue their point — even with authority figures. <br>➤ Exhibit a competitive nature—they won't back down to save face and may not be good at expressing emotions. | Learners with feeling style <br>➤Might immediately show displeasure upon hearing a sad story or experiencing unfair treatment in class. <br>➤ Might show concern for those who fail. <br>➤ Won't do the assignments given by that teacher if they feel the teacher doesn't like them. <br>➤ May need feedback and encouragement—"Teacher, am I doing this right?" <br>➤ Will learn more from them if tasks assigned to them are related to human needs. <br>➤ Might interpret any criticism as a sign that others dislike them. |

Continued table

| Judging style and perceiving style: What is the student's lifestyle like? ||
|---|---|
| Learners with judging style<br>➤ May rush to complete tasks hastily and never revise once done.<br>➤ May not explore new sources of information or investigation methods.<br>➤ Can get upset if unexpected situations or changes occur in agendas or planned activities.<br>➤ May be too quickly confined by certain frameworks or concepts.<br>➤ Seem to approach everything based on established plans, goals, or memoranda (perhaps internalized rather than written down).<br>➤ May become increasingly anxious due to overwork and hope to finish before others can show their achievements.<br>➤ Likely appreciate clear expectations from others. | Learners with perceiving style<br>➤ May have done something with no tangible results, such as reading a book without taking notes, being unable to report, or engaging in a discussion without reaching any conclusions.<br>➤ May underestimate or overestimate the time needed to complete a task.<br>➤ Can be delighted when unexpected situations arise or changes occur in the class schedule, and may struggle to settle on a topic, research plan, or methods to use, continually exploring instead.<br>➤ May work until the last minute or request an extension and are always amazed by how quickly time passes.<br>➤ May surprise parents with the materials used (poster boards, 3D models, etc.) even though the task was assigned days ago.<br>➤ Too many expectations seem to be a hindrance to them. |

## 8.5.2 Rod and Frame Test

**Rod and Frame Test** (RFT) is a method to test cognitive style, which was designed by Herman Witkin, and the test instrument is the rod and frame apparatus. There is a slant light frame on a dark background. A bright rod is in the frame but independent of the frame surface and can be rotated. When the test starts, the subject is required to adjust the rod to what they perceive as vertical while being surrounded by a tilted frame. This test measures an individual's visual perception and orientation in relation to external visual cues. High scores indicate a greater reliance on internal cues (field independence), while low scores suggest a greater reliance on external cues (field dependence). The RFT helps researchers understand individual differences in perceptual styles and has applications in fields like psychology, education, and sports science (Witkin, H., Goodenough, D. R., Oltman, D. M., & Cox, P. K., 1977).

The RFT is currently used in the field of education to assess individuals' perceptual and cognitive styles. By presenting participants with a tilted frame and asking them to adjust a rod to match the perceived vertical line, educators can gain insights into students' ability to perceive spatial orientation. This information can be valuable for tailoring teaching strategies to accommodate different cognitive styles, helping educators better understand students' learning preferences and needs. Additionally, the RFT can aid in identifying students who may benefit from specific interventions or accommodations to optimize their learning experience.

### 8.5.3 Group Embedded Figures Test

**Group Embedded Figures Test** (GEFT), also known as the group hidden figures test, is a psychological assessment tool developed by Albert F. Chapin (1955). It aims to measure an individual's psychodynamic instability by analyzing their responses to abstract geometric figures. It helps identify cognitive styles, such as tendencies toward stability or instability in perception and thinking processes. Participants are presented with a series of ambiguous images and asked to interpret them (Figure 8-4). The test typically consists of a series of visual tasks where participants must locate simple shapes embedded within more complex designs. There are usually around 25 to 30 items in the test. The main focus of the test is to investigate participants' ability to distinguish embedded figures from the background, which reflects their cognitive style in terms of field dependence or field independence. Their interpretations are then analyzed to reveal underlying cognitive patterns and tendencies. Those who can eliminate the interference of background factors and quickly and easily perceive the designated simple figure from the complex figure belong to the field-independent type; those who find it more difficult to complete the task belong to the field-dependent type.

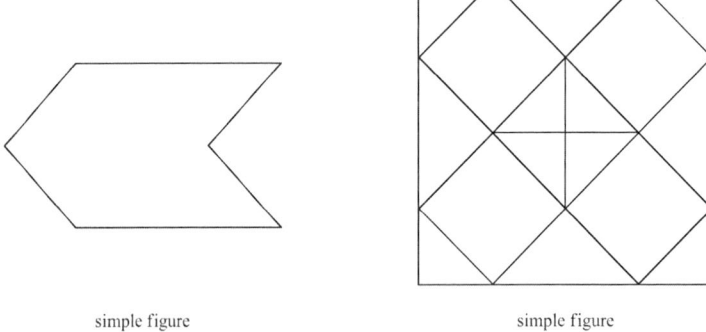

**Figure 8-4 Cognitive style figure test**

In educational settings, the GEFT can assist educators in understanding students' cognitive preferences and learning styles and aid in the development of tailored teaching strategies. By recognizing individual differences in cognitive processing, educators can adapt instructional methods to better suit students' needs and improve learning outcomes.

### 8.5.4 Scales and questionnaires

In the 1970s and 1980s, researchers began to study the measurement tools of learning styles, which mainly are scales and questionnaires as follows.

1. **Learning Style Inventory (LSI)**

Learning Style Inventory (LSI), compiled by the Dunns (1978), is primarily used to assess individuals' preferred learning styles. It is designed to identify how individuals process information and learn best, helping educators tailor teaching methods to suit different learning preferences. The LSI is suitable for a wide range of populations, including students, educators, and professionals engaged in learning and training activities.

The inventory typically consists of a series of questions or statements that respondents rate or rank based on their agreement or preference. The number of items in the LSI can vary depending on the specific version or adaptation used, but it usually contains around 20 to 30 items.

The main issues explored by the LSI include how individuals prefer to receive and process information (e. g., visual, auditory, kinesthetic), their preferred pace and structure of learning activities, their attitudes toward collaborative and independent study, and their comfort levels with various learning environments (e. g., quiet, interactive, hands-on). Overall, the LSI aims to provide insights into individuals' learning preferences and styles to inform instructional design and facilitate personalized learning experiences.

2. **Learning Style Profile**

Learning Style Profile (LSP), developed by Keefe (1982), is primarily used to assess individuals' learning preferences and styles. It is applicable to learners of various ages and educational backgrounds. It is designed to identify how individuals process information, interact with learning materials, and approach learning tasks. The LSP is suitable for a wide range of individuals, including students, educators, and professionals. It typically consists of a set of questions or statements that participants respond to, aiming to uncover their preferences in various aspects of learning, such as sensory preferences, learning environment preferences, social interaction preferences, and cognitive processing preferences. The number of items in the LSP may vary depending on the specific version or application, but it generally covers a comprehensive range of questions to provide a detailed profile of an individual's learning style.

### 3. Learning Style Questionnaires

Learning Style Questionnaire (LSQ), developed by Honey and Mumford (1982), is primarily used to assess an individual's preferred learning style. It is designed to identify how individuals learn best and how they prefer to approach learning tasks. The LSQ is suitable for a wide range of individuals, including students, professionals, and anyone interested in understanding their learning preferences. The questionnaire typically consists of a series of questions or statements, and the number of items can vary depending on the specific version of the questionnaire being used. The questions generally aim to investigate how individuals prefer to engage with learning tasks, their attitudes toward different learning strategies, and their tendencies in problem-solving situations.

### 4. Cognitive Style Analysis

According to McKenna and Austin (1969), Cognitive Style Analysis (CSA) is primarily used to measure cognitive styles along two dimensions: holistic-analytic and verbal-imagery. It aims to assess individuals' preferred ways of processing information and problem-solving strategies. The target audience typically includes individuals from various fields such as education, psychology, and organizational development. The CSA questionnaire typically consists of a series of items or statements designed to evaluate participants' preferences for holistic versus analytic thinking and verbal versus imagery processing. The questionnaire assesses how individuals approach tasks, solve problems, and perceive information. It may include questions related to how participants prefer to organize information, their preferred learning strategies, and their tendencies in problem-solving.

### 5. Solomon Learning Style Self-test

Solomon Learning Style Self-test, developed by Barboro A. Solomon (1992), aims to assess individuals' learning styles. The questionnaire is designed to help individuals understand their learning preferences and methods, enabling them to learn more effectively and adapt to various learning environments. The test is suitable for individuals of all ages and educational backgrounds. It typically consists of a set of questions or statements that respondents answer to identify their preferences in learning activities, approaches to problem-solving, information processing, and interaction with learning materials and environments. By evaluating individuals' preferences and tendencies in different learning aspects, the questionnaire can provide targeted learning advice and guidance.

## 8.6　Individualized instruction according to learning styles

Since each learning style has its positive and negative aspects as well as advantages and disadvantages, the effective utilization of students' learning styles also involves "promoting strengths" and "making up for weaknesses".

### 8.6.1　Individualized teaching guidance strategies

Individualized teaching guidance strategies are tailored approaches to instruction that cater to the unique needs, strengths, and learning styles of individual students. These strategies involve personalized learning plans, targeted interventions, and differentiated instruction to support each student's academic progress and development.

**1. The matching strategy of "promoting strengths"**

The matching strategy refers to the approach that teachers adopt in designing and implementing teaching methods, aligning them with the strengths of students' learning styles, in order to fully utilize the learning styles in which students excel. When a student's learning style fits well with the teacher's teaching style and other factors in the learning process, their academic performance (scores) is better. If the teacher's teaching style does not match the student's learning style and is not adjusted in a timely manner, it is easy to lead to style conflicts, causing students not to concentrate and resulting in poor exam results, gradually developing a sense of disinterest in learning, and ultimately losing interest in the course. The emotions and confidence of both teachers and students will also be affected (Dunn R., Dunn, K., & Price, G., 1982). When students' field orientation matches their teacher's, their learning outcomes are more favorable (Packer & Bain, 1978). The match of field-independent teachers with field-independent students is the best combination (Saracho, 1981). When teachers align their teaching styles with students' learning styles, students not only learn more easily but also experience greater success.

**2. The mismatching strategy of "making up for weaknesses"**

The mismatching strategy means that teachers intentionally adopt strategies that do not align with the learning styles that students excel in during teaching design and implementation, according to the negative aspects and disadvantages of students' learning styles, in order to make up for some deficiencies and disadvantages of students' learning styles. Students face a variety of learning tasks and developmental requirements, and their preferred learning style is often not sufficient to meet the requirements of teaching and training goals, so it is necessary to promote the continuous improvement of their learning style by "making up for weaknesses." *For example, field-independent school children can be assigned to participate in tasks that require social sensitivity, while field-dependent school children can also be assigned to perform tasks that require the application of analytical skills to be completed independently* (Chen Qi, Liu Rude, 2007). When school children realize that certain aspects of their learning styles are not compatible with teaching and training objectives, it is particularly important to exert their subjective initiative to compensate for certain deficiencies and disadvantages in their learning style.

In order to make comprehensive use of the two basic teaching strategies of "promoting strengths" and "making up for weaknesses", teachers should effectively master and flexibly use a variety of teaching methods, so as to alternate or cross-transform various teaching methods according to different types of learning styles in the process of teaching, and implement balanced matching teaching strategies and intentionally mismatching teaching strategies for different styles. If teachers cannot effectively master and flexibly use a variety of teaching methods but just use their own preferred teaching methods, it may lead to the polarization of students' learning in the corresponding courses.

### 8.6.2 Individualized teaching guidance modes

Differentiated teaching guidance modes can be designed for students with different learning styles in collective teaching: simultaneous matching (mismatching) mode and successive matching (mismatching) mode (Mo Lei, 2007).

**1. Simultaneous matching mode**

Simultaneous matching (mismatching) mode refers to matching or mismatching different types of learners at the same time. The basic procedure is as follows (Figure 8-5):

1) Conduct whole-class instruction. The teacher presents learning objectives and requirements to the entire class, teaching the most fundamental knowledge using a unified approach.

2) Proceed with differentiated instruction based on classification, allowing students to self-study in their preferred ways while the teacher supervises and guides. After each group of students has completed their learning tasks, the teacher gathers the entire class for summarization and asks each group to introduce their learning methods respectively, fostering mutual inspiration and assigning the next stage of learning tasks.

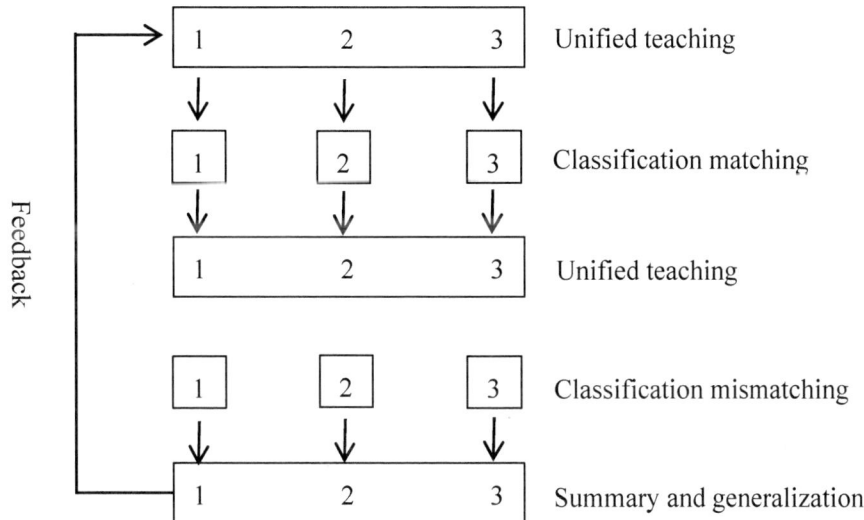

Figure 8-5  Simultaneous matching (mismatching) mode diagram

Source：莫雷,《教育心理学》,教育科学出版社,2007,第298页.

3) Proceed with mismatching, instructing each group to learn the new task in a non-preferred way.

4) Gather the whole class for summarization, pointing out the issues that must be noted when utilizing various learning methods.

In this mode, regardless of the type of student learning style, they can receive both matching and mismatching at the same time, hence termed the simultaneous matching (mismatching) mode (Refer to Appendix 1).

2. Successive matching mode

Successive matching (mismatching) mode refers to alternating matching or mismatching different types of learners at different times, as shown in Table 8-9. "+" indicates matching in the table, and "-" indicates mismatching.

Stage 1. The teaching method adopted by the teacher matches the first type of students' learning style but mismatches with the second and third types.

Stage 2. The teaching method matches the second type of students' learning styles while naturally mismatching with the first and third types.

Stage 3. The teaching method matches the third type of students' learning style, naturally mismatching with the first and second types.

The opportunities for matching and mismatching are equal for different types of students' learning styles in different teaching modes. In both simultaneous matching (mismatching) and successive matching (mismatching) modes, these two strategies are used simultaneously or interchangeably, allowing for continuous improvement and refinement of different students' learning styles, leading to a more comprehensive development of learning capabilities (Refer to Appendix 2).

Table 8-9  Successive matching (mismatching) mode

| Matching (Mismatching) Mode / Teaching stage / Learning style | Students with the first learning style | Students with the second learning style | Students with the third learning style |
| --- | --- | --- | --- |
| Stage 1 | + | − | − |
| Stage 2 | − | + | − |
| Stage 3 | − | − | + |

Learning styles vary from person to person. Some students are visual learners, while others prefer auditory or kinesthetic approaches. Understanding your own learning style can help you study more effectively and achieve better results. Students exhibit diverse approaches to learning, which can be broadly categorized into different styles. These styles encompass various preferences in acquiring knowledge, processing information, and engaging with educational materials. By recognizing and accommodating these differences, educators can create more effective learning environments tailored to individual needs. Whether they are visual, auditory, kinesthetic, or other styles, each student's unique learning profile influences how they comprehend and retain information. Therefore, fostering inclusive approaches that acknowledge and respect these differences can enhance student engagement, motivation, and overall academic success. Ultimately, embracing diverse learning styles promotes a more holistic and equitable educational experience for all learners.

# Ⅰ. Review and reflection

learning styles
the Dunn's model and theory
Keefe's model and theory
Curry's onion model
Sternberg's theory of mental self-government
Riding's theory of two-dimensional structure
social factors
physiological factors
psychological factors

cognitive style
field independence
field dependence
impulsive learning style
holistic type
serial type
deep processing
surface processing
convergent cognitive style
divergent cognitive style
simultaneous cognitive style

successive cognitive style
extroversion and introversion
sensing and intuition
thinking and feeling
judging and perceiving
rod and frame test
group embedded figures test
Learning Style Inventory
Learning Style Profile
Learning Style Questionnaire (LSQ)
Cognitive Style Analysis
Solomon Learning Style Self-test
the matching strategy
the mismatching strategy
simultaneous matching (mismatching) mode
successive matching (mismatching) mode

## II. Design a high school science class according to simultaneous matching mode.

## III. Design an English lesson according to successive matching mode.

(Refer to Appendixes I and II)

# Appendix Ⅰ

**Answers to Questions of Material Analysis of Every Chapter.**
**Chapter 1 Ⅱ. Material Analysis**
This curve shows that forgetting starts immediately after learning, and the forgetting speed is very fast in the initial time. With the elapse of time, the forgetting speed gradually slows down, and forgetting almost no longer occurs after a long time. It can be seen that the process of forgetting is uneven, and its trend is fast first and slow then, more first and less then and shows a negative acceleration. After nine hours, the rate of forgetting slows down nine hours later and continues to decline even after the passage of many days.

**Chapter 2 Ⅱ. Material Analysis**
The performance of the girl described in the poem usually takes place in pre-operational stage according to Piaget's cognitive-stage theory.

According to Piaget's cognitive-stage theory, the cognitive development is composed of 4 stages: sensorimotor stage, pre-operational stage, concrete operational stage (concrete operations), and formal operational stage (formal operations).

In the pre-operational stage (2 to 7 years), the child develops a representational system and uses symbols to represent people, places, and events. Language and imaginative play are important manifestations of this stage. Thinking is still not logical.

"妾"means the child in the poem is a girl. "妾发初覆额"means that the girl's age is about 4-6 years old or so, belonging to the pre-operational stage. According to Piaget, imaginative play are important manifestation of this stage. So,"折花门前剧" suggests that the characteristic of the girl of this stage—she likes playing games. And "郎骑竹马来,绕床弄青梅" suggests the game she plays is imaginative; and their thinking is illogical.

In a word,"长干行"describes children's cognitive development of thinking and imagination.

**Chapter 3 Ⅱ. Material Analysis**
Zhang Shuo **likes to argue** due to the development of abstract logical thinking, which has advantages and disadvantages.

Due to the development of abstract logical thinking, adolescents' views on themselves and the surrounding environment have undergone great changes, and their behavior has also undergone various changes. **Middle school children like to argue.** Once adolescents acquire the new way of thinking of formal operations, they always want to practice, consolidate, and improve it. A child who used to be very obedient now likes to argue and talk back to his parents after entering middle school because, at this time, he realizes that his parents' opinions are not always right. Even if they are right, things might have been better done using other methods (he thinks of other possibilities and can collect various facts to prove his hypothesis). The reason why he doesn't argue with his parents is that he just doesn't want to argue, and the sly smile on the corner of his mouth has already explained everything. In short, as he thinks deeper, he discovers the essence behind the phenomenon that he did not see in the past.

Wise parents who know that their child's tendency to argue is a sign of maturity will accept this kind of disobedience happily. Whenever an argument arises, they focus on the principle aspect of the problem rather than escalating into meaningless arguments. If the child's opinion is correct, parents should sincerely accept it. If it's not right, through equal discussion, parents should let their children have a deeper understanding of the complexity and diversity of things, as well as the reasons behind the parents' claims. If children cannot understand for a while, parents should be patient and give them enough time to think and make judgments.

Chapter 4 Ⅱ. Material Analysis

According to Asubel's learning theory, kindergarteners are very different from middle school students in learning the poem. The kindergarteners' learning is the rote learning and the middle school students' learning is meaningful reception learning.

The rote learning refers to the failure of learning materials to establish artificial and substantial connection with original cognitive structure. The meaningful reception learning refers to the learning materials linked with original knowledge in non-artificial and substantial way.

The kindergarteners learn the poem by reading many times, so they can recite the poem, but they do not understand it. The learning process of kindergarteners does not link the poem with their own original knowledge in the substantial way. They just learn the literal poem.

The middle school students learn the poem by understanding the meaning of the poem. It's not the rote learning. They connect the poem with their own cognitive structure in non-artificial and substantial way. They learn the internal meaning of the poem.

Above all, kindergarteners' learning process is rote learning and middle school students' learning process is meaningful reception learning.

### Chapter 5 Ⅱ. Material Analysis

1. According to Maslow, basic human needs are divided into five kinds: physiological needs, security needs, love and belonging needs, respect needs and self-actualization needs. Maslow divided the five needs into deficiency needs and growth needs. Among them, the first four kinds of needs are deficient needs, which are necessary for human beings to maintain survival activities. After they are satisfied, the intensity will be reduced. The need for self-actualization belongs to the need for growth, and it can never be satisfied. In other words, the need for self-actualization will not decrease with the satisfaction, but will be enhanced with the satisfaction, so the pursuit of knowledge is endless.

Learning belongs to theself-actualization need which belongs to the growth need, and the self-actualization need will not decrease with the satisfaction, so learning is endless.

2. According to knowledge view and student view of constructivism, *readers* with different experience who read *Hamlet will construct* different Hamlets.

Constructivism believes that knowledge can't exist outside the individual in the form of entity. Although we give knowledge a certain external form through language symbols, learners still understand and construct their own knowledge based on their own experience background.

Constructionism holds that learners can often form the explanation of problems based on relevant experience and cognitive ability when learning new information and solving new problems, and this explanation derived from their empirical background. As a result of the difference of experience background, students' understanding of the problem is often different.

According to knowledge view and student view of constructivism, as a result of the difference of experience background, readers' understanding of the problem is often different. Readers still understand and construct their own knowledge based on their own experience background. Different *readers* with different experience who read *Hamlet will construct* different Hamlets.

### Chapter 6 Ⅱ. Material Analysis

Xiaoqiang's confusion between the English alphabet and Chinese *pinyin* can be attributed to the concept of negative transfer within learning transfer theory. Learning transfer theory explores how prior learning experiences influence subsequent learning. There are two main types of transfer: positive transfer, where prior knowledge aids in new learning, and negative transfer, where prior knowledge interferes with or hinders new learning.

In Xiaoqiang's case, negative transfer has occurred due to the similarities and differences between the English alphabet and Chinese *pinyin*. Both systems share a number of similar-looking characters (e. g. , b, p, m, f, d, t, n, l, etc.) and have similar phonetic representations, albeit within different linguistic contexts and pronunciation rules. This similarity creates interference as Xiaoqiang's brain tries to distinguish between the two systems, particularly during the initial stages of learning the English alphabet.

Additionally, the sequence and usage of these characters in *pinyin* and the English alphabet might differ, causing further confusion. For instance, while *pinyin* is primarily used for representing sounds in Mandarin Chinese and follows specific tone rules, the English alphabet is used to construct words with varying phonetic combinations and grammar structures. This difference in application and function exacerbates the interference, making it challenging for Xiaoqiang to switch seamlessly between the two systems.

Therefore, Xiaoqiang's confusion arises from the overlapping yet distinct characteristics of the English alphabet and Chinese *pinyin*, leading to negative transfer where his prior knowledge of *pinyin* actually impedes his ability to master the English alphabet effectively. Strategies to mitigate this confusion could include explicit instruction highlighting the differences between the two systems, practicing in isolated contexts to build distinct associations, and engaging in activities that reinforce the unique properties of each alphabet.

Chapter 7 Ⅱ. Material Analysis

The effect of the prosodic syllable method is better than that of traditional method.

According to Memory Retention Percentage that Figure 1 shows, poems are the least to forget, and meaningless syllables are the easiest to forget.

Some students memorize "introduce, produce, reduce, induce and deduce" in the traditional method like this: i-n-t-r-o-d-u-c-e, p-r-o-d-u-c-e, r-e-d-u-c-e, i-n-d-u-c-e, d-e-d-u-c-e, and they belong to meaningless syllables, which are the easiest to forget. According to Figure 2, memorizing the words is just like reciting a poem, and if middle school students use the prosodic syllable method to remember these words, the effect is more effective.

All in all, according to the above analysis, the effect of the prosodic syllable method is better than that of the traditional method.

# Appendix II

**Case Study: Simultaneous Matching (Mismatching) Mode in a High School Science Class**

Context:

In a high school biology class, the teacher, Ms. Johnson, aims to teach the topic of cellular respiration. Her students exhibit diverse learning styles, including visual, auditory, and kinesthetic preferences.

Step 1: Whole-Class Instruction

Ms. Johnson begins the lesson with a whole-class instruction session. She presents the learning objectives and explains the fundamental concepts of cellular respiration using a PowerPoint presentation, which includes diagrams and videos. This unified approach ensures that all students receive the same foundational knowledge.

Step 2: Differentiated Instruction

After the introduction, Ms. Johnson divides the class into small groups based on their learning preferences:

—Group A (Visual Learners): They are given colorful charts and infographics to study the process of cellular respiration.

—Group B (Auditory Learners): They listen to a podcast that discusses the topic in detail and engages in a group discussion afterward.

—Group C (Kinesthetic Learners): They participate in a hands-on activity where they model the process using physical materials.

While the students engage in their preferred methods of learning, Ms. Johnson circulates among the groups, providing guidance and answering questions.

Step 3: Mismatching Instruction

After the groups have completed their tasks, Ms. Johnson introduces a mismatching phase. She instructs each group to switch to a non-preferred learning method:

—Group A (Visual Learners): Now must listen to a lecture on cellular respiration without visual aids.

—Group B (Auditory Learners): They are tasked with creating a visual poster summarizing the key points of the lecture.

—Group C (Kinesthetic Learners): They are required to write an essay explaining the process in detail.

This phase challenges students to adapt to different learning styles, fostering flexibility and resilience.

**Step 4: Summarization**

Finally, Ms. Johnson gathers the entire class for a summarization session. Each group presents their findings and reflects on their experiences with both matching and mismatching methods. Ms. Johnson points out the advantages and challenges of each approach, emphasizing the importance of being versatile in learning.

Outcome:

By utilizing the simultaneous matching (mismatching) mode, Ms. Johnson effectively engages her students with diverse learning styles. They benefit from both tailored instruction and the challenge of adapting to new methods, leading to a deeper understanding of cellular respiration and enhancing their overall learning experience.

# Appendix Ⅲ

**Teaching Case: Successive Matching (Mismatching) Mode in an English Lesson**
Topic: Vocabulary Development
Objective: Students will learn new vocabulary words related to emotions and practice using them in sentences.
Class Duration: 45 Minutes
Class Level: Intermediate English Learners
Materials Needed:
—Flashcards with vocabulary words and images
—Audio recordings of sentences using the vocabulary
—Whiteboard and markers
—Worksheets for sentence construction

**Lesson Plan**

1. Introduction (5 minutes)
—Activity: Mr. Johnson introduces the topic of emotions and explains the importance of vocabulary in expressing feelings.
—Matching: He starts with a brief visual presentation of emotions using flashcards, which matches the visual learners in the class.

2. Visual Learning Phase (10 minutes)
—Activity: Students are divided into pairs and given flashcards with images representing different emotions (e.g., happy, sad, angry, excited).
—Task: Each pair discusses the emotions depicted in the images and writes down sentences using the corresponding vocabulary words.
—Outcome: This phase engages visual learners effectively.

3. Auditory Learning Phase (10 minutes)
—Activity: Mr. Johnson plays audio recordings of sentences that use the vocabulary words in context.
—Mismatching: While auditory learners thrive in this phase, visual learners may find it challenging since they are not visually engaged.
—Task: After listening, students are asked to turn to a partner and discuss what they heard, focusing on the emotions conveyed in the sentences.

4. Kinesthetic Learning Phase (10 minutes)

—Activity: Students participate in a "Human Emotion Charades" game where they act out the vocabulary words without speaking.

—Mismatching: This phase primarily caters to kinesthetic learners, while auditory and visual learners may find it less engaging.

—Task: After acting, students write down sentences describing the emotions that were acted out, reinforcing their understanding through movement.

5. Consolidation and Reflection (10 minutes)

—Activity: Mr. Johnson gathers the class back together and asks students to share their sentences.

—Matching: He encourages visual learners to illustrate one of the emotions while auditory learners read their sentences aloud.

—Discussion: Mr. Johnson facilitates a class discussion on how each learning style contributed to their understanding of the vocabulary.

## Conclusion

By incorporating successive matching (mismatching) modes throughout the lesson, Mr. Johnson effectively engages students with different learning styles. Each phase allows students to experience varied methods of learning, enhancing their vocabulary acquisition and retention. The lesson concludes with a reflection on how recognizing and accommodating diverse learning styles can lead to a more inclusive and effective educational experience.

# Appendix IV

## Comprehensive Examination I

| 题号 | I | II | III | IV | V | 总分 |
|---|---|---|---|---|---|---|
| 得分 | | | | | | |

| 得分 | |
|---|---|
| 评卷人 | |

### I. Blank Filling. (20 points in total, 2 points for each)

Directions: *Fill in the blanks with the correct answers, and then please write them on your answer sheet.*

1. In psychological research, individual psychological activities are generally divided into three categories: processes, individual psychology and _____ states.
2. By _____ we can get information about the individual properties of things, such as the color, softness and hardness, taste, tone of things, etc.
3. _____ is the process of interpreting sensory information, which reflects the overall properties of things, e.g., a coat, a flag, a house, etc.
4. According to Bruner's cognition-discovery theory, learning includes three processes: _____, transformation and evaluation.
5. _____ is the engine of behavior, a force that stimulates, maintains and directs behavior toward a specific purpose.
6. In the actual learning process, there are many kinds of motivation factors for learning, among which there are three common ones: _____ drive, external incentive and external pressure.
7. _____ refers to a psychological state in which an individual feels lacking in learning activities and tries to seek satisfaction.
8. Maslow divided basic human needs into five kinds, in which _____ needs are the lowest level of needs.
9. _____ is highly curious, highly engaged in learning, and less concerned with the impact of failure.
10. _____ refers to the influence of one kind of learning on another kind of learning, and can also refer to the influence of acquired experience on the completion of other activities.

Ⅱ. **Multiple Choice.** (20 points in total, 2 points for each)

**Directions:** *Choose the best answer to each question from the four choices given, and write it on your answer sheet.*

( )11. What characteristics of perception does the following picture show us?

    A. Perceptual selectivity.      B. Perceptual wholeness.
    C. Perceptual constancy.      D. Perceptual development.

( )12. What characteristics of perception does the following picture show us?

    A. Perceptual selectivity.      B. Perceptual wholeness.
    C. Perceptual constancy.      D. Perceptual development.

( )13. _____ emphasizes genetic factors, neglect of the environment and education.
    A. Environmental determinism      B. Neo-Piagetian
    C. Genetic determinism      D. Interactive determinism

( )14. _____, concept, cultural level, educational mode, educational ability, will directly or indirectly affect the cognitive development of students.
    A. Father's education      B. Mother's education
    C. Parents' education      D. Teachers' education

( )15. A teacher went across a river with his students. He said that although there was no bridge in front of him, there were large pieces of stone in the river. The teacher jumped on the stone first and then asked the students to find their way. The students were looking for different stones and taking different paths, and they all cross the river. The theoretical basis of this teaching approach is _____.
    A. the butterfly effect      B. the conformity theory
    C. the Matthew effect      D. the zone of proximal development

( )16. According to Gagne, learning can be divided into five types. Which of the following does not belong to the five types?

  A. Secure skills.      B. Intellectual skills.

  C. Cognitive strategy.     D. Speech skills.

( )17. Which of the following Chinese idioms is used to express conditioned response?

  A. 杯弓蛇影    B. 耳濡目染    C. 朝三暮四    D. 乐不思蜀

( )18. Which of the following Chinese idioms does not belong to conditioned response?

  A. 闻风丧胆    B. 一帆风顺    C. 惊弓之鸟    D. 谈虎色变

( )19. Lu Xun said: "There are two trees in front of my house. One is a jujube tree, the other is still a jujube tree." What psychological characteristics does what Lu Xun said reflect?

  A. Aender differences.     B. Age differences.

  C. Personality differences.    D. Learning attitude differences.

( )20. "Love me, love my dog" belongs to what kind of psychological phenomenon?

  A. Law of extinction.

  B. Law of stimulation differentiation.

  C. Law of stimulation acquisition.

  D. Law of stimulation generalization.

## Ⅲ. True or False. (20 points in total, 2 points for each)

Directions: *Please judge whether the following statements are true or not according to the principles of psychology. If you think it is true, write "T" in the corresponding position on your answer sheet, and if false, write "F".*

21. ( ) Vygotsky believes that cognitive development is a process in which individuals, under the influence of environment and education, gradually transform their lower psychological functions into higher psychological functions.

22. ( ) The word "learning" is a well-known term; it's an activity that people do all their lives.

23. ( ) Watching television may impede attentional development.

24. ( ) Modern psychology holds that learning, in a broad sense, is the process of making more lasting changes in behavior or behavioral potential as a result of experience.

25. ( ) Evasive conditioning and escaping conditioning are two types of negative

reinforcement.

26. (      ) Constructionists stress that students don't walk into a classroom with an empty head.
27. (      ) Constructivism learning theory proposed the student-centred teaching instead of teacher-centred teaching.
28. (      ) According to constructivism learning view, learning is not a process in which teachers simply pass knowledge to students, but a process in which students construct knowledge themselves.
29. (      ) Internal incentives refer to external factors that have positive significance to individuals and attract individuals to engage in learning activities.
30. (      ) Friendship belongs to esteem need.

Ⅳ. **Explanation of Psychological Terms.** (**20 points in total, 5 points for each**)

Directions: *Explain the following psychological terms and write the answers on your answer sheet.*

31. cognition
32. ZPD
33. classical conditioning
34. assimilation

Ⅴ. **Answer Questions Briefly.** (**20 points in total, 10 points for each**)

Directions: *Please give appropriate answers to the following questions based on psychological principles, and then write them on your answer sheet.*

35. What is the significance for normal university students to learn the subject—Psychology of School Children's Cognition and Learning?
36. What are the steps of the scaffolding construction?

### Scoring Criteria for Comprehensive Examination Ⅰ

Ⅰ. Blank Filling. (20 points in total, 2 points for each)

1. psychological    2. feeling/sensory    3. Perception    4. acquisition
5. Motivation    6. internal    7. Learning need    8. physiological
9. Success-orienteer    10. Learning transfer

评分标准:填对,每道题得 2 分,单词写错不得分,大小写问题不扣分。

Ⅱ. Multiple Choice. (20 points in total, 2 points for each)

11—15 ABCDD  16—20 AABCD

评分标准:选对,每道题得2分,选择错误不得分。

Ⅲ. True or False. (20 points in total, 2 points for each)

21—25 TTTTF  26—30 TTTFF

评分标准:判断正确,每道题得2分,判断错误不得分。

Ⅳ. Explanation of Psychological Terms. (20 points in total, 5 points for each)

31. **Cognition** refers to the process that people acquire knowledge or apply knowledge or the processes of information processing, which is the most basic mental process of people, including feeling, perception, memory, thinking, imagination and language.

32. **ZPD**, that is Vygosky's term of the Zone of Proximal Development, refers to the gap between what they are already able to do by themselves and what they can accomplish with assistance. (Zone of Proximal Development [ZPD] refers to the gap between the children's actual level of problem solving and the potential level to solve the problem under the guidance of adults or cooperate with the competent partner.)

33. **Classical conditioning** refers to conditioned response in which a person learns to make a reflex, or involuntary, response to a stimulus that originally did not bring about the response. (Classical conditioning refers to the learning based on associating a stimulus that does not elicit a response with another stimulus that does elicit the response.)

34. **Assimilation** is the integration of external factors into a structure that is forming or has been formed, that is, the integration of environmental factors into the existing schema or structure of the organism, so as to strengthen and enrich the subject's actions.

评分标准:根据心理学原理诠释以上术语,或者给予例证。

  1. 句子通顺,解释正确得5分(33题两种答案都可以得分);

  2. 句子通顺,解释不完整,根据具体情况,得1—4分;

  3. 解释完全不正确,完全不合题意,得0分;

  4. 单词拼写错误1处,扣0.5分,以此类推,同一个拼写错误不重复扣分。

Ⅴ. Answer Questions Briefly. (20 points in total, 10 points for each)

35. 1. It is helpful for normal university students to use children's cognitive development characteristics in the future to improve the teaching effect. (3分)

    2. It is helpful for normal university students to grasp the learning rules and

characteristics of middle school students in the future, solve their learning problems and improve their learning effect. (3分)

3. To help teachers to combine education practice to carry out education and teaching research and promote teachers' professional growth. (3分)

评分标准：

　　1) 每个要点3分,该题得9分,如果句子通顺,没有错别字,卷面整洁另外加1分；否则,酌情扣分；

　　2) 少一个要点扣3分,以此类推,扣完为止,不倒扣分；

　　3) 如果答题的要点部分不正确,酌情扣1—2分；

　　4) 如果某一个要点全部不正确,得0分；

　　5) 单词拼写错误1处,扣0.5分,以此类推,同一个拼写错误不重复扣分。

36. Steps of scaffold construction are：

　　① Determine ZPD(2分)；② Build scaffolding (2分)；③ Enter the situation (2分)；④ Cooperative learning (2分)；⑤ Effectiveness evaluation (2分)。

评分标准：

　　1) 该题共5个要点,每个要点2分,如果句子不通顺,有错别字,酌情扣分；

　　2) 少一个要点扣2分,以此类推,扣完为止,不倒扣分；

　　3) 如果答题的要点部分不正确,扣1分；

　　4) 如果某一个要点全部不正确,得0分；

　　5) 单词拼写错误1处,扣0.5分,以此类推,同一个拼写错误不重复扣分。

# Appendix V

## Comprehensive Examination II

| 题号 | I | II | III | IV | V | 总分 |
|---|---|---|---|---|---|---|
| 得分 | | | | | | |

| 得分 | |
|---|---|
| 评卷人 | |

I. Blank Filling. (20 points in total, 2 points for each)

Directions: *Fill in the blanks with correct answers, and then please write them on your answer sheet.*

1. Psychological process is the dynamic process of a person's psychological phenomenon, including _____ process, emotional process and volitional process.

In psychological research, individual psychological activities is generally divided into three categories: psychological processes, individual psychology and _____ states.

3. The experience of perception is stored in the mind of the individual in need. That's what psychology calls _____.

4. _____ learning theory proposed the student-centred teaching instead of teacher-centred teaching.

5. In the actual learning process, there are many kinds of motivation factors for learning, among which there are three common ones: internal drive, _____ incentive and external pressure.

6. Maslow divided basic human needs into five kinds, in which _____ needs are the highest level of needs.

7. _____ has a high opinion of their abilities, but this opinion is highly susceptible to the experience of failure. They tend to have perfectionist tendencies, put too much pressure on themselves, and are in constant fear.

8. _____ recoils and reacts passively to academic challenges. They are not proud of their success and they are not ashamed of their failure.

9. Learning transfer can be divided into three types, namely, positive transfer, negative transfer and _____ transfer, according to the different nature of

migration or the different effects of migration.

10. Learning transfer can be divided into two types, namely, forward transfer and backward transfer, according to the chronological order. "Draw inferences from one example" refers to the _____ transfer.

Ⅱ. **Multiple Choice.** (**20 points in total, 2 points for each**)

**Directions**: *Choose the best answer for each question from the four choices given, and write it on your answer sheet.*

( )11. What characteristics of perception does the following picture show us?

  A. Perceptual selectivity.    B. Perceptual wholeness.
  C. Perceptual constancy.    D. Perceptual development.

( )12. What characteristics of perception does the following picture show us?

  A. Perceptual selectivity.    B. Perceptual wholeness.
  C. Perceptual constancy.    D. Perceptual development.

( ) 13. _____ emphasizes external behavior and its reinforcement and feedback, ignoring internal psychological processes.
  A. Genetic determinism    B. Neo-Piagetian
  C. Environmental determinism   D. Interactive determinism

( )14. According to Gagne, learning can be divided into five types. Which of the following does not belong to the five types?
  A. Speech skills.    B. Intellectual skills.
  C. Cognitive strategy.    D. Secure skills.

( )15. Which of the following Chinese idioms does not belong to conditioned response?
  A. 画饼充饥    B. 一朝被蛇咬,十年怕井绳
  C. 风声鹤唳,草木皆兵    D. 周郎妙计安天下,赔了夫人又折兵

(   )16. Which of the following Chinese idioms is used to express conditioned response?

  A. 望梅止渴  B. 耳濡目染  C. 朝三暮四  D. 乐不思蜀

(   )17. "杯弓蛇影"belongs to what kind of psychological phenomenon?

  A. Law of stimulation generalization.

  B. Law of extinction.

  C. Law of stimulation acquisition.

  D. Law of stimulation differentiation.

(   )18. Lu Xun said:"There are two trees in front of my house. One is a jujube tree, the other is still a jujube tree." What psychological characteristics does what Lu Xun said reflect?

  A. Gender differences.  B. Personality differences.

  C. Age differences.  D. Attitude difference.

(   )19. What kind of experiment does the picture show us?

  A. Tolman's classic experiment.

  B. Kohler's classic experiment.

  C. Thorndike's puzzle cage experiment.

  D. Brunner's operant conditioning experiment

(   ) 20. What of the following pictures is Skinner's operant conditioning experiment?

A. 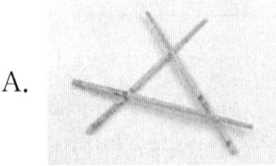  B.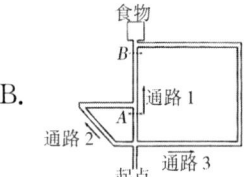

C.   D.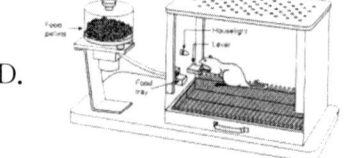

## III. True or False. (20 points in total, 2 points for each)

Directions: *Please judge whether the following statements are true or false according to the principles of psychology. If you think it is true, write "T" in the corresponding position on your answer sheet, and if false, write "F".*

21. (     ) In the narrow sense, learning refers to the process of relatively lasting changes in the behavior, ability and psychological tendency of individuals in their social practice activities by taking language as an intermediary and accumulating experience through thinking activities.

22. (     ) Constructionists stress that students don't walk into a classroom with an empty head.

23. (     ) Motivation is the engine of behavior, a force that stimulates, maintains and directs behavior toward a specific purpose.

24. (     ) External pressure refers to the requirements of the external environment on learners, forcing them to engage in learning activities.

25. (     ) Sex intimacy belongs to love and belonging need.

26. (     ) Sunshine belongs to physiological need.

27. (     ) Success orienteer is highly curious, highly engaged in learning, and less concerned with the impact of failure.

28. (     ) Failure avoider is afraid of challenges and the consequences of failure. Therefore, they will adopt a variety of self-defense strategies and attribute the failure to factors beyond the control of the outside world.

29. (     ) The representative of formal training theory is Köhler.

30. (     ) Cognitive structure theory is a new theory of learning transfer proposed by Wolff.

## IV. Definition of Psychological Terms. (20 points in total, 5 points for each)

Directions: *Explain the following psychological terms and write the answers on your answer sheet.*

31. cognition
32. escape conditioning
33. schemes
34. learning scaffolding

| 得分 | |
| --- | --- |
| 评卷人 | |

V. **Answer Questions Briefly.** (20 points in total, 10 points for each)

Directions: *Please give appropriate answers to the following questions based on psychological principles, and then write them on your answer sheet.*

35. According to Gagne, learning can be divided into eight different levels from simple to complex different degrees. What are they?
36. Please make a brief explanation of "Learning is endless" using Maslow's hierarchy of needs theory.

## Scoring Criteria for Comprehensive Examination Ⅱ

Ⅰ. Blank Filling. (20 points in total, 2 points for each)

1. cognitive    2. psychological    3. memory    4. Constructivism
5. external    6. self-actualization    7. Overachiever    8. Failure taker
9. zero    10. forward

评分标准：填对，每道题得2分，单词写错不得分，大小写问题不扣分。

Ⅱ. Multiple Choice. (20 points in total, 2 points for each)

11—15 ABCDD    16—20 AABCD

评分标准：选对，每道题得2分，选择错误不得分。

Ⅲ. True or False. (20 points in total, 2 points for each)

21—25 TTTTT    26—30 TTTFF

评分标准：判断正确，每道题得2分，判断错误不得分。

Ⅳ. Explanation of Psychological Terms. (20 points in total, 5 points for each)

31. **Cognition** refers to the general, typical, and essential age characteristics of school children in cognitive activities such as perception, memory, thinking and imagination.
32. When the aversive stimulus or unpleasant situation occurs, the organism makes a certain response, thus escaping the aversive stimulus or unpleasant situation, and the probability of the reaction occurring in similar situations in the future increases. This type of conditioning is called **escape conditioning.**
33. **Schemes** are Piaget's term of organized patterns of thought and behavior used in particular situation. (The scheme is Piaget's term of an organized pattern of thought and behavior used in particular situation.)
34. **Learning scaffolding** refers to a state, that is, the various forms of learning bracket provided by the teacher; it also refers to a process in which the teacher provides the learning scaffold according to the original ZPD of the learner, and then gradually removes the scaffolding to promote the learner to realize

independent learning and get rid of the original ZPD.

评分标准:根据心理学原理诠释以上术语,或者给予例证。
1. 句子通顺,解释正确得 5 分(33 题两种答案都可以得分);
2. 句子通顺,解释不完整,根据具体情况,得 1—4 分;
3. 解释完全不正确,完全不合题意,得 0 分;
4. 单词拼写错误 1 处,扣 0.5 分,以此类推,同一个拼写错误不重复扣分。

Ⅴ. Answer Questions Briefly. (20 points in total, 10 points for each)

35. According to Gagne, learning can be divided into eight different levels from simple to complex degrees. They are:(2 分)
1) signal learning (1 分); 2) stimulate-response learning (1 分); 3) chain learning (1 分); 4) speech association learning (1 分); 5) discrimination learning (1 分); 6) concept learning (1 分); 7) rule learning (1 分); 8) learning how to solve problems (1 分)

评分标准:
1. 该题共 8 个要点,每个要点 1 分,这样共得 8 分,导入语 2 分;
2. 少一个要点扣 1 分,无导入语扣 2 分,以此类推,扣完为止,不倒扣分;
3. 如果某一个要点全部不正确,得 0 分;
4. 单词拼写错误 1 处,扣 0.5 分,以此类推,同一个拼写错误不重复扣分。

36. According to Maslow, basic human needs are divided into five kinds: physiological needs, security needs, love and belonging needs, respect needs and self-actualization needs. (2 分) Maslow divided the five needs into deficiency needs and growth needs. (1 分) Among them, the first four kinds of needs are deficiency needs, which are necessary for human beings to maintain survival activities. (1 分) After they are satisfied, the intensity will be reduced. The need for self-actualization belongs to the need for growth, and it can never be satisfied. (2 分) In other words, the need for self-actualization will not decrease with the satisfaction, but will be enhanced with the satisfaction, so the pursuit of knowledge is endless. (2 分)

　　Learning belongs to theself-actualization need which belongs to the growth need, and the self-actualization need will not decrease with the satisfaction, so learning is endless. (2 分)

评分标准:
1. 该题共 6 个要点,每个要点分值已经给出,如果句子不通顺,酌情扣分;
2. 少一个要点,按分值扣分,以此类推,扣完为止,不倒扣分;
3. 如果答题的要点部分不正确,扣 1—2 分;
4. 如果某一个要点全部不正确,得 0 分;
5. 单词拼写错误 1 处,扣 0.5 分,以此类推,同一个拼写错误不重复扣分。

# References

1. ALLOWAY T P. How does working memory work in the classroom? [J]. Educational research and reviews, 2006, 1(4): 134-139.
2. AMSEL E, GOODMAN G, SEVOIE D, CLARK M. The development about reasoning about casual and noncasual influences on levers [J]. Child development, 1996, 67(4): 1624-1646.
3. ANGLIN J M. Knowing versus learning words [J]. Monographs of the society for research in child development, 1993, 58 (10): 176-186.
4. ANGLIN J M. Vocabulary development: A morphological analysis [J]. Monographs of the society for research in child development, 1993, 58 (10): 1-166.
5. ATKINSON J W. An introduction to motivation [M]. Princeton, NJ: Van Nostrand, 1964.
6. AUSUBEL D R, ROBINSON, F G. School learning: An introduction to educational psychology [M]. New York: Holt, Rinehart & Winston, 1969.
7. BADDELEY A, HITCH G J, BADDELEY D. Working memory[M]//BOWER G H. The psychology of learning and motivation: Advances in research and theory. New York: Academic Press, 1974: 47-89.
8. BADDELEY A D. Working memory [M]. Oxford: Oxford University Press, 1986.
9. BANDURA A. Social foundation of thoughts and actions: A social cognitive theory [M]. Englewood Cliffs, NJ: Prentice Hall, 1986.
10. BERGRMANN P G. Introduction to the theory of relativity [M]. New York: Prentice-Hall, Inc,1942.
11. BOOTH J L, SIEGLER R S. Developmental and individual differences in pure numerical estimation[J]. Developmental psychology, 2006, 41(6): 189-201.
12. BRANSFORD J D, SHERWOOD R D, HASSELBRING T S, KINZER C K, WILLIAMS S M. Anchored instruction: Why we need it and how technology can help [M]//NIX D, SPIRO R J. Cognition, education, and multimedia: Exploring ideas in high technology. Hillsdale, NJ: Lawrence Erlbaum Associates, 1990: 115-141.
13. BRONFENBRENNER U. Ecological models of human development[M]//Husen

T, Postlethwaite T N. International encyclopedia of education. 2nd ed. Oxford: Elsevier Science, 1994:1643-1647.
14. BRONFENBRENNER U. Ecology of the family as a context for human development: Research perspectives [J]. Developmental psychology, 1986, 22 (6): 723-742.
15. BRONFENBRENNER U, MORRIS P A. The ecology of developmental processes[M]//DAMON W, LERNER R, DAMON W. Handbook of child psychology: Theoretical models of human development. 5th ed. Hoboken, NJ: John Wiley & Sons, 1998: 1; 993-1028.
16. BRONFENBRENNER U. The ecology of human development [M]. Cambridge, MA: Harvard University Press, 1979.
17. BROPHY J E. Motivating students to learn [M]. London:Routledge, 2004.
18. BROPHYJ. Teacher praise: A functional analysis [J]. Review of educational research, 1981, 51(1): 5-32.
19. CARBO M, DUNN R, DUNN K. Teaching students to read through their individual learning styles [M]. Englewood Cliffs, NJ: Prentice Hall, 1986.
20. CHOMSKY C S. The acquisition of syntax in children from five to ten [M]. Cambridge: MIT Press, 1971.
21. COLLINS A, BROWN J S, HOLUM A. Cognitive apprenticeship: Making thinking visible[J]. American educator, 1991, 15(3): 6-11; 38-46.
22. COOPER L A, SHERPARD R N. Chronometric studies of the rotation of mental images[M]//CHASE W G. Visual information processing. New York: Academic Press, 1973: 75-176.
23. COVINGTON M C, CRUTCHFIEND R S, DAVES L B, OLTON R M. The productive thinking program: A course in learning to think [M]. Columbus, Ohio: Charles E. Merrill, 1974.
24. COVINGTON M V. The motive for self-worth[M]//AMES R, AMES C. Research on motivation in education. Vol 1: Student motivation. San Diego, CA: Academic Press, 1990:3-21.
25. CRAIK F I M, LOCKHART R S. Levels of processing: A framework for memory research [J]. Journal of verbal learning and verbal behavior, 1972, 11 (6): 671-684.
26. CRAWFORD J. The decline of bilingual education: How to reverse a troubling trend? [J]. International multilingual research journal, 2007, 1(1): 33-37.
27. Curry L. An organization of learning style theory and construct[M]// Curry L. *Learning style in continuing education for the health professions*. Ottawa:

Canadian Medical Association, 1983, pp. 115-131.
28. DANSEREAU D F. Learning strategy research[M]//SEGAL J, CHIPMAN S, GLASER R. Thinking and learning skills: Relating instruction to basic research. Hillsdale, NJ: Lawrence Erlbaum Associates, 1985: 209-239.
29. DECI E L, RYAN R M. Intrinsic motivation and self-determination in human behavior [M]. New York: Plenum Press, 1985.
30. DEMBO M H. Applying educational psychology[M]. 5th ed. New York: Longman Publishing Group, 1994.
31. DERRY S J, MURPHY D A. Designing systems that train learning ability: Form theory to practice [J]. Review of educational research, 1986, 56 (1): 1-39.
32. DEVINE T G. Teaching study skills: A guide for teachers[M]. 2nd ed. Boston: Allyn & Bacon, 1987.
33. DUNN R, DUNN K, PRICE G. Manual: Productive, environmental reference survey[M]//SHERMAN R FREDMAN N. Handbook of measurements for marriage and family therapy. New York: Routledge, 1987.
34. DUNN R, DUNN K, PRICE G E. Learning styles inventory [M]. Lawrence, KA: Price Systems, 1998.
35. DUNN R, DUNN K. Teaching secondary students through their individual learning style: Practical approaches for grades 7-12 [M]. Boston: Allyn & Bacon, 1993.
36. EBBINGHAUS H. Memory: A contribution to experimental psychology [M]. New York: Teachers College Press, Columbia University, 1913.
37. EVANS T D. Encouragement: The key to reforming the classrooms [J]. Educational leadership, 1996, 54(1): 81-85.
38. FELDMAN R S. Understanding psychology[M]. 11th ed. Beijing: The People's Posts and Telecom Press, 2015.
39. FLAVELL J H. Meta-cognitive aspects of problem solving[M]//RESNICK L. The nature of intelligence. Hillsdale, NJ: Lawrence Erlbaum Associates, 1976: 231-235.
40. GAGNE R. The conditions of learning[M]. 3rd Ed. New York: Holt, Rinehart & Winston, 1977.
41. GALOTTI K M, KOMATSU L K, VOELZ S. Children's differential performance on deductive and inductive syllogisms [ J ]. Development Psychology, 1997, 33(1): 70-78.
42. GATHERCOLE S E, ALLOWAY T P. Working memory and learning: A

practical guide [M]. Thousand Oaks, CA: Sage Publications, 2008.
43. GREENO J G, COLLINS A M, RESNICK L R. Cognition and learning[M]// BERLINER D C, CALFEE R C. Handbook of education psychology. New York: Macmillan. 1996: 15-46.
44. GREGORC A F. An adult's guide to style [M]. Columbia, CT: Gregorc Associates, 1989.
45. GREGORC A F. Learning/Thinking styles: Classroom interaction [M]. West Haven, CT: National Education Association, 1990.
46. HAKUTA K, BUTLER Y G, WITT D. How long does it take English learners to attain proficiency? [R/OL]. (2020-01-01)[2024-03-26]. https://www.doc88.com/p-0099786926570.html? id=5&s=rel
47. HARNISHFEGER K K, POPE R S. Intending to forget: The development of cognitive in directed forgetting [J]. Journal of experimental child psychology, 1996, 62(2): 292-315.
48. HELMS D B, TURNER J S. Exploring child behaviour [M]. Philadelphia: W. B. Saunders Company, 1976.
49. HONEY P, MUMFORD A. The manual of learning styles [M]. Maidenhead: Peter Honey Publications, 1982.
50. HURLOCK E B. An evaluation of certain incentive used in schoolwork [J]. Journal of educational psychology, 1925, 16(3): 145-159.
51. INHELDER B, PIAGET J. The growth of logical thinking from childhood to adolescence [M]. New York: Basic Books, 1958.
52. JAMES W. The principles of psychology [M]. Elk Grove, CA: Franklin Classics, 2018.
53. JANOWSKY J S, CARPER R. Is there a neural basis for cognitive transitions in school-age children? [M]// SAMEROFF A J, HAITH M M. The five to seven year shift: The age of season and responsibility. Chicago: The University of Chicago Press, 1996: 33-56.
54. Jere B,Teacher praise: A functional analysis[J]. Review of educational research, 1981,51(1):26.
55. JUDD C H. The relationship of special training to general intelligence [J]. Educational review. 1908, 36(4): 28-42.
56. Kantowitz B H & Sorkin R D. Human factors: Understanding people-system relationships[M]. New York: John Wiley & Sons, 1983.
57. KAGAN J S, ROSMAN B L, DAY D, ALBERT J, PHILLIPS W. Information processing in the child: Significance of analytic and reflective attitude [J].

Psychological monographs: General and applied, 1964, 78 (1): 1-37.

58. KEEFE J W. Learning styles profile handbook: Accommodating conceptual study and instructional preferences [M]. Reston, VA: NASSP, 1989.

59. KEEFE J W. Assessing and guiding classroom learning [M]. Boston, MA: Allyn & Bacon, 1982.

60. KOHLER W. The mentality of apes [M]. Alcester: Read Books, 2011.

61. KOHLER W. The place of value in a world of facts [M]. New York: Liveright Publishing Corporation, 1976.

62. KOLB D A. Experiential learning: Experience as the source of learning and development [M]. Englewood Cliffs, NJ: Prentice Hall, 1984.

63. KRASHEN S, MCFIELD G. What works? Reviewing the latest evidence on bilingual education [J]. Language learning, 2005, 1(2) : 7-34.

64. KREUTZER M A, LEONARD C, FLAVELL J H, HAGEN J W. An interview study of children's knowledge about memory [J]. Monographs of the society for research in child development, 1975, 40 (1): 1-60.

65. LORSBACH T C, REIMAR J F. Developmental changes in the inhibition of previously relevant information [J]. Journal of experimental child psychology, 1997, 64(3): 317-342.

66. LUNA B, GARVER K E, URBAN T A, LAZAR N A, SWEENEY J A. Maturation of cognitive processes from late childhood to adulthood [J]. Child development, 2004, 75(5): 1357-1372.

67. MACAN T M, SHAHANI C, DIPBOYE R L, PHILIPS A P. College students' time management: Correlation with academic performance and stress [J]. Journal of educational psychology, 1990, 82(4): 760-768.

68. MAYER R E. Educational psychology: A cognitive approach [M]. New York: Little, Brown and Company, 1987.

69. MCKEACHIE W J, PINTRICH P R, Lin Y G, SMITH D A F, SHARMA R. Teaching and learning in college classroom: A review of the research literature [M]. Ann Arbor: The University of Michigan, 1987.

70. MILLER G A. The magical number seven plus or minus two: Some limits on our capacity for processing information [J]. Psychological review, 1956, 63(2): 81-97.

71. MILLERPH, WEISS M G. Children's attention location, understanding of attention, and performance on the incidental learning task [ J ]. Child development, 1981,52 (3): 583-590.

72. MYERS I B, BRIGGS K C. Gifts differing: Understanding personality type [M].

Palo Alto: Davies-Black Publishing, 1995.

73. NELSON-LE GALL S. Help-seeking behavior in learning [M]//Gordon W. Review of research in education. Washington D C: American Education Research Association, 1985: 55-90.

74. OWENS R E. Language development [M]. 4th ed. Boston: Allyn & Bacon, 2001.

75. OXFORD R L. Language learning strategies: What every teacher should know [M]. Boston: Heinle & Heinle Publishers, 1990.

76. PACHER J, BAIN J. Cognitive style and student-teacher compatibility [J]. Learning and individual differences, 1998, 10(2): 197-212.

77. PAPALIA D E, FELDMAN R D. Experience human development [M]. 12th ed. Beijing: The People's Posts and Telecom Press, 2014.

78. PASK G. Conversational techniques in the study and practice of education [J]. British journal of educational psychology, 1976, 46(1): 12-25.

79. PASK G. Learning strategies, teaching strategies, and conceptual or learning style [M]//SCHMECK R R. Learning strategies and learning styles. New York: Plenum Press, 1988: 197-219.

80. PIAGET J, INHELDER B. The child's conception of space [M]. London: Routledge & Kegan Paul, 1956.

81. PIAGET J. The language and thought of the child [M]. London: Routledge & Kegan Paul, 2001.

82. PIAGET J. The origins of intelligence in children [M]. New York: The International University Press, 1952.

83. RESNICK L B. Developing mathematical knowledge [J]. American psychologist, 1989, 44(2): 162-169.

84. RIDING P, RAYNER R, ZHOU J. Cognitive styles analysis: Understanding means of representation [M]. London: David Fulton Publishers, 1997.

85. RIDING R H. Cognitive style: A review [M]//RIDING RH, RAYBER SH. International perspectives on individual differences: Cognitive style. New Jersey: Ablex Publishing Corporation, 2000: 315-344.

86. RIDING R H. On the nature of cognitive style [J]. Educational psychology, 1997, 17(12):29-49.

87. RIDING R J. Cognitive styles analysis: A learning styles model for understanding different perceptions and learning techniques [J]. Educational psychology, 1991, 11(3 4): 193 215.

88. SARACHO O N, SPODEK B. Teacher's cognitive style and the educational

applications [J]. Educational forum, 1981, 45(2): 153-159.
89. SIEGLER R S, Booth J L. Development of numerical estimation in young children [J]. Child development, 2004, 75(2) : 428-444.
90. SIEGLER R S, OPFER J E. The development of numerical estimation: Evidence for multiple representations of numerical quantity [J]. Psychological science, 2003, 14(3): 237-243.
91. SLAVIN R E. Educational psychology: Theory and practice [M]. 7th ed. Beijing: Beijing University Press, 2004.
92. SLAVIN R E. Educational psychology theory and practice [M]. 10th ed. Beijing: The People's Posts and Telecom Press, 2017.
93. SOLOMON B A. The learning style self-test [M]. New Jersey: Prentice-Hall, 1992.
94. SORLIE S. Adolescent life and labour [M]. Chicago, IL: The University of Chicago Press, 1926.
95. STERNBERG R J, LUBART T I. Defying the crowd: Cultivating creativity in a culture of conformity [M]. New York: Free Press, 1995.
96. STERNBERG R J, STERNBERG K. The psychologist's companion: A guide to scientific writing for students and researchers [M]. Cambridge: Cambridge University Press, 2003.
97. STERNBERGR J, SPEAR-SWERLING L. Teaching for thinking: A program for school improvement through teaching critical thinking across the curriculum [M]. Washington, D. C. : American Psychological Association, 1996.
98. STERNBERG R J. Thinking styles [M]. Cambridge: Cambridge University Press, 1999.
99. SUTHERLAND K, WEHBY J, COPELAND S. Effect of rates of varying behavior-pacific praise on the on-task behavior of students with EBD [J]. Journal of emotional and behavioral disorders, 2000, 8(1): 2-8.
100. THOMAS J W, ROHWER W D. Academic studying: The role of learning strategies [J]. Educational psychologist, 1986, 21 (1-2): 19-41.
101. THOMAS S L, ROBINSON H A. Improving reading in every class: A sourcebook for teachers [M]. Boston: Allyn & Bacon, 1972.
102. THORNDIKE E L, WOODWORTH R S. The influence of improvement in one mental function upon the efficiency of other functions [J]. Psychological review, 1901, 8(3): 247-261.
103. TORRANCE E P. Guiding creative talent [M]. Englewood Cliffs: Prentice Hall, 1962.

104. VOSNIADOU S. Children and metaphors [J]. Child development, 1987, 58(3): 870-885.
105. VYGOTSKY L S. Mind in society: The development of higher psychological processes [M]. Cambridge, MA: Harvard University Press, 1978.
106. WEINBERG S. Gravitation and cosmology [M]. New York: John Wiley and Sons, 1972.
107. WEINSTEIN C E, UNDENWOOK V L. Learning strategy: the how of learning [M]//SEGAL J W, CHIPMAN S F, GLASER R. Thinking and learning skills. Hillsdale NJ: Lawrence Erlbaum Associates, 1985: 187-223.
108. WITKIN H A, MOORE C A, GOODENOUGH D R., COX R. W. Field-depend and field-independent cognitive styles and their educational implications [J]. Review of Educational Research, 1977, 47(2): 1-64.
109. 陈辉. 短时记忆容量的年龄特点及材料特点 [J]. 天津师范大学学报(社会科学版), 1988 (4): 25-30.
110. 陈琦, 刘儒德. 当代教育心理学 [M]. 北京: 北京师范大学出版社, 2007.
111. 程灶火, 耿铭. 儿童记忆发展的横断面研究 [J]. 中国临床心理学杂志, 2001, 9 (4): 255-259.
112. 董奇. 论元认知[J]. 北京师范大学学报(社会科学版), 1989(1): 68-74.
113. 冯忠良. 教育心理学[M]. 北京: 人民教育出版社, 2000.
114. 冯忠良, 伍新春, 姚梅林, 等. 教育心理学[M]. 2版. 北京: 人民教育出版社, 2010.
115. 何心勇. 英语词经（初级版）[M]. 北京: 中国科学文化音像出版社有限公司, 2024.
116. 何心勇. 英语词经（中级版）[M]. 北京: 中国科学文化音像出版社有限公司, 2024.
117. 何心勇. 英语词经（高级版）[M]. 北京: 中国科学文化音像出版社有限公司, 2024.
118. 教育部教师工作司. 教师教育课程标准(试行)解读 [M]. 北京: 北京师范大学出版社, 2013.
119. 教育部人事司, 教育部考试中心. 教育心理学考试大纲 [M]. 北京: 北京师范大学出版社, 2002.
120. 梁启超. 饮冰室文集点校 [M]. 吴松, 卢云昆, 王文光, 段炳昌点校. 昆明: 云南教育出版社, 2001.
121. 孔子等. 图解论语(插图本)[M]. 南京: 凤凰出版社, 2012.
122. 林崇德, 杨治良, 黄希庭. 心理学大辞典 [M]. 上海: 上海教育出版社, 2003.
123. 凌光明. 小学低年级学业不良儿童的有意注意稳定性研究[D]. 苏州: 苏州大学,

2001.
124. 刘电芝. 学习策略研究 [M]. 北京：人民教育出版社，1999.
125. 刘电芝，黄希庭. 学习策略研究概述 [J]. 教育研究，2002(2)：78-82.
126. 路海东. 教育心理学 [M]. 长春：东北师范大学出版社，2002.
127. 卢家楣. 心理学：基础理论及其教学应用 [M]. 上海：上海人民出版社，2004.
128. 罗伯特. 教育心理学：理论与实践 [M]. 7 版. 姚梅林，徐守森，王雁，译. 北京：人民邮电出版社，2004.
129. 莫雷. 教育心理学 [M]. 广州：广东高等教育出版社，2002.
130. 庞维国. 自主学习——学与教的原理和策略 [M]. 上海：华东师范大学出版社，2003.
131. 彭小虎，王国峰，朱丹. 儿童发展与教育心理学 [M]. 上海：华东师范大学出版社，2013.
132. 山香教师招聘考试命题研究中心. 河南省教师招聘考试专用教材教育理论基础 [M]. 北京：首都师范大学出版社，2015.
133. 邵瑞珍，皮连生. 教育心理学(修订本) [M]. 上海：上海教育出版社，1997.
134. 邵瑞珍，皮连生，吴庆麟，等. 教育心理学参考资料选辑 [M]. 上海：上海教育出版社，1990.
135. 史耀芳. 学习策略及其培养 [J]. 江西教育科研，1994(2)：36-38.
136. 索里，特尔福德. 教育心理学 [M]. 高觉敷，刘范，林传鼎，等译. 北京：人民教育出版社，1982.
137. 孙长华，吴志平，吴振云，等. 7－19 岁时期记忆的发展研究 [J]. 应用心理学，1992，7(1)：15-21.
138. 夏惠贤. 论邓恩学习风格模型及其教学意蕴 [J]. 外国中小学教育，2006(6)：1-7.
139. 杨治良，郭力平. 认知风格的研究进展 [J]. 心理科学，2001，24 (3)：326-329.
140. 叶奕乾，祝蓓里. 心理学 [M]. 上海：华东师范大学出版社，1988.
141. 尹可丽，闵卫国，周泓. 中小学生认知与学习 [M]. 北京：高等教育出版社，2014.
142. 张春玲. 学习风格：因材施教的新视域 [J]. 当代教育论坛，2009(5)：7-8.
143. 张世富. 心理学 [M]. 北京：人民教育出版社，2016.
144. 朱秀芳，沈坚，吴玉芝. 小学儿童教育心理学 [M]. 北京：人民教育出版社，1986.
145. 朱智贤. 儿童心理学 [M]. 6 版. 北京：人民教育出版社，2018.